Springer Studies in Alternative Economics

This book series offers an outlet for cutting-edge research in alternative, heterodox and pluralist economics. It features scholarly studies on various schools of thought beyond the neo-classical orthodoxy, including Austrian, Post Keynesian, Sraffian, Marxian, Georgist, Institutional-evolutionary, as well as feminist, radical, social, green, and ecological economics. It aims to promote pluralism of economic ideas, methodological approaches, and topics.

The series also welcomes works that seek to develop alternative visions of the economy, economic structures and new approaches that aim to serve society, for example by embedding the economy within the ecosystem, or to enrich economic thought by advancing diversity, gender, race, and social equality. All titles in this series are peer-reviewed.

Carmine Gorga

Concordian Economics, Vol. 2

Some Applications

Springer

Carmine Gorga [iD]
The Somist Institute
Gloucester, MA, USA

ISSN 2731-5908 ISSN 2731-5916 (electronic)
Springer Studies in Alternative Economics
ISBN 978-3-031-54641-9 ISBN 978-3-031-54642-6 (eBook)
https://doi.org/10.1007/978-3-031-54642-6

© The Editor(s) (if applicable) and The Author(s), under exclusive license to Springer Nature Switzerland AG 2024

This work is subject to copyright. All rights are solely and exclusively licensed by the Publisher, whether the whole or part of the material is concerned, specifically the rights of translation, reprinting, reuse of illustrations, recitation, broadcasting, reproduction on microfilms or in any other physical way, and transmission or information storage and retrieval, electronic adaptation, computer software, or by similar or dissimilar methodology now known or hereafter developed.
The use of general descriptive names, registered names, trademarks, service marks, etc. in this publication does not imply, even in the absence of a specific statement, that such names are exempt from the relevant protective laws and regulations and therefore free for general use.
The publisher, the authors, and the editors are safe to assume that the advice and information in this book are believed to be true and accurate at the date of publication. Neither the publisher nor the authors or the editors give a warranty, expressed or implied, with respect to the material contained herein or for any errors or omissions that may have been made. The publisher remains neutral with regard to jurisdictional claims in published maps and institutional affiliations.

This Springer imprint is published by the registered company Springer Nature Switzerland AG
The registered company address is: Gewerbestrasse 11, 6330 Cham, Switzerland

Paper in this product is recyclable.

To

My Mother,
Luisa Capuano in Gorga

Whose works
Apparently small
Were intense and continuous

Never idle. Never bored. Here is a short list of what my mother knew how to do: she knew how to make us all talkative at the table. She knew how to cook consistently savory meals—without the help of a recipe. On Sundays and Holy Days, she created a Table of Plenty. There was always an extra plate for friends who would drop in.

During and after the war we suffered a lot. But she never made me feel poor; on the contrary, once she made me feel rich. We went to visit some of her friends; they were eating the *skins* of their potatoes. We never did. (And now potato skins are considered an exotic succulent treat.)

She could transform wool into woolen threads; she knew how to weave woolen sweaters and socks; she knew how to mend sweaters and socks; she knew how to make beautiful works with the crochet needle, and beautiful embroidery of any fashion, with no patterns on hand; she prepared the dowry for sister and instructed her on how to run a house; she knew how to bake bread; she knew how to raise chickens and a small pig (we were not living on a farm, but at the outskirts of a town). In Rocca, we had a wall wooden oven. Of course, she knew how to bake dark grain bread that would last us a month. I believe her specialty was to make *friselle*, crunhy little things... I had to Google them up: "*This Italian Friselle is baked once then toasted to perfection. Topped with fresh tomatoes, this simple twice-baked bread is packed with flavour. Serve it as an appetizer or snack either way you will enjoy it.*" Who knew! I knew only that they lasted three months perhaps, and we were having breakfast with them. We added olive oil.

And of course she knew how to make sausages, and preserve for the long run all parts of the small pork that was killed in our house every year; prosciutto was one of her products; she knew how to preserve tomato juice and tomato concentrate for the winter; she knew how to buy all necessary ingredients for a balanced diet; indeed, she knew how to administer our small family budget. She knew how to make my father happy; he called her Luisella. And she knew how to raise children, all five of us. La Signora Gorga was loved by her friends.

The strongest punishment she would put me through? A pinch on the upper arm. I never heard her raise her voice.

When I showed her Moona, my wife, she said; "Ma chesta e' proprio na creatura" (But this is just a little girl). Joan wears every day one of the two bracelets my mother gave her as a wedding gift.

She would make us pray together, whenever she could; my father, who was not too strong a believer, would just listen in. My mother had an abiding, forceful, vital faith in God. With the cupboard empty and no money in the wallet, she said once: "I have to go shopping." She returned announcing that she had found a 10,000 Italian Lire bill on the street.

She would ask deep philosophical questions—without expecting an answer.

Preface

Fifty years of research and publication, plus the experience of having lived through Mussolini's Italy and the devastation of World War II, do *not* make me more clairvoyant than anyone else. But personal experience does have its value.

Short term, we are at a fork in the road. One path leads to ruin; the other leads to a brilliant future—a brilliant future for everyone.

If we are in danger of losing it all today, it is because we have set the haves against the have-nots, gender against gender, race against race, money against nature. We have twisted our reasoning in knots. This is a world that leads to ruin for everyone. How long will those canned foods in fully armored bunkers last? And what will the survivors, the remnant find when they come out of the bunkers?

Let us focus on the long term; it might help us solve many problems in the short term. A brilliant world will come; a brilliant world will come. It is unavoidable. It will gradually come, and we might even avoid the precipice on whose brink we are so irresponsibly teetering today, as soon as we enter the new/old intellectual world of Concordian economics.

Deep inside, Concordian economics is not a theory that wants or needs to remain on the shelves. Rather, it is a pratice that comes to full fruition when it is enmeshed with the lives of We the People. And the lives of the people are enmeshed in a series of concentric circles; they are best described by appropriate theories: economics, sociology, jurisprudence, political science, and on and on. Is this enough of a justification for the starting point repetitions that the Reader will encounter in this presentation? Besides, not every Reader reads a book cover to cover.

To be highfalutin, Concordian economics might be called the Theory of Interdependence.

Hence, the beginning, the continuation (?) of the "story" can be found in 2023 Maria Popova's Christmas Morning insertion of the individual person in the Universe. And that is not the full treatment of Interdependence yet. One really ought to start from the equivalence of matter to energy to spirit. It is sprit that connects everything to Spirit.

Accordingly, I have grouped some possible applications of this work into four parts titled respectively (a) *Intellectual Interdependence*; (b) *Financial Interdependence*; (c) *Physical Interdependence*; and (d) *Human Interdependence*.

Intellectual Interdependence. Under this heading are examined, first, some of the current relationships between modern economics and politics; thereafter, we go deeper into the social relationships that will likely exist during the acquisition of Concordian economic rights and responsibilities; ultimately, the relationships that count most are those that Concordian economics will likely create in the political economy of the future. A major bone of contention will be eliminated: Rather than primacy, we will discover a relationship of complementarity between Keynes and Hayek, between the Government and the Market.

Financial Interdependence. This heading will give us a chance to understand the role that money used to play in the past, the role it is playing in the present, and the role it might play in the future. Not only that, but we will also explore what is money, where it comes from, and how it ought to be produced and distributed. We will thus have an opportunity to recommend the creation of a new monetary system that, if and when it becomes operational, will offer us a fundamental paradigm shift from money controlling people *to people controlling money*. At the end of this section there is "Project Financial Independence," a project that can come true only in a regimen of full social, economic, and political *interdependence*. Personal Financial Independence is a sore need in our lives. Without Financial Independence, all calls to efficiency and all calls to morality are quite hollow.

Physical Interdependence. An examination of this issue will offer us rich opportunities to discover ways to build a physical environment vastly different from the one we are living in today: The gamut ranges from downtown development through racial harmony to some futuristic designs in urban development. In the end, we might achieve the "integral ecology" that Pope Francis, among many other futurists, clearly envisages.

Human Interdependence. An examination of the reality of human interdependence offers us the possibility to settle some old scores. Is there scarcity in the world? Scarcity of What? Do the rich make us poor? Interested in knowing who the creators of poverty are? Read on.

One more chapter deals with a self-explanatory topic: "Ethics in Concordian Economics." This is not so much a theoretical but a practical result of Concordian economics. Skipping the horrific conditions of the world of today, with Concordian economics we are connecting with the old—two-thousand-years-old—doctrine of *economic* justice. Extending into the future the theoretical and practical roots of this doctrine, a doctrine founded on the tween traditions of freedom and morality, we have a great opportunity of turning economics from a Science of Discord to the Economics of Concord, namely Concordian economics.

The book concludes with an extension of the Three Rules of Concordian Monetary Policy—by applying them to the international world. One result of this extension is a proposed Bancor International Order (BIO). This is the international order that, no doubt, in the end Keynes was trying to create with his suggestion to use the Bancor, not as a world currency, but as an accounting creature to ease international trade. It is easier to deal with Digits than with Dollars. My hope is that through the creation of this institution, BIO, we will create a friendly, democratic world currency. Then we might be able to exchange the end of the US Dollar Hegemony, a great desire of President Putin, for ending hostilities in Ukraine. The US Dollar Hegemony is creating an unpleasant result for us in the United States after all: When foreign nations liquidate their dollar hoards, they purchase our real assets. Even Italy is controlling Chrysler these days.

Proposed is a Grand Bargain: fickle dollars for steady peace.

Gloucester, MA, USA
January 2024

Carmine Gorga

Acknowledgements

As stated in Vol. 1, a book like this conceived and brought to life in the course of many years is due to many influencers. I hope not to miss too many of them. The framework is uniquely due to 27 years of exhaustive probing by Franco Modigliani and by Meyer L. Burstein for 23 years. This work was set on its way by a powerful suggestion by my dissertation adviser, Vittorio de Caprariis and by Francesco Compagna. Earlier still I received my clarity of mind through the teaching of Rosalia Scarlata. Robert A. Mundell, Mitchell S. Lurio and Norman G. Kurland have been great teachers. Much encouragement was provided by Alan Reynolds, Raymond G. Torto, and John K. Skank. Otto Eckstein, Frank L. Cooper, Steve H. Hanke, and Harry G. Johnson were the first economists to confirm that the revised Keynes' model was consistent. Helpful comments, suggestions, and recommendations were tendered by Michael E. Brady, William J. Baumol, Stephen Thornton, Michele Boldrin, Jeroen C. J. M. van den Bergh, Kevin P. Gallagher, William J. Toth, William R. Collier, Jr., Damon Cummings, Veljko Milutinovic, and John Opuda-Asibo. Selective portions of this analysis have been endorsed by John K. Galbraith, Buckminster Fuller, Mark Perlman, Roger H. Gordon, Francesco Forte, Augusto Graziani, Alberto Tarchiani, Aldo Garosci, Giorgio Spini, Gerald Alonzo Smith, Charles T. Wood, Norman A. Bailey, Rosanna Marini, Gordon Richards, Rudy Oswald, Steve Kurtz, Ernest Kahn, Louis J. Ronsivalli, Howard Zinn, Robert F. Drinan, Thomas J. Marti, Cassian J. Yuhaus, James E. Hug, Richard John Neuhaus, John J. Neuhauser, Irving Kristol, Michael J. Naughton, Robert G. Kennedy, John C. Rao, Stefano Zamagni, and Laurence J. Kotlikoff, among others. Thanks for editorial assistance go to Janis D. Stelluto, Ralph Cole Waddey, Anne Jones, Jonathan F. Gorga, and David S. Wise. Special thanks go to Peter J. Bearse, for his invaluable editorial assistance, deep insights, and clarification of the figures by suggesting the transformation of short lines into directional arrows. My work has also greatly benefited from the patient review and exhaustive suggestions by many anonymous referees.

Special thanks are owed to the editors of the following websites, who have given generous hospitality to much of my work:

EconCurrents and *EconIntersect*, under the editorship of Dr. John B. Lounsbury, an econometrician. *EconIntersect* is among the 100 Top Websites for Enlightened Economists.

TalkMarkets, under the editorship of Boaz Berkowitz, the Founder and CEO of TalkMarkets with a brilliant career in financial affairs.

Mother Pelican: A Journal of Solidarity and Sustainability, under the editorship of Luis T. Gutierrez, Ph.D. in Industrial and Systems Engineering.

OpEdNews (OEN) under the editorship of Rob Kall, the author of *The Bottom-Up Revolution: Mastering the Emerging World of Connectivity* (2019). OEN is a technorati top 100 site.

Social Science Research Network (SSRN) has given hospitality to much of my work. My SSRN All-Time Author Citations ranking is 21,224. One published paper deposited on this platform recently made its Top Ten List.

ResearchGate, a professional network for scientists and researchers. On this platform, at last reading, I have received 10,440 reads and scored a Research Interest of 92.1, which is higher than 64% of ResearchGate members.

Google Scholar is keeping track of most of my work. And *Academia.edu*, in addition to hosting much of my work, has published a couple of my articles.

To the editors of my journal articles and published books, enormous heartfelt thanks.

Last but not least I would like to acknowledge a debt of gratitude to Harry Bego for allowing me to use his TExtract program.

Contents

1 Opening Our Minds to Concordian Economics 1
   1.1   A Prequel 1
   1.2   Introduction 2
   1.3   The Role of Hoarding: *An Ancient Problem, Ignored for Centuries* 5
        1.3.1   Hoarding, Investment, Growth, Poverty 6
        1.3.2   Hoarding and Inflation 6
        1.3.3   Hoarding and Deflation 7
        1.3.4   How to Deal with Hoarding 7
        1.3.5   Looking Forward 7
   1.4   How to Stop Inflation Cold 8
        1.4.1   Concordian Labor Policy 8
        1.4.2   Concordian Monetary Policy 9
        1.4.3   Concordian Fiscal Policy 11
        1.4.4   Concordian Industrial Policy 11
        1.4.5   Concordian Debt Policy as Mosaic Debt Jubilee 12
        1.4.6   A Couple of Final Points 13
        1.4.7   Creation of Jobs 13
        1.4.8   Jobs Without Disruptions 14
        1.4.9   Access to National Credit 14
        1.4.10 Cost of Capital Expenditures 14
        1.4.11 Consumer Share of Ownership 15
        1.4.12 Capitalism Is NOT the Real Problem 15
        1.4.13 A Final Plea 18
   1.5   Conclusion 18
   References 19

Part I Intellectual Interdependence

2 Politics and Economics 23
   2.1   What Is Being Done 23

		2.1.1	Politics with Meager Economics	23
	2.2	The Invisible Fault Line		25
		2.2.1	Some Invisible Consequences of Politics with Poor Economics	25
	2.3	What Ought to Be Done		27
		2.3.1	Politics Rich with Good Economics	27
	2.4	Conclusion		30
	References			31
3	**The Interdependence of Economic Rights and Responsibilities**			**33**
	3.1	Introduction		33
	3.2	A Web of Words		34
	3.3	A Nation Divided by Privileges		34
	3.4	A Nation United by Rights		35
	3.5	Once upon a Time		35
	3.6	Some Content of the *Doctrine* of Economic Justice		36
	3.7	A Bit on the Transition to the Modern World		37
	3.8	Toward the Reconstruction of Society		38
	3.9	From Mainstream Economics to Concordian Economics		39
	3.10	From the Doctrine to the Theory of Economic Justice		40
	3.11	A New Transition: From an Abstract to a Concrete Theory of Economic Justice		41
	3.12	The Resources of the Nation Are Potentially Infinite		41
	3.13	Four Economic Rights		42
		3.13.1	The Right of Access to Land and Natural Resources	42
		3.13.2	The Right of Access to National Credit	43
		3.13.3	The Right to Own the Wealth One Creates	44
		3.13.4	The Right to Protect What One Owns	45
	3.14	Who Are the Opponents?		46
	3.15	An Organic Policy		47
	3.16	The Larger Context		47
	3.17	Toward a Grand New World		47
	3.18	Conclusion		47
	Appendix: Some Nuances of Land Tax Values			48
	References			49
4	**A Peaceful March Toward Concordianism**			**51**
	4.1	Adieu Keynes, Adieu Hayek		51
		4.1.1	Introduction	51
		4.1.2	The Beginning	52
		4.1.3	End Points	53
		4.1.4	Concordian Economics as the Bridge to Reality	54
		4.1.5	Toward the Resolution of the Crisis	55
		4.1.6	There Is Nothing New	55

	4.1.7	From Two European to Four American Economists	56
	4.1.8	We Have Met Our Four American Economists	57
	4.1.9	Basic Rationale for the Four Macro Policies	58
	4.1.10	Conclusion	60
4.2	A Gentle Walk Away from 1% Capitalism and Marxism. Adieu Locke, Adieu Marx		61
	4.2.1	Introduction	61
	4.2.2	History, Oh History: The History of Economic Justice	61
	4.2.3	Three Fundamental Mistakes in Marx's Analysis	63
	4.2.4	The Emptiness of Property Rights	64
	4.2.5	How to Eliminate Blatant Injustices from Many Existing Property Rights?	65
4.3	Welcome Concordianism		66
	4.3.1	Introduction	66
	4.3.2	A Bit of Recent History	66
	4.3.3	Role of Governments	67
	4.3.4	Hints About the Transition	68
	4.3.5	A General Comment	68
	4.3.6	A Recap: Few Specifics About Economic Rights and Responsibilities	69
	4.3.7	Economic Rights and the Theory of Justice	71
	4.3.8	Four Horses of Inequality	71
	4.3.9	Inequality Benefits no One	72
	4.3.10	Conclusion	72
Appendix: A Few More Observations on Marxism			73
References			74

Part II Financial Interdependence

5	**King Cash**		79
5.1	Introduction		79
5.2	The Importance of Cash		80
5.3	Past: The Old American Way		80
	5.3.1	The Use of Cash	80
5.4	Present: Cash-Back—A Silver Lining		82
	5.4.1	Cash-Back	82
5.5	Future: Those Lazy Workers—They Are Gaming the System		84
	5.5.1	Those Lazy Workers	84
5.6	An Innovative Program		86
	5.6.1	All-Labor Reward Program	86
	5.6.2	Conclusion	89

5.7		Appendix: Some Considerations About Men's and Women's Work	89
5.8		Jobs—and Money—Through Financialization	90
	5.8.1	About Financialization	90
5.9		The Lender Is not a Hoarder. And What Is Interest?	92
	5.9.1	The Lender Is not a Hoarder	92
	5.9.2	What Is Interest?	93
	5.9.3	A Fruitful Curb of the Power of the Lender	95
	5.9.4	Conclusion	96
References			96

6 Whence Money … 99

6.1		How to Use Public Policy to Guide Accumulation Toward Virtuous Ends	99
	6.1.1	Summary of Section 6.1	99
	6.1.2	The Core of the Issues	100
	6.1.3	Structure of Section 6.1	101
	6.1.4	Aristotle's Criticism of Plato's Position	102
	6.1.5	Aristotle's Analysis of the Use of Money in Virtue Ethics	103
	6.1.6	Adam Smith and the Institution of Central Banking	104
	6.1.7	The Pessimistic Interlude	105
	6.1.8	The Greater Specificity of Concordian Monetary Policy	105
	6.1.9	The Greater Generality of Concordian Monetary Policy	106
	6.1.10	The Greater Rationality of Concordian Economics	106
	6.1.11	Some Cultural Consequences of Slavery	109
	6.1.12	A Discontinuity in the Conception of the Creation of Money	110
	6.1.13	Oresme: The Lost Link	111
	6.1.14	Conclusion	111
6.2		Money, Banking, and the Economic Process	113
	6.2.1	Introduction	113
6.3		Concordian Economics	114
	6.3.1	A Review of the Economic Process in the History of Economics	115
6.4		Money	115
	6.4.1	The Creation of Money	116
	6.4.2	The Government Keeps a Monopoly on the Creation of Cash	118
	6.4.3	Origin of Cash in the United States	119
6.5		Rules for the Creation of Money	119

	6.6	Pricing Policy	120
	6.7	Concluding Comments	120
	References	....	123
7	**Where-To Money**		125
	7.1	The Current State of Affairs	125
		7.1.1 Where Does Money Go in a Stock Market Crash?	125
		7.1.2 The State of Unpreparedness of the Economics Profession	125
		7.1.3 A Continuing State of Crisis	126
		7.1.4 How Can We Ever Get Out of the Current Spectrum of Opinion?	128
		7.1.5 What Is Amiss with All Current National Monetary Systems?	129
	7.2	What Can the Private Sector Do	130
		7.2.1 Operation "Defuse the Bomb"	130
		7.2.2 Who Are the Potential Supporters of This Proposal?	132
		7.2.3 Some Further Recommendations	133
	7.3	What Can the Central Bank Do	134
		7.3.1 Operation "Mend the Fed"	134
		7.3.2 A Bit on the Rationale of This Proposal	135
		7.3.3 Some Expected Effects of Both Operations	140
	7.4	From Money Controlling People to People Controlling Money	147
		7.4.1 Oh, the Rich	147
		7.4.2 Time Is Running Short	149
	References	....	151
8	**Project Financial Independence**		153
	8.1	Introduction	153
	8.2	How to Obtain Financial Independence?	156
	8.3	A Bit of Politics	158
	8.4	Time is Running Out	159
	8.5	Three Fundamental Reasons for the Urgency of Financial Independence	160
	8.6	One More Effect	161
	8.7	Conclusion	161
	References	....	161

Part III Physical Interdependence

9	**Toward Economic, Ecological, and Human Interdependence**		167
	9.1	Some Ecological Effects of Concordian Economics	167
		9.1.1 Introduction	167

		9.1.2	On Ecological Effects of Concordian Monetary Policy	168
		9.1.3	On Ecological Effects of Fiscal Policy: Present and Future	169
		9.1.4	On Ecological Effects of Kelsonian/Concordian Labor Policy	173
		9.1.5	On Ecological Effects of Concordian Industrial Policy	174
	9.2	A Reverse Perspective		176
		9.2.1	Some Tasks Ahead of Us in Community Development	176
		9.2.2	Coronavirus and Economic Interdependence	179
		9.2.3	A Deep Cultural Shift	184
		9.2.4	A Few Issues About Fluoridation	185
	9.3	Appendix		188
		9.3.1	Rebuild the Downtown Through Racial Harmony	189
		9.3.2	Why Wall Street Ought to Favor a Gradual Decline in the Cost of Land	191
		9.3.3	Why Countries Shouldn't Sell Their Natural Resources to Foreigners	194
		9.3.4	Conclusion	200
		9.3.5	Functional Integration of Management Tasks	200
	References			204
10	Two Published and Two Unpublishable (?) Urban Plans			207
	10.1	Introduction		207
	10.2	First Published One		208
	10.3	Second Published One		208
	10.4	A First Unpublishable (?) Plan		209
	10.5	A Second Unpublishable (?) Plan		210
	10.6	And then… A Proposal by My Nephew Gianni Papa to Use Marine Water		211
	10.7	The Proposal		211
		10.7.1	Component Parts of the Mechanical System	212
		10.7.2	A Field of Possible Innovations	212
		10.7.3	Broad Cost Estimates	213
		10.7.4	Who Will Be the First to Create Such a System?	213
	10.8	Our Survival		213
	References			213

Part IV Human Interdependence

11	Ethics in Concordian Economics		217
	11.1	Introduction	217
	11.2	Ethics in Concordian Economic Theory	218

		11.2.1	An Addendum on Ethics and the Theory of Distribution of the Values of Ownership Rights	220
	11.3		Ethics in Concordian Economic Policy	221
	11.4		The Content of Economic Justice	222
	11.5		Justice and Charity	223
	11.6		Ethics in Concordian Economic Practices	224
	11.7		Lack of an Existing Tool Kit	224
	11.8		New Tools to Control Economic Practices	225
	11.9		Conclusion	230
	References			231
12	**Whence Poverty**			**233**
	12.1		Introduction	233
	12.2		Scarcity and Fear of Scarcity	233
	12.3		Fear of Scarcity as the Mother of All Evil	236
	12.4		How the Rich Make Themselves Richer	237
	12.5		The Poor Make Us Rich	239
	12.6		The Creators of Poverty	239
	12.7		The Rich Are *Not* the Creators of Poverty	240
	12.8		Were I Wicked	243
	12.9		The Rich Are *Not* the Creators of Jobs	243
	12.10		Sundry Consequences	243
	References			245
13	**Oh, the Bancor**			**247**
	13.1		Introduction	247
	13.2		Let Us not Pervert Keynes' Thought	247
		13.2.1	How to Set Things Right	248
	13.3		Two Crucial Issues in Foreign Trade	248
		13.3.1	Who Pays for the Tariffs?	249
		13.3.2	Who Benefits?	249
		13.3.3	Long Run Issues	249
		13.3.4	Effects on the Balance of Payments	249
		13.3.5	Two Crucial, Hidden Issues	250
	13.4		Fish Stocks and Our Balance of Payments	251
		13.4.1	Why This Imbalance?	251
	13.5		How to Solve the Many Money Woes of the World Using the Bancor	255
		13.5.1	When Should the xBancor Be Created?	255
		13.5.2	What Value Should Be Assigned to the xBancor?	256
		13.5.3	What Is the Role of the IMF and the World Bank in a Bancor Regimen?	256
		13.5.4	What Are the Benefits of Creating Bancors?	256
		13.5.5	Short-Term Effects	256
		13.5.6	Long-Term Effects	257
		13.5.7	Is There an Ecological Side to This Proposal?	257

	13.6	Conclusion	258
	References		258
14	**Economics of Justice and Peace in the World**		**259**
	14.1	The National Scene	259
	14.2	The Bancor as an Instrument of National Peace	261
	14.3	The International Scene	262
	14.4	The Grand Bargain	263
	14.5	The Bancor International Order as the End of the Unipolar World	263
	14.6	AGAIN: The Price of U.S. Dominance of World Markets	264
	14.7	Louis D. Brandeis on Compromise	265
	14.8	An Unexpected Benefit	265
	14.9	Can the Bancor International Order Be Created?	265
	14.10	A Look Forward	266
	Appendix on Immigration		266
	References		266

Conclusion 269

Index 273

About the Author

Carmine Gorga is President of The Somist Institute and a Fulbright Scholar. He is the founder of Concordian economics.

The Federal Reserve System has graciously suggested that his proposal for the creation of a new monetary system ought to be presented to state and federal representatives. He has been described as an economist for the modern world.

During 50 years of research and publication, 27 of them powerfully assisted by Prof. Franco Modigliani, a Nobel Laureate in economics at MIT, and for 23 years by Prof. M. L. Burstein, Dr. Gorga has developed a new system of thought in which everything is logically and harmoniously related to everything else. This is a system that allows us to pass from Rationalism to Relationalism. Concordian economics sits at the core of Relationalism.

He holds a Ph.D. in Political Science from the University of Naples and an M.A. in International Relations from the John Hopkins School of Advanced International Studies (SAIS) in Washington, DC. The University of Naples is the University of Thomas Aquinas and Benedetto Croce, the first university to establish a separate chair for economics (separate from the moral sciences).

He is a naturalized American citizen, born in the Deep South of Southern Italy under Mussolini. He is trying all that he can not to die under an autocrat.

He was born in the year of the Lord, as they used to say, 1935. That was in the midst of the Great Depression, which was soon followed by WW2—when the hoarding of basic foodstuff went rampant. The smell of burned flesh is still in his nostrils; and the pains of hunger too widespread to discuss. Clearly, he has deep reasons to be a practicing economist and a pacifist.

Chapter 1
Opening Our Minds to Concordian Economics

Abstract If we mention any topic in economics nowadays, we find a crisis lurking somewhere on its way. Either Concordian economics is capable of solving these crises or it is not worth the paper it is written on. To make the best use of it, we must keep three concerns constantly in mind. The system must minimize Hoarding, minimize Inflation, and it must create as many Jobs as requested by the population. To observe these goals in action, we need a kaleidoscopic view of the economic system: moving our point of view just a little bit, we see a completely different universe, but always an integrated universe. Looking at it another way, if we engage in true dialogue we discover that there is nothing new under the sun. Only the trends have accelerated their pace. It is this acceleration that has brought us to the brink of disaster. Whether we have enough time to avoid the precipice or not, in this volume we will study a number of recommendations on what needs to be done—for the benefit of everyone. The wise Benjamin Franklin knew it all along: "If we do not hang together, we shall surely hang separately."

1.1 A Prequel

How to start this book? This might be an opportune moment to contemplate the Declaration of Economic Interdependence, a document that I prepared in 2012 for the United Nations Rio+20 Conference:

Fully appreciative of the many blessings of the Declaration of Independence, it might now be an appropriate time to draft.

For this reason, interspersed through some unavoidable repetition, the Patient Reader will discover many new wrinkles, new intuitions, and important analyses in the construction of Concordian economics. The patient Reader will discover that most repetitions serve to obtain a slightly different view, a more comprehensive view of any topic. A cause might have effects on a variety of fields. We will not examine all the effects of a cause. We will do our best. Besides, if only we already had economic justice as a social, economic, and political operating system, many of the recommendations expressed in this book would already be implemented; they would already be with us, rather than being a possible distant envisioned world.

A Declaration of Economic Interdependence

Whereas the Declaration of (Political) Independence has, without open discussion, been transformed into a Declaration of Personal Independence,

Whereas this ideology has given rise to the Age of Entitlements, an age dominated by the conception that there can ever be rights without responsibilities,

Whereas the lack of personal and civic responsibility has generated the conception of Life as One-Against-All,

Whereas this emphasis on our own welfare—independent, if not at the expense, of the welfare of our fellow citizens—has created economic insecurity for everyone, rich and poor alike,

We affirm that our greatest political need is to build a society in which the reality of **Economic Interdependence** is fully acknowledged.

In this society, we declare,

the fundamental conception of Life is

One-With-All

and we trust that the effect will be economic jubilation for all.

In order to build such a society

we are called upon to realize the political ideals of

Liberty, Justice, and Goodwill toward one and all.

In order to build such a society, our challenge is to deny

all structures of individual and societal selfishness and

to affirm

The Principles of Economic Justice.

Put another way, Concordian economics brings to fruition the analysis of economic matters started by Aristotle, Augustine, Aquinas, Adam Smith, and Keynes and Hayek (**combined**). In the immortal words of Prof. Mario Rizzo, we might say that all modern economics is a footnote.

In the process, we will untie as many knots in our reasoning as possible.

1.2 Introduction

O Reader, please, close your eyes. No one exists around you. Not even you.

It is now time to reconstruct the world to our liking. You exist. All set to spring into this wondrous world: you think, you feel, you love. You are ready to enjoy all the beauty of the universe: the stars, the birds, a rose, the majestic trees, the savannas, the dolphins, Baby girls, Baby boys, Books.[1]

---

[1] What does it mean to be in love with all these things and many more? It means to be emotionally in close relation with them. No, this is not a vacuous appeal. This is the root of true ecology. And it means to be faithful to the equivalence of matter to energy and to spirit. Personally, I feel that I am a guest here in the universe paying no rent.

1.2 Introduction

Would you not like to have people around you who feel the same way? Enjoy the world the same way you do? Wonder of wonders, you talk and people respond appropriately.

A "realistic" view of things today convinces us that the world is not like that at all. Frank Ramsey put it in an elegant rhetorical form. The ancient wisdom of my hometown, Roccadaspide, puts it this way. To the question "Where are you going?" Most interlocutors answer: "I carry onions."

The world is infested with discord. Where did we go wrong?

This is not a new vision or a new pleading. "In everything you do, act without grumbling or arguing; prove yourselves innocent and straightforward, children of God beyond reproach in the midst of a twisted and depraved generation—among whom you shine like the stars in the sky." This was Paul to the Philippians (2:14–15). Was Paul's exhortation a retrieval of the ancient wisdom of Psalm 4: "O men, how long will your hearts be closed,/ will you love what is futile and seek what is false"?

Hope springs eternal. Concordian economics will help us create the best possible world that we have ever desired. No, this is not a personal idiosyncratic view. Professor William J. Baumol, reviewing one of my papers in a personal communication wrote: "You are certainly striking out boldly in new directions and your work promises to yield new insights and results." This is not a singular assessment. Reviewing the same paper, Prof. Michele Boldrin remarked: "I find admirable your effort to combine insights from so varied and different areas of research into a new and fascinating picture."

Volume 1 has given us the tools to create a new world. The world does need our help. Let us work together and see what happens.

* * *

Let us give a quick look at what we are leaving behind. Modern scientific economics offers us little more than a Money Mystery. How can we ever liberate ourselves from the tentacles of the Money Mystery?

Modern scientific economics is made up of money only. Money, mind you, never defined; never quite understood. What we know, or pretend to know, is what money does, the functions, not the definition of money. And money does an awful lot of awful things. How do we get rid of this Money Monster?

Technically speaking, at the core of modern economics there is a widely acknowledged "black box." Nothing, really.

Obviously, what needed to be done and what we did was to fill that "black box." We filled it with the analysis of the economic process.

Therefore, abandoning the poverty of the current "monetary discourse " we can now joyfully plunge into the richness of the Concordian universe, the richness of the economic process, which results from an integration of the Production of real wealth, Distribution of the economic value of ownership rights over the wealth as it is created, and the Consumption or expenditure of monetary wealth to purchase real wealth. An image helps (Fig. 1.1).

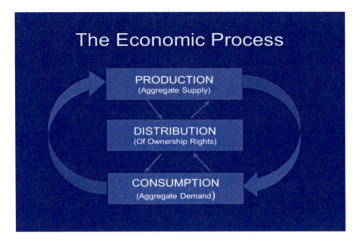

Fig. 1.1 The Economic Process

Taking a leaf from Galileo, we can plaintively ask whether we could have ever put those things—real wealth, ownership rights, and money—in the economic process. Real wealth is not just a name. Its apperception creates a mental framework that will allow ecologists and physicists to work in tandem with economists. Our last best hope. If the collaboration of such powerful minds will not save us from ecological disaster, nothing will.

Ownership of the wealth that we produce is not just a rich verbal expression. Its recognition creates a framework of mind that yields concord in our daily discourse about production and distribution of wealth. A Concordian monetary system will grant us a paradigm shift from money controlling people to *people controlling money*.

But why extoll the virtues of Concordian economics any longer; let us roll up our sleeves and put those promises into our daily reality: There are three "big" interrelated issues that form the substratum of our work: Hoarding, Inflation, and Jobs (H.I.J.). They challenge us with problems that have to be resolved. Concordian economics can resolve them either directly or indirectly, both in theory and practice. We have to keep levels of Hoarding and Inflation as low as possible, and we have to create as many Jobs as necessary. Collaboration of the reader is required to keep these strictly interrelated issues constantly in the back of our minds—even when they are not explicitly mentioned in the pages that follow. Again, to observe the operation of these goals in action, we need a kaleidoscopic view of the economic system: moving our point of view just a little bit, we see a completely different universe, but always an integrated universe. Hoarding, for instance, has direct effects on the accumulation of wealth, hence on poverty; but then it also has an effect on the resistance to any form of debt jubilee as one possible attack against inflation. It is less evident perhaps, but does not inordinate accumulation of land and industrial capacity in a few hands have a negative effect on jobs? Let us get to work.

1.3 The Role of Hoarding: *An Ancient Problem, Ignored for Centuries*

From Moses to Locke, everyone knew about Hoarding. Ever since Adam Smith, nobody does; see, e.g., Gorga (2010). Locke successfully canceled our understanding of economic justice, whose key content is represented by a vigilant struggle against Hoarding; see, e.g., Gorga (2009). Explicitly, ever since the days of Adam Smith, economists have been under formal obligation not to utter the word Hoarding. Their economic models do not, and indeed cannot, include Hoarding. Their models say that all wealth that is not consumed is saved—and saving equals investment. Therefore, no room is left for Hoarding in their models. Hence, economists have to maintain that Hoarding does not exist.

And yet, the daily reality tells us otherwise. Since the Great Financial Crisis of 2008, for instance, we have seen headlines such as Europe banks hoarding ECB cash, threatening credit crunch (2012), Banks across Europe are considering taking a drastic step to avoid negative rates (2016), and Bank of America Clients Hoard Cash at Highest Level in Two Decades (2022). This ancient problem first became an outsized problem in the US during the Dot.com Crash (2001)—if not during the Great Depression—and the Global Financial Crisis (GFC) of 2008, and then shifted to Europe. After all this time, we might have acquired a more dispassionate, a more controlled, a more scientific view of the issue. But the third reference above shows the problem of hoarding money persists. Besides, it is not only money that can be hoarded: everything can. Gold, for sure; but also land. And foodstuff? The immediate effect of hoarding of any item in the supply chain is manifested by an increase in prices. Do you feel the pain of a penniless mother who is trying to feed her baby?

Having captured Hoarding in Volume 1 and made it an integral constituent part of the structure of economic theory, see, also Gorga (2023), we can now try to subdue its existence in real life.[2] Hoarding is an **ineradicable part of the human existence**. We all **fear scarcity**, and Hoarding is supposed to create a cocoon of security for us.

It is of these presumptions that we *have to disabuse* men's and women's minds. The theory and practice of Interdependence assures us that we can have economic security only if **all human beings have security**. *Security for all is assured by a reduction of Hoarding to the lowest amount possible.*

Revolution!

With Concordianism there is no longer going to be a struggle of any one against everyone else, but our own **internal struggle** against each one of us.

---

[2] Professor M. L. Burstein, one of the sharpest minds in economics, used to call me the "Hoarding Maven."

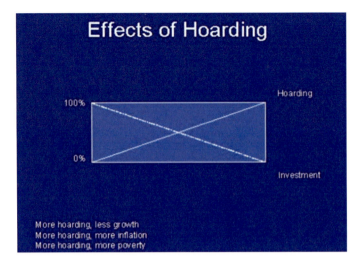

Fig. 1.2 The Hoarding-Investment Nexus

1.3.1 Hoarding, Investment, Growth, Poverty

For contravening all the rules of logic, we have freed the economic discourse of the relation of "equality" between saving and investment. In Volume 1 we analyzed a new relation, a relation of complementarity between Hoarding and Investment. This relation allows us to recover a more comprehensive understanding of hoarding. A great tool to this effect is the well-known Lorenz diagram. As it can be seen from the diagram below, the relation between Hoarding and Investment allows us to make three fundamental observations: More hoarding in the economy, less growth; more hoarding, more inflation; more hoarding, more poverty.

More hoarding clearly equals less investment—hence, less economic growth. Again, the relationship between hoarding and poverty is of immediate comprehension: more is accumulated by the few, less is available to the many (FIg. 1.2).

1.3.2 Hoarding and Inflation

The explanation of why when there is more hoarding there is more inflation resides in this simple fact. When one buys property and keeps it in a passive state, the money used to buy that wealth remains in circulation and creates an imbalance with the amount of wealth that is for sale in the market. Hence, prices rise. That is the seed of inflation.

1.3.3 Hoarding and Deflation

The difficult nature of hoarding is revealed by this simple fact. At times when financial and industrial corporations hoard cash, hoarding performs a deflationary function. This is a peculiar function that, apart from few aberrant cases (and the general case of economies with insignificant financial institutions), occurs only at the bottom of any crisis and is quantitatively miniscule when put in relation to the value of the economic system over the entire business cycle.

1.3.4 How to Deal with Hoarding

Rather than remaining on these fascinating issues, which are treated at some length in my work, I would like to stress the key conclusion that can be reached on the basis of the new paradigm. Professor Michael Emmett Brady (2007), one of the clearest minds in economics these days (full disclosure, I am the junior author of a paper we published together[3]), points out in his review of one of my books that the phenomenon of hoarding is not new. Hoarding is at least four thousand years old. Michael Brady highlights: "Keynes states this on pp. 241–42 and 351–52 [of the *General Theory*] but does not emphasize it for his economist audience. G[orga] emphasizes it and convincingly identifies it as the main problem" of "a destabilizing boom-bust business cycle over time."

The key conclusion of my work is this. *Do not try to fight hoarding head-on.* You will lose, because hoarding is rooted in an essential human characteristic: the instinctive search for economic security. Fight, instead, all those **institutions** that increase economic insecurity and compel human beings to hoard wealth in order to find some personal, individual sanity in a crazed world.

1.3.5 Looking Forward

The complexity of the issues is revealed by the circularity of events: the more people hoard, the more destabilized the economic system becomes. But the individual, alone, is left with no rational alternative. **It is society as a whole that creates insecurity, and society alone can break the vicious circle**.

How? Here's a hint: **By running the economy to the tune of justice**.

To admit to the existence of hoarding and to include this phenomenon into macroeconomic models is the easy part. The hard part is to find the right economic policy to keep hoarding always at the lowest possible level. A brief introduction to these policies follows.

---

[3] Brady and Gorga (2009).

1.4 How to Stop Inflation Cold

Over the years, I have written in many venues about the extreme importance of four economic rights and responsibilities and their transformation into four Concordian economic policies. My writings on this topic have consistently received the most readers, all over the world.

To my unending surprise, spurred by our immediate needs I have recently discovered another major—**major**—ability of Concordian economics; see, Gorga (2022). Here it is: With the policies offered by Concordian economics, we can stop inflation cold.

Let us see how.

1.4.1 Concordian Labor Policy

For its expected immediate results, the key, most immediate policy to institute—ideally, all over the world—is the Concordian Labor Policy.

Labor unions and politicians, all over the world, must stop pushing for "higher" wages.

I know, at first look this policy appears to be cruel and capitalistic.

Labor unions and politicians must instead push for **equity distribution** of the value of the wealth created by workers and employees. Before looking at the advantages of this proposed policy, let us acquire a deeper knowledge of the negative consequences of the push for higher wages.

1.4.1.1 Some Negative Consequences of the Push for Higher Wages

What are some of the immediate consequences of the push for higher wages? Corporations do sooner or later raise their prices. Most of them will have to raise their prices if they want to survive in business. With higher prices, inflation raises its ugly head; the flames of inflation devour the temporary benefits of high wages.

Much damage is inflicted upon humankind from the push for high wages. People who are not in the labor force, people on fixed income are forced to pay higher prices, all the while they receive no personal benefit from higher wages, which at least temporarily are enjoyed by people in the labor force.

The push for higher wages carries indeed cruel consequences for the poor; they become automatically poorer by the moment.

Not the least negative consequence from the push for higher wages is the negative effects in relation to competition from abroad. This is the reason why we in America have ceded our manufacturing power to foreign nations. Again, low-income people and the poor who badly need a job to survive are punished the most.

1.4.1.2 Some Benefits of Fair Equity Distribution

Legally, workers today are "consultants" to the corporation for which they work. This is the practical import of the labor contract. Whatever wages they receive, that is all they can expect. The owners of the corporations, instead, benefit from the capital appreciation of their stocks. It is this value that needs to be more equitably distributed. Capitalists do not deserve it. They get a bad name just for this misappropriation of wealth that is not created by them, but by workers and employees of the corporation.

Today, especially in the United States, thanks to the genius of Louis O. Kelso, there is a legal mechanism through which workers can share in the fair division of capital appreciation: this is the fabled Employee Stock Ownership Plan (ESOP).

There are many advantages to the use of this tool. There are fiscal benefits for the corporation, and workers acquire stocks without having to spend a cent of their scarce supply of money.

There is a positive outcome for everyone. Workers who are now part owners of the corporation in which they work tend to work harder and more imaginatively to create more value for everyone. Not the least benefit of this policy is its ability to take fire out from the conversation between capitalists and socialists. From a poisonous ground, this policy moves people to positions of reciprocal respect.

Labor unions must link their membership dues to the apportionment of equity in the distribution of stock ownership.

American capitalists and American workers know a good thing when they see it. During the last few years, the number of workers belonging to ESOPs has surpassed the (declining) number of workers belonging to labor unions.

Academic economists seem to be unaware of the existence of ESOPs and those economists who are aware of them often disparage them.

Can we imagine the day in which ESOPs gain widespread recognition and acceptance?

1.4.2 Concordian Monetary Policy

This is a second tool to stop inflation cold. Concordian Monetary Policy calls for the Fed, and every Central Bank in the world, to follow these three basic rules for the creation of loans:

1. issue loans only to create real wealth;
2. issue loans only to individual entrepreneurs, to corporations with ESOPs, and to local public agencies with taxing power;
3. issue loans at cost.

The first rule will stop inflation of the value of financial assets cold. We have to stop feeding the monster of financialization. If the price of financial assets grows to the sky, the entire chain of economics is unavoidably affected. See the parallel increases in the cost of houses. (*Pace* the current definition of inflation as affecting only some consumer goods.)

Withdrawing public funds from financial institutions, no damage will be done. The value of financial assets might still continue to grow if the source of credit is restricted to the private market.

1.4.2.1 Make Loans at Cost

The distinction between public and private financial markets automatically makes it clear that any public agency like the Fed ought not to make a profit out of its operations. Thus, such loans must be issued at cost. And when such loans are issued at cost, a whole slew of positive consequences follows: credit becomes affordable on Main Street; by obtaining loans at cost, local economies will flourish; these activities will acquire an immediate competitive advantage. In some cases, the competitive advantage will be such that local enterprises will be competitive again in relation to foreign enterprises, which generally benefit from their lower local labor costs.

And speaking of labor costs, if unions favor the policy of equity distribution mentioned above, with the Fed's restraint of issuing loans only to enterprises that produce real wealth of tables and chairs, the manufacturing power of the United States will be restored to its former glory.

Environmentalists fear not. One of the many implications of the policies advocated here is that financially secure people will reduce waste and degradation of our natural resources. Production for no other purpose than to repay debts will come to a screeching halt.

In a manifestation of moral fortitude, the Fed has given a nod of approval to this policy. In a personal communication to this writer, the Fed has suggested that I should present this proposal ("for the creation of a new monetary system") to my "state and federal representatives."

1.4.2.2 Creation of Money

Last but not the least point to be made about a Concordian monetary policy is that this is the fulfillment of the hopes and efforts of our beloved Benjamin Franklin. It is he who gave the Government, rather than the bankers, the power to create and distribute public money.

Unfortunately, Alexander Hamilton led the country to a surreptitious counter-revolution when he created the first Bank of the United States on the model of the Bank of England.[4]

It is high time, as William Jennings Bryan advocated long ago, that we restore the "money of the Constitution." The full sentence is pregnant of more meaning: "…when

---

[4] For the many nuances in this transition and later developments of American monetary policy, see, e.g., Brown (2023).

1.4 How to Stop Inflation Cold   11

we have restored the money of the Constitution, all other necessary reforms will be possible, and… until that is done there is no reform that can be accomplished."

How true is this realization still today is an issue that is conveniently placed under wrap.

Concordian Monetary Policy ought to be instaurated any time soon. It must be instaurated the day after a major crash in the Stock Market, if we want to minimize the devastation that generally flows from such crashes.

1.4.3 *Concordian Fiscal Policy*

As Henry George and the Georgists recommend, as soon as possible we ought to raise taxes, no longer on income and capital appreciation, but on the basis of the market value of land and natural resources. We would then stop penalizing enterprise and initiative.

This policy will have two major deflationary effects: the cost of government will be reduced, and the price of land will be abated.

The first condition becomes apparent as soon as it is considered that, with the application of Concordian Economic Policies, the functions of government will naturally and organically be shrinking. Who will beg for a hand-out, when the cupboard is full?

Taxes on land will convince owners of latifundia, the large estates strangling our cities and towns (let alone the large tracts of land in downtown areas), to sell some of their lands: An increase in the supply of land will induce a reduction in the price of the land. Homes will become more affordable—for benefits of home ownership, see, e.g., Sodini et al. (2023). Horrible problems associated with homelessness will be abated; see. e.g., Kristof (2023).

All enterprises will be affected by deflationary trends in the costs of land and natural resources; everyone will benefit. (Landowners will benefit from lower costs of doing business if they are in business as well as lower cost of consumer goods.)

The discourse about the history of natural resources is even more eventful. How did oil and mineral extractors ever succeed in getting subsidies for resource exhaustion (depletion allowances) rather than compensating the "community" for the extraction of the public's **common** resources, our common wealth?

1.4.4 *Concordian Industrial Policy*

The application of the Brandeis Rule will do its part in reducing the flames of inflation. The immediate effect will be a freeze in the price of assets of the largest corporations: Since they cannot be bought or sold, their value will stabilize around their true worth. This effect will have deflationary influences.

Most of all, those financial—and human—resources that today are devoted to buying and selling other corporations will be directed toward the internal needs of corporations. If these resources are devoted to stabilizing the cost of labor and materials, the deflationary effect will not take long to be felt.

Do consider the ensemble: market wages, not high wages; loans at cost, rather than loans at interest; lower income taxes and corporate income taxes; concentration of human and financial resources on the internal needs of corporations.

Is this a dream? An impossible dream? Or is it a near-eternal quest to create the polis, a social organization in which, as Martin Luther King, Jr. so magistrally put it, men and women "will not be judged by the color of their skin but by the content of their character."

1.4.5 Concordian Debt Policy as Mosaic Debt Jubilee

> Should We Cancel Student Debt?
> No!
> We Should Cancel All Debt.

Most kings and emperors worthy of their robes declared a debt jubilee upon elevation to the throne. It seems that the Israelites practiced a debt jubilee every seven years. This policy hides all sorts of wisdom and suffers only from an apparent loss in the value of money.

Money has value when it can be exchanged for real goods and services. When such correspondence does not exist, what one holds is a hot succession of zeros. These zeros kill the enterprise and initiative of way too many people.

If debts are not repaid within seven years (this is true especially for business loans), it means that the incurring—and the granting—of a loan was a mistake. Perpetuating a mistake does not do any good to anyone. Implied here is a nuance: loan makers must share a responsibility in the execution of loans. (Too many loans are granted for the satisfaction of immediate greed both on the part of the borrower and the lender.)

There is another not too subtle distinction in a debt jubilee. Capital loans ought to be encouraged; consumer loans ought to be discouraged at all costs. Capital loans have the potential of creating economic freedom for debtors and creditors; consumer loans definitely enslave the borrower. They also foster an inappropriate manifestation of a desire for immediate gratification.

Let us stress here something very important. For a faithful application of the Mosaic Debt Jubilee, we should follow the practices of the best Credit Unions. We need an institutional change in our financial practices—and a thorough reconsideration of our current consumer credit habits. We need to avoid lending money with terms exceeding seven years. We should have a hard evaluation of mortgages extending over 20, 30, 40 years. We need above all refrain from issuing loans for the purchase of consumer goods and especially loans that have a fairly certain likelihood of default.

1.4.6 A Couple of Final Points

To this short list, we must now add the damage that inflation is causing to the reputation of politicians and bankers in addition to the reputation of economists.

To paraphrase Brandeis, it is economists who need Concordian economics most.

Rather than going blind into the future, why don't we reconnect with a tried-and-true tradition, the tradition of the American Progressive Movement?

Instead of following any longer two flawed European economists, Keynes and Hayek, *unless we study their positions as necessarily complementary,* why don't we listen to four powerful American voices? Benjamin Franklin, Henry George, Louis D. Brandeis, and Louis O. Kelso are their names. They never met, but together they offer a powerful system of economic thought.

With them, morality does not take second place to efficiency. And notice that efficiency generally refers solely to financial efficiency. Morality is shunted aside.

1.4.7 Creation of Jobs

Soon after the abatement of the effects of Hoarding and Inflation in our H.I.J. program, we recognize that what the world craves most is the creation of Jobs. So, let us pay some undivided attention to the topic. Economic development has become a synonym for job creation. And it is indeed essential to create jobs. As I have mentioned here and there, jobs are essential to preserve the dignity of individual human beings. Dignity granted by others, for sure; dignity granted to oneself is perhaps at the center of a civilized society.

The creation of jobs has become a bane of our existence. Some people ask for—and obtain—sumptuous subsidies so they can create jobs. Some people ask for—and obtain—deep disruptions of our urban environment so they can create jobs. Some people ask for—and obtain—permission to burn ancestral woods and forests so they can create jobs. The details of these processes are too gruesome to be noted here. Sneak peep: Does not corruption of our political environment travel on such premises?

Here, we will rather attempt to give an answer to the fundamental question: "So, how can we create jobs without such disruptions?"

The deepest long-term effect of controlling Hoarding is the opportunity to create jobs without disruptions. This is indeed a deep issue, rarely observed, rarely analyzed. Somehow, we have been led to believe that it is OK to disrupt our social, economic, and ecological environment if the result is "the creation of jobs." Well, no. Concordian economics *has* the capacity to create jobs without such pitiful disruption.

1.4.8 Jobs Without Disruptions

Many presidents attempt to create jobs throughout the world through tariff controls—and subsidies. While jobs must be created in each state, disruptions are likely to occur in world trade and make net positive effects of this policy option all but uncertain. But, certainly, world trade patterns must be studied to make sure that there are no unfair trade deals in existence. If found, these deals must be repaired.

Nothing special to add about subsidies, except emphasizing that we ought to put a stop to them: most often subsidies are offered, but jobs are hard to materialize.

Beyond that, Concordian economics offers many ways of creating jobs without accompanying disruptions—especially through better performance of necessary policies.

A reverse policy is also being explored in Concordian economics: **receiving income without performing a job outside the home**, but *not as an entitlement*, which implies no responsibilities—rather as a right, a right that ensues through the performance of interesting responsibilities.

1.4.9 Access to National Credit

The monetary policy advocated by Concordian economics is not supposed to be created in a vacuum. Access to national credit is made available only to individual entrepreneurs, to cooperatives, and to corporations with an Employee Stock Ownership Plan (ESOP) in their governance. ESOPs, by themselves, offer a major competitive advantage: ESOPs tend to keep wages low. Employees who are owners of the corporations for which they work know that wages are payment in advance of profits. By keeping wages as low as possible, they create competitive advantages for their corporations that make the pot of profits at year-end that much sweeter. The most important effect of this type of financing is that employees/owners are unlikely to tolerate such disruptions as poisoning the aquifers or producing consumer products that in the long run ruin the health of the population. ESOPs preserve and produce jobs, mostly without disruptions.

1.4.10 Cost of Capital Expenditures

Sacrifices of quick and dirty profits will become more tolerable in a regimen of Concordian monetary policy because, by issuing loans at cost, the cost of capital expenditures will be lower than it is at present.

Most certainly, the reduction in the cost of capital expenditure will make it much easier not only for private entrepreneurs, but for cities and towns and state governments to afford the creation of new infrastructure jobs: bridges are more likely to be repaired; new roads, new airports, new schools will be created.

If necessary jobs are created, the demand for unnecessary disruptive jobs will be automatically lowered.

1.4.11 Consumer Share of Ownership

Concordian economics also recommends that access to national credit be granted only to corporations that have a Consumer Ownership Plan (CSOP) in their governance. Concordian economics recognizes that it is consumers who keep corporations alive during an entire fiscal year. Thus, these corporations ought to grant their customers a share of the profits at year-end. Actually, this expense ought to be calculated as cost of doing business. Hence, profits will be distributed only after taking care of this obligation of the firm. Sales slips will determine how much is owed to each customer. Let us imagine a world in which Burger King, and Macy's, and—indeed—Visa and Master Card distribute a certain percentage of their profits to their customers at the end of the year. Is that not a completely new economic world? And it is a world that is fast coming along via a great variety of cash-back programs, no need to create unnecessary jobs.

And such a disbursement of income occurs via a set of responsibilities: the responsibility to buy products from such and such a corporation; the responsibility to preserve the sales slips and to keep good accounting practices.

The road to CSOPs is paved with a set of major promises. When CSOPs are displayed in full vigor, there will not be any more any need to create unnecessary jobs—or to distribute entitlements, of course—to sustain people's lives; such jobs too often only disrupt our ecology.

In the course of our examination of the likely effects of the application of Concordian economics, we will meet an even more exciting form of creation of income with payment for work done in existing jobs: **housework**. The day will come when the person who performs the work will present the bill, not to husband or wife, but to the Government. A peek into the substance of the issue: how much wealth did Steve Jobs' mother create?

Indeed, there are many more effects that flow from Concordian economic policies. As a whole, the Government can reduce its intrusion into economic affairs, because the Market will provide. Good capitalism will then be in full bloom.

1.4.12 Capitalism Is NOT the Real Problem

It is 1% Capitalism that is the Problem; see, Gorga (2021b).

It is NOT the "best economy ever" generally acquired at the cost of keeping unions weak and the environment degraded? Are there not people who want to work, and cannot find a job? Due to the peculiar statistics about employment and unemployment, we don't even know how many millions of them there are. Nor are trade wars something to write home about.

Two more conditions explain the status of the current economy: steady, high budget deficits and stratospheric infusions of *our* money into the financial system through operations of the Federal Reserve System.

No, it is not Capitalism that is creating such horrible conditions as the ones in which people in the upper and middle classes die by overwork, and the poor die horrible deaths for lack of work.

It is the 1% Capitalism.

It is economic inequality that is the rot at the core of our lives.

I should qualify that. In our heart of hearts, we common mortals know that. Even card-carrying members of the One Percenters, from Warren Buffet down, know that the problem is economic inequality.

It is the rear guard composed of economists who do NOT seem to know that.

I should qualify this, too. The economics profession bifurcates. Some say that inequality is a Law of Nature about which there is nothing to be done; some even say that inequality is GOOD for us, otherwise we would not have—what? The "economy"? Not too many economists go that far, but certainly many maintain that inequality is good for GROWTH.

No, I should qualify this too. Even card-carrying members of the economics profession know that inequality is the rot at the core of 1% Capitalism. Inequality is the tree; 1% Capitalism is the fruit.

Indeed, the literature produced by economists on this topic uses untold terabytes of data. I feel the pain of computers groaning under that weight.

Trouble is that this brave phalanx of economists searches for inequality EVERYWHERE—BUT IN THE ECONOMY.

Thus, the spread of pixie dust that obfuscates the reality becomes a necessity. Some economists, aided and abetted by sociologists, even blame either the character or the intelligence of the 99 Percenters.

Enough already. When will economists look into the economy to find the sources of inequality?

Trouble is that if they look into the libraries of mainstream economics or even Austrian economics *et hoc genus omne*, they cannot find the answers. They can only get confused.

A strong plea: Do stop reading Keynes and Hayek, and the literature, all the literature, grafted on their inchoate, partial, and partisan thoughts. At my last check, they are two dead economists—and I mean mentally dead, not physically dead. Of the warring factions feeding on the separate thought of these two giants, there is only one question to ask: Has there ever been a Government without a Market, or a Market without a Government?

Here is the literature that economists should absorb: First, a paper written by Benjamin Franklin, yes the same Benjamin Franklin who instigated the War of Independence—and helped us win it, only to lose it to Alexander Hamilton, who created the Bank of the United States on the model of the Bank of England, whose requests had created the need for the insurrection of the Colonists in the first place.

Yes, it is Benjamin Franklin who worked indefatigably for the proclamation of the United States Constitution in whose Article 1, Sect. 8, we find that members of Congress, the representatives of the people, have the (implicitly exclusive) power to "coin Money" and "regulate the Value thereof."

Not only Oresme, the writer of the first treatise on money in the fourteenth century, the first creator of Gresham's Law that bad money drives good money out of the economy by hoarding it; it is not only Oresme who declared that "coinage belongs to the public, not to the prince." Even Adam Smith believed that the effective control of money and loans by an independent, Central Bank should create an institution that could promote the fortunes of those who are charitable (the sober people) while penalizing/neutralizing those who are greedy (the prodigals, projectors, and imprudent risk takers).

Did not Adam Smith also say:

> All for ourselves and nothing for other people, seems, in every age of the world, to have been the vile maxim of the masters of mankind.

Is not this a streak of Adam Smith's thought that is kept strictly under wrap?

The second set of literature and commentaries that economists must absorb if they want to get out of the "haze," to use Keynes' word, in which they are tightly enveloped, concerns *Progress and Poverty* by Henry George—and the vast literature created by Georgists in the four corners of the world.

The third set of literature is the output of Louis D. Brandeis.

The fourth set of literature can be found in and about some of the books of Louis O. Kelso, especially his delightful, extremely important essay titled "*Karl Marx: The Almost Capitalist.*" What will economists, moralists, and the literati find in this literature, a literature that, to use the eminent Alan Blinder's words, is not couched in "*theoretical drivel, mathematically elegant but not about anything real* "?

They will find the four horses of inequality, namely.

1. Low taxes on land and natural resources foster vast land holdings;
2. (Legal) appropriation of capital appreciation that ought to belong to the creators of wealth grows into vast accumulations of real and financial wealth in the hands of the few;
3. The concentration of national credit in the hands of prime dealers, rather than its judicious dispersal among the people who are the ultimate creators of the value of our national credit, generates an imbalance whereby, beyond the satisfaction of needs for real wealth, the few accumulate financial multiples of zeros, while the many starve; and
4. The practices of the Pac Man Economy give rise not to internal harmonious growth, but to zombie corporations that are "too big to fail." These ventures must be allowed to fail—when they fail.

How to tame these wild horses? Well the solutions roll out of this list by themselves—and these solutions can be truly understood if put into the new/old paradigm of Concordian economics:

A. Raise taxes on land and natural resources;
B. Use equity sharing programs (cash-back programs are very promising);
C. Create money:
   (1) only to fund the production of new real wealth, not financial assets;
   (2) issue loans to qualified people and corporation with ESOPs, cooperatives, and public entities with power of taxation so to assure the repayment of the loan;
   (3) issue loans at cost;
D. Let corporations be free to grow internally as large as they are able to, but sternly prohibit the Pac Man Economy: growth by purchase; external growth by mergers and acquisitions. I like to call this the Brandeis Rule;
E. Let us give serious consideration to the Mosaic debt jubilee. There are hidden jewels there. Let us be wise; let us be brave.

1.4.13 A Final Plea

Sternly apply these four (actually, five) policies, and in ten years or so we will redress all the evils of inequality; in the process, we do not beg for one cent out of the affluent (no IRS compulsion; no moral extorsion); we deflate the power of politicians to take economic decisions for us; we prevent the next collapse of the Stock Market, and if applied the very first day the Stock Market collapses, the damage to the real economy will be minimal, if nonexistent.

> Let us be wise; let us be brave. Vincent Ferrini (2002), our first Gloucester Poet Laureate, reviewing my book on the economic process for the Gloucester Daily Times, caught the essence of this work. Concordian economics, he wrote, offers "the answers to universal poverty and the anxieties of the affluent."

1.5 Conclusion

The application of Concordian economics *automatically* plunges us into Concordianism. (That is the beauty of Culture; it makes us do things without our awareness, without even our assent.) With Concordianism in action, there will no longer be Individualists and Collectivists, but Somists, men and women well integrated into the social context; there will no longer be Capitalists and Socialists, but Concordians. There will no longer be a view from the left and a view from the right. Ideology will disappear, and room will be made to search for Truth.

References

Brady, M. E., & Gorga, C. (2009). Theory of effective demand into Keynes's decision theory: Toward a new (and Final?) interpretation of the general theory. *International Journal of Applied Economics and Econometrics, 17*(3), 195–235.

Brady, M. E. (2007). A dynamic system's (the economic system as a complex, evolving process) reinterpretation of Keynes's Y= C+ I model. (A review of *The Economic Process: An Instantaneous Non-Newtonian Picture* by Carmine Gorga), July 8, at http://www.amazon.com/Economic-Process-Instantaneous-Non-NewtonianPicture/dp/0761821562/ref=cm_cr_dp_orig_subj

Brown, E. (2023). Three presidents who made thanksgiving a national holiday—And what they were celebrating. *ScheerPost,* November 23. Available at https://scheerpost.com/2023/11/23/ellen-brown-three-presidents-who-made-thanksgiving-a-national-holiday-and-what-they-were-celebrating/. Accessed 23 November 2023.

Ferrini, V. (2002). Gorga worthy of note. *Gloucester Daily Times*, December 11, p. A6.

Gorga, C. (2009). The economics of jubilation—Blinking Adam's fallacy away. *Social Science Research Network* (*SSRN)*, October 15. Available at The Economics of Jubilation - Blinking Adam's Fallacy Away by Carmine Gorga: SSRN.

Gorga, C. (2010). Hoarding and most economists. In *History news network*. Colombian College of Arts and Sciences, George Washington University. Available at https://historynewsnetwork.org/article/129965. Accessed on 6 November 2023.

Gorga, C. (2015). Two proposals in the form of two petitions designed to stabilize the monetary system. *The Somist Institute,* December 3. Available at The Somist Institute. Accessed 28 September 2023.

Gorga, C. (2017). A comprehensive analysis of the graham-Cassidy bill, through concordian economics 101. *TalkMarkets*, September 22. Available at https://talkmarkets.com/contributor/carmine-gorga/blog/a-comprehensive-analysis-of-the-graham-cassiidy-bill-through-concordian-economics-101?post=150362. Accessed 28 September 2023.

Gorga, C. (2021a). Jobs Without Disruptions Through Concordian Economics." *EconIntersect*, September 6. Available at Jobs Without Disruptions Through Concordian Economics—Global Economic Intersection (econintersect.com). Accessed on 7 November 2023.

Gorga, C. (2021b). Neither Trumpism Nor Capitalism Is The Real Problem." *EconIntersect*, September 6, 2021. Available at Neither Trumpism Nor Capitalism Is The Real Problem - Global Economic Intersection (econintersect.com). Accessed on 7 November 2023.

Gorga, C. (2022). How to stop inflation cold. *EconCurrents,* March 24. Available at How To Stop Inflation Cold - EconCurrents. Accessed on 3 November 2023.

Gorga, C. (2023). Economics and Hoarding. *EconCurrents,* January 28. Available at Economics and Hoarding—EconCurrents. Accessed on 2 November 2023.

Kristof, N. (2023). Houston shows how to tackle homelessness. *The New York Times*, November 26. Section SR, pp. 8–9. Available at https://www.nytimes.com/2023/11/22/opinion/homeless-houston-dallas.html. Accessed 27 November 2023.

Sodini, P., Van Nieuwerburgh, S., Vestman, R., & von Lilienfeld-Toal, U. (2023). Identifying the Benefits from Homeownership: A Swedish Experiment. *American Economic Review, 113*(12), 3173–3212.

Part I
Intellectual Interdependence

Chapter 2
Politics and Economics

Abstract The road to perdition for the United States, the Last, Best Hope of Earth, is paved with the *poverty of our current political discourse.* The discourse is composed of politics **without** economics. And when economics is included, the content is meager indeed. We have to reach the stage at which the political discourse is rich with good economics—ideally throughout the world, but let us start with the United States. This chapter is divided into three parts: Section 1 gives a look at what is being done; Section 2 gives a look at the hidden, widening fault line that exists in society today; Section 3 gives a look at what ought to be done. Concordian economics helps.

2.1 What Is Being Done

2.1.1 Politics with Meager Economics

I am not much of a reader of "Politics," so I will refrain from generalizing too much. But an analysis I did once of the Graham-Cassidy healthcare bill revealed some interesting features of modern politics, (Gorga, 2017).

Premise: Started by Otto von Bismarck (1815–1898), social security progams are a great modern innvation. They do what an individual person is not able to do. They agglomerate small contributions into massive Funds that smoothen out many finanial hardships for the great majority of people.

I was naively expecting that, since funding for Medicare is mostly done through payroll taxes, politicians, especially conservative politicians, would refuse to even discuss the issue. Barring that self-restraint, I was naively expecting an in-depth conversation about the pockets from which the money materializes and how much money could/should be distributed among patients, so *they would select the best possible care* for themselves and their families. A healthy population ought to be a concern of civil governments. After all, immunities are few; pandemics spread easily.

Perhaps I expected proposals to reinforce existing Medicare (and Medicaid) programs or ways to fund some sort of specialized—new, imaginative—national medical insurance program. Any idea? Apart from futuristic solutions that might use AI, for instance, two practical solutions easily come to mind: (1) The creation of a private insurance company that sets up a profit sharing program among its employees; (2) An insurance company that reduces premiums as insured people increase their personal health improvement programs.

What a shock.

The call is for privatization, for sure; but, the call is for "classic" privatization: the creation of private corporations that can spill as much profit from their constituents—to the exclusive benefit of management and the **few** owners of such corporations. And when the discussion revolves around taxes, the concern is to **reduce taxes** for wealthy taxpayers.

Worse. In a superficial reading and understanding of the Bill, voters seem to be purposefully given the impression that the government spends money for the *financial* benefit of patients.

This is a gross misconception.

Even with Medicaid, which is funded by "government" money, patients are a convenient humanitarian *reason* to spend money—however raised, whether through taxes or debt. Patients never see the money. Even in the case of smaller co-pay and insurance subsidies, patients do *not* receive money. *They simply spend less of their money.*

Those who receive money are doctors and nurses, the administrative staff of hospitals, and the administrative staff of insurance companies. Profits, if any, also accrue to the owners of for-profit hospitals (and administrators of some non-profit hospitals as well) and owners of insurance corporations. Unseen also in this discussion are all intermediaries engaged as suppliers and consultants to hospitals and insurance corporations who perform services not available in-house such as services of lawyers and planners and even engineers, in case of new construction or renovation of hospitals and nursing homes.

These are the people who stand to *lose* money, if Medicaid and Medicare programs are cut down.

What is the central characteristic of this type of legislation, then? The jostling is about who shall get benefits out of a list of constituents. Patients are nowhere to be seen.

Since real people like patients are nowhere to be seen, the **topic of discussion** really ought to be classified *not* about *patients,* but about the transfer of *money*; and not even money itself, but the *transfer* of money from one set of constituents to another. The concern is about money, not patients.

The politics of the right generally advocates a reduction of expenses for social programs so that taxes might be reduced.

What is the likely consequence of such an advocacy?

The central point of our discussion is that, for most taxpayers who stand either to lose their jobs, or to receive less income, puff: All financial gains promised from potential reductions of taxpayers' burden disappear; they are balanced by real financial losses that appear from reductions in employment income and even profits.

This is the magic of comprehensive economic accounting, as contained in Concordian economics.

Only the pain of untreated patients remains.

In the final analysis, who stands to gain from an eventual implementation of legislation like the Graham-Cassidy healthcare bill? This much seems to be clear: wealthy taxpayers and corporations will see their taxes reduced.

But wait. The multiplier suggests that losses—and gains—are never quite equal to the initial input. If the overall production process is affected, widespread losses might affect even the richest taxpayers.

Legislation of this sort does not offer rich political or economic fare. We are left with not even a scent of understanding of what money is, where money comes from, and where money goes. It is all magic mirrors.

Is not this poverty of the political discourse a major cause of the evident disillusionment of too many people toward "politics" these days?

2.2 The Invisible Fault Line

2.2.1 *Some Invisible Consequences of Politics with Poor Economics*

Politics as usual has become a huge distraction. Cynics might say that the distraction is willed in high places, as a form of modern "Bread and Circuses"—the Roman technique to keep the "masses" happy. If so, one curt reminder is appropriate: the Roman Empire collapsed.

Politics "as usual" is absorbing too much of our time and energy. We are concentrating on gossip, vitriol, impossible dreams, and more and more imaginative conspiracy theories. What are the consequences of this type of "politics"? The price is that we are neglecting the most urgent needs of our country. An in-depth analysis reveals something quite unexpected, we are neglecting the hidden, ever-widening fault line that is splitting our country, as well as many parties, into two factions fighting for **two negatives**. Extremists are taking over, very clearly in the Republican Party, somewhat unobtrusively in the Democratic Party in the United States as well. These are tendencies that, under different names perhaps, exist the world over. One says no to the Government; the other says no to the Market.

What are the most urgent political needs of our country? The consequences of the actions of the Masters of Mankind—Adam Smith's words—have been felt *most* by those who today are identified as Make America Great Again (MAGA) People. Were they not traditionally associated with the Democratic Party in the USA—and now their hopes are mostly with the remnants of the Grand Old Party, the Republican Party? Their swing votes represent the core of our political and economic problem, Gorga (2021).

There is much more than words that our political leadership owes our country men and women—and children. There is a whole array of injustices that have to be set aright. Set these injustices right and you unify the country. We must realize that, while MAGA People are at the forefront of the affront of injustices, no section of the population escapes scot-free.

The affections that hold MAGA People together are the resentments and the afflictions that society inflicts upon them. Their lives are being eviscerated by the latifundia; yes, who knows about the latifundia any longer? Ever since Constantine converted to Christianity, latifundia have disappeared from polite political imagination; but vast tracts of land—whether in the wilderness, in dilapidated downtowns, or in the undeveloped band of land that strangles the cities—are still controlled by few people and some big corporations. As a consequence, MAGA People tend to be corralled into crowded lots.

And there is more, much more. MAGA People's lives are being eviscerated when money is lent to people with money **on easy terms** and the people without money are left to pay outrageous interest—mostly to purchase necessary consumer items.

MAGA People's lives are being eviscerated whenever two mega corporations are glued together; then the few gain more power and the people within and without both corporations suffer many afflictions.

MAGA People's lives are being eviscerated by robots that take their jobs, their livelihood, away.

No, economic oppression is not due to the ill will of anyone. It is systemic; it springs from the system, a system that we have built helter-skelter, adding a patch here and a patch there. No one has designed it. There has never been any real understanding of the economic process as a whole—only understanding of parts of the elephant. In its development we have overlooked many essential elements. It is now past time to put it all together.

We have built a system that ultimately affects negatively everyone. Do we ever consider the condition of the billionaire who goes to bed at night with the fear that he or she will wake up to the news that, due to the collapse of the Stock Market somewhere in the world, this poor soul has lost a good chunk of the wealth so painfully accumulated over the years? And what if the money was mostly borrowed? The window is a way out.

Have we ever considered the psychological reflection on the affluent when our society opts for a "preferential treatment for the poor"? If we are going to love the poor so much, to the extent of giving them a preferential treatment, don't we implicitly say that we hate the rich—or at least that we have less love for the rich?

Have we, indeed, seriously considered that we have built a society of beggars? While the poor beg for food and shelter, the middle classes beg for a job. And the affluent are constantly begging for a subsidy and/or a tax reduction.

Yes, these are the horrible conditions that weigh so heavily on the life of nearly everyone today; these are the conditions that are splitting the country—and indeed the world—into smithereens; these are conditions that can and must be changed.

2.3 What Ought to Be Done

2.3.1 *Politics Rich with Good Economics*

The center must hold. Realizing that the many failed revolutions *from the left* during the past few centuries were followed by counterrevolutions *from the right*, it has lately occurred to me that the time perhaps has come to have a **revolution from the center.** All we need to do is to create the Republican Party of Concord, by isolating those who insist on extreme right positions.[1] Ideally, soon to be followed is the creation of the Democratic Party of Concord by jettisoning positions advocated by the extreme left.[2] See, Gorga (2016).

These recommendations seem to apply to much of the rest of the world.

---

[1] The most objectionable positions of the extreme right are racism and sexism. Are cures available?

[2] The most objectionable positions of the extreme left are an indiscriminate defense of abortion and homosexuality. IMHO, the cure for the one is the *duty* to carry pregnancy to term—a duty that by definition excludes any government intervention; the cure for the intolerance of homosexuality can be found only in the *love* for every human being. The danger of homosexuality lies in the confusion engendered by non-homosexuals.

2.3.1.1 The Road Ahead

The center must hold. We must make our own position clear. Essentially, reduced to a bare bone presentation, this is the reality. No, we will not stand for the demise of the Market; no, we will not stand for the demise of the Government.

The sad truth is *not* that these factions are wrong. The tragedy is that they are *both* right. The problem is that they think they are absolutely right.

This is an economic ideology of the right and an economic ideology of the left. Is not this a strong indication that there is something rotten in Denmark? Is not economics supposed to be a science? The economic theory of the right and the economic theory of the left do not allow politicians—and economists as well, for that matter—to see the limitations of their positions. Those are complementary positions; one does not stand without the other.

We need both the Market and the Government; we need Concordian economics.

2.3.1.2 The Core of Concordian Economics

As we move along, we shall see that applying the same *Three Rules* of Concordian monetary policy for the creation and distribution of money both locally, through *Local Independent Banks* and globally, through the *Bancor International Order* (BIO), will grant us a world of peace and justice. Russia will be induced to stop the war in Ukraine, and China might be inclined to change some of her most irksome practices. A few more ingredients are required; major among them is a systematic debt jubilee every seven years.

I presented the Three Rules of Concordian monetary policy to the Federal Reserve System (the Fed), see Gorga (2015), and the Fed graciously responded: "Given your proposal, I suggest that you contact your state and federal representatives." See, Attachment.

Must I emphasize, "your proposal for creating a new monetary system"?

For lack of time and financial resources, I have pursued this directive only fitfully. Is finally this the right time to collectively concentrate our energy on actually creating a Concordian monetary system? Is this a good time to create an organization that might be called "Friends of Concordian economics (FoCe)"? FoCe is a nice Italian word: it means "spring."

2.3 What Ought to Be Done

BOARD OF GOVERNORS OF THE FEDERAL RESERVE SYSTEM
WASHINGTON, DC 20551

September 14, 2016

Carmine Gorga, Ph.D.
Polis-tics Incorporated
87 Middle Street
Gloucester, MA 01930

Dear Dr. Gorga:

Thank you for your most recent correspondence to Federal Reserve Board Chair Janet Yellen in which you emphasized the need for creating a new monetary system.

It is important to know that the Chair receives a great number of letters and emails daily. As a public figure with many daily responsibilities, she is unable to reply to all of those letters and emails personally. However, she welcomes insight and observations from the public.

With regard to your suggestion about the creation of a new monetary system, it is important to know that the Constitution, under Article 1, Section 8, Clause 18, grants the U.S. Congress the power "to make all laws which shall be necessary and proper for carrying into execution" enumerated powers. These provisions give Congress comprehensive authority over the currency and the monetary system of the United States. Only Congress may declare what shall be money and may regulate its value under Article 1, Section 10. Congress was exercising this constitutional power when it passed the Federal Reserve Act of 1913.

Given your proposal, I suggest that you contact your state and federal representatives.

Again, we thank you for taking the time to write.

Sincerely,

Jean Durr
Public Affairs Office

Ideas in books on the shelves do no good to anyone.

Concordian economics also offers rather concentrated expressions of a fiscal policy, a labor policy, and an industrial policy. These are policies built to satisfy the needs of the four—not three—factors of production: land, labor, financial capital, and physical capital.

These are, no doubt, the most important possible applications of Concordian economics. Yet, as we shall see, there are many others. They vary from developing the downtown through racial harmony to the recognition and respect of the panoply of interdependencies in which our physical and human world is so richly enmeshed.

Dear Reader, do not take this as a Pollyannaish exercise. It deals with the whole reality of the economic process. O Men of little faith. Will you remain of little faith even with the evidence of the Fed's readiness to accept the wisdom of Concordian monetary theory? You still have doubts? Why should you assume that the Fed—and all other Central Banks—will not implement Concordian proposals? Why should you assume that the Fed, and all other Central Banks of the world, will not have a profound interest in serving the public good—when they know how to serve it?

Why do you assume that Central Bankers like what they are doing today?

In any case, should the Fed refuse to follow Concordian monetary rules, Congress has the constitutional power and the duty to instruct the Fed to adopt those rules. And if the Congress should refuse? Well, the traditional recourse is a well-established one: We shall throw the "rascals" out and elect true representatives of the will and the interests of all We the People.

Underneath it all, what becomes painfully evident? An age-old truth becomes manifest: We have met the enemy and it is us. We the People have to agree as to what is that we want. Today we all have our favorite solutions to our problems. We must stop fighting each other and agree on what comes first. We must do it. We will do it; because God—or Nature—has so created us that we eventually accept a good thing when we see it.

2.4 Conclusion

The essential characteristic of Concordian economics is *Interdependence*: Without any doubt. The basic model of Concordian economics itself, the economic process, is full of interdependencies. Just to remain on essentials, Money, Real Wealth, and Ownership Rights over money and wealth do not have a life independent of each other but are in full interdependent relations. Even Economic Right do not stand alone but are dependent on Economic Responsibilities.

In addition to monetary policies, are not Concordian fiscal, labor, and industrial policies full of interdependencies? Do they not form interrelationships that build the fabric of our modern social, economic, and political existence?

And Human Beings, they are not aloof observants of Concordian economics. Rather, they are going to become the Agents; the Implementers; the Creators of Concordian economics. Any special characteristics of these Agents? With Concordian economics in the saddle, people are in command of economics. Their *will* to implement economic rights and responsibilities is so powerful that they are themselves transformed in the process—from a set of *Independent Human Beings, or Individuals,* as it is devoutly advocated today, they become *interdependent* **Somists** and **Concordians.**

Very likely, God Himself/Herself/Itself is *not* a man or a woman but a Somist.

Most certainly, God is a Concordian.

People who are not religious, even pure "materialists" perhaps, have to remember that Nature is full of interdependencies. John Muir famously discovered: "When one tugs at a single thing in nature, he finds it attached to the rest of the world."

References

Gorga, C. (2015). Two proposals in the form of two petitions designed to stabilize the monetary system. The Somist Institute, December 3. Available at The Somist Institute. Accessed 28 September 2023.

Gorga, C. (2016). A revolution from the center. OpedNews, November 21. Available at https://www.opednews.com/articles/A-Revolution-from-the-Cent-by-Carmine-Gorga-Ph-Bankers_Corporations_Economic_Justice-161121-738.html. Accessed 29 November 2023.

Gorga, C. (2017). A comprehensive analysis of the graham-cassidy bill, through concordian economics 101. *TalkMarkets*, September 22. Available at https://talkmarkets.com/contributor/carmine-gorga/blog/a-comprehensive-analysis-of-the-graham-cassiidy-bill-through-concordian-economics-101?post=150362. Accessed 28 September 2023.

Gorga, C. (2021). Three steps to unify the country. *EconIntersect*, September 6, 2021. Available at https://econintersect.com/pages/opinion/opinion.php/post/202001190038. Accessed 28 September 2023.

Chapter 3
The Interdependence of Economic Rights and Responsibilities

Abstract In order to eliminate any possible doubt that Concordian economics might be a theoretical construction unable to sustain a close encounter with daily reality, we will focus a bit of our attention on a few key aspects of the central components of Concordian economics: economic rights and economic responsibilities. We will observe some of the relations that they establish: 1. Between individual human beings and thus in relation to the opponents of rights; the forces of privilege, 2. Their position in relation to society as a whole, namely how did they evolve over time, and 3. In relation to economic theory as well as the theory of economic justice. Economic rights and economic responsibilities are not dislocated entities, some belonging to individual human beings and some to society, for instance. We shall see that they are both lodged in the same human being. This is the chain established by the responsibilities: my responsibilities establish my rights and make your rights possible; your responsibilities establish your rights and make my rights possible. It is this set of interrelationships that determines their potential to create Social Renewal through Economic Justice for All, as a fundamental aspiration of civilized society. This was the title of the first presentation of the issues. Theoretically, economic rights and responsibilities are born out of this sequence: Concordian economic theory, Concordian economic policy, and Theory of Economic Justice. Hence they are born through the transformation of the millenarian *Doctrine* of Economic Justice into the **Theory** of Economic Justice. This transformation, so far, has only been accomplished within the realm of Concordian economics.

3.1 Introduction

Hard to think that thirty years have gone by since the original publication of part of this work, Gorga (1994). Problems that existed then have only become worse. And they could be incredibly ameliorated if the rich suggestions of Concordian economics were systematically implemented. The fault does not lie with the occasional Reader—all over the world. The fault for the lack of implementation of these rights lies with the writer. Let me try to be more direct, then. All economic problems we experience today arise from the lack of economic justice, and more specifically, from the lack of implementation of four economic rights and responsibilities.

Allow me to put it still another way, the converse way. If we want to solve any of the existing economic problems of the day, we have to systematically implement a set of universal unalienable rights that are essential to the life, liberty, and happiness of all citizens of a nation.

Piecemeal implementation—with astonishing positive results—of these economic rights and responsibilities has been going on almost forever; it is their systemic implementation that is sorely missing. Piecemeal results have been consistently excellent, but not sustained and widespread. These results have been recorded especially in the voluminous literature offered by the implicit or explicit followers of Benjamin Franklin, Henry George, Louis D. Brandeis, and Louis O. Kelso. We will savor a tiny bit of this literature especially in the Appendix of all places.

To realize the importance of economic rights and responsibilities, we have to place them in the context of the forces they have to oppose in order to assert themselves. The opponents of rights are not some vague and unidentifiable forces. The opponents of rights are the active forces of privilege.[1] The essential differentiation between rights and privileges is this: Rights unite; privileges divide.

3.2 A Web of Words

Unfortunately, we are in a field in which confusion reigns. We will cut through the web of words: rights, property rights, economic rights, economic privileges, entitlements, justice, economic justice, social justice, fairness, and equity. We will steer away from confusion by concentrating our attention on rights, specifically economic rights. Why? Because rights indeed unite, while privileges divide.

An incisive observation by Amy Edmondson (2017), a Professor at the Harvard Business School, is most appropriate here: "[I]t's hard to learn if you already know. And unfortunately, we're hardwired to think we know." No further comment is necessary.

3.3 A Nation Divided by Privileges

The dynamics of privilege become apparent in nearly every morning newspaper. We know the headlines by rote: this group wants a tax reduction or a subsidy; that group wants an increase in services. The dynamics are all there. Privileges, since they are not due to us, are always acquired to the detriment of other people. Hence,

---

[1] The early American colonists and those who freely followed them in an ever widening procession from every corner of the world were propelled upon these shores by the same desire: to escape from the iron clasp of privilege. I must know something about it; I am one of the late comers.

the recurring struggle of wills. No issue is ever settled. No one is ever secure about anything.

Based upon such quicksand, there are never enough resources to satisfy the grab for privileges.

Hence it takes force to extract privileges. But once the privilege is obtained, its use fosters passivity: there is nothing to do but enjoy the privilege until the next challenger comes around. By then, the will and the strength of the user of privilege have generally been so enfeebled that surrender is near.

Certain it is, the dispossessed will eventually rise again.

3.4 A Nation United by Rights

Rights unite us all. They make us all equal.[2] The magic of rights is this. Rights are part and parcel of a culture, a way of life, an understanding of life. Hence, once a right is asserted in one particular case, it is asserted for all. (It is the extension of the application of rights that often is a horrendously slow process.) The opposing political will must be broken. The opposing will is more easily broken, it has quite recently been understood, if the request is advanced in a reasonable fashion, hence the success of nonviolent political movements and if the request makes it absolutely clear that the privileged group is *not* going to be denied the exercise of the right that is proposed. The right must be universal. Once the opposing will is broken, the right is exercised by all, and it is exercised actively. As opposed to privileges, it takes a continuous act of the will to exercise that right. The right then implies a duty; the first duty is to exercise the right.

Where are our rights today? We have none. The field is a true wasteland.

No one has any rights today. There are only privileges and entitlements. How did we reach this stage?

3.5 Once upon a Time

Once upon a time, for a long time, for a couple of millennia actually, we were all living under the aegis of the Doctrine of Economic Justice. Then came Locke, and unobtrusively, he abandoned the *Doctrine* of Economic Justice in favor of a highfalutin proposition, a proposition that appeared to be concrete and straightforward, but it actually is far from simple and direct. This proposition concerns the *justice of property rights*.

---

[2] To be equal in front of the law does not mean to be identical. To be equal means that no one has privileges. To be equal means that everyone has the same rights.

What an epochal change. A change that, under the guise of being opposed to, has actually been riotously reinforced by Marx, his predecessors, and his followers through an examination of the *injustice* of property rights.

It is out of this vise that we have to extricate ourselves. Somehow we have to reconnect with the long lost Doctrine of Economic Justice. History helps.

3.6 Some Content of the *Doctrine* of Economic Justice

The Doctrine of Economic Justice ruled the Western World for about two thousand years; see Wood (2002). As Aristotle formulated it and Thomas Aquinas, followed by the Doctors of Salamanca, corroborated it, the doctrine was composed of two planks, the plank of Distributive Justice and the plank of Commutative (commutation = exchange of wealth) Justice. The plank of Distributive Justice talked of fairness in the distribution of wealth as it was created; the plank of Commutative Justice established the principle of equivalence—already implicit in Aristotle—as the objective measure of what was given and what was received. Since prices are rather elastic entities, the Doctors of Salamanca determined that the *just* price is the fair market price.

The doctrine was never static; at a glacial pace, perhaps, there was a constant attempt to improve the value of its content; the effort to establish better methods to determine the fairness of weights and measures was constant. Certainly, from the very beginning of Greek mythology, the Goddess of Justice, Athena, was conceived as the goddess of civilization, knowledge, wisdom, and crafts at the same time; more technically, perhaps, Themis was conceived as the *personification* of justice (justice herself), goddess of wisdom and good counsel, and the interpreter of the gods' will. Themis was generally represented as a lady holding an old-style scale (the blindfold is a modern addition); the scale has two identical plates falling from a central pillar (a la Gaudi); the third item in the equivalence concretely is the pillar itself, more abstractly it is the *relation* between the respective *weights* placed on the two plates. Was it not this a perfect depiction of the objective measure called for by the principle of equivalence?

Much scholarship, much beyond the ability and the interest of this writer will have to prove or disprove the validity of these assertions. One result might be sufficient for the time being. No tenant or sharecropper—and no society—under that doctrine would have tolerated the scale of distribution of wealth prevailing today: some corporate officers receive compensation 350 times larger than that of the average worker. Talk of the sources of inequality.

This ancient conception of economic justice was supported by an entire culture of moderation. Usury was legally prohibited; it took President Nixon to destroy the last vestiges of that tradition in 1971. Even in ancient Greece, the commons were the last resort for free laborers: they could go there to gather berries and wood or to offer pasture to their one or two sheep; once the commons were enclosed, to recover the value of the *sums given to the Kings*, buyers brought 100 sheep to those lands, and the ecology of the **enclosures** collapsed—what collapsed were the enclosures, as Garrett

Hardin later admitted, but the truth has never been favored by fanatical extremists. Debt jubilees were common. Monasteries functioned as not-for-profit corporations; they created employment for the laborer class at fair wages; their product was made available to the poor free of charge. Surplus wealth in the community-at-large *legally* belonged to the poor; see, Tierney (1959: 22–44) and was distributed to the poor, not through any of the verbal bludgeons used by Karl Marx, or administrative nightmares of our welfare system, but by voluntary disposition by the owners of that wealth. More extended discussions of these issues, as well as detailed sources of information, can be found in many venues, of course, but also in some publications of this writer; see, for example, Gorga (2011).

These propositions might remain a bit abstract; let us anchor them more closely into history.

3.7 A Bit on the Transition to the Modern World

Three portentous, internally related events occurred in 1776 as effects of Locke's emphasis on property rights. Thomas Jefferson, in drafting the Declaration of Independence, literally *erased* the word "property" from the famous Lockean synthesis of "life, liberty, and property"; this was the formula that encapsulated much remote history. All in favor of the pursuit of happiness; all in favor of a world of entitlements, if not a world of rights without responsibilities. All to preserve the union, while tolerating the original sin of slavery.

On the other side of the pond, Adam Smith published his *Wealth of Nations* in that same year. While the emphasis has, properly, been placed on the positive content of that masterpiece, its negative content has been passed under silence. Yet, one is more powerful than the other. Without understanding the negative content of the *Wealth of Nations* we are literally deprived of the understanding of the negative forces ruling the modern world today. Two such forces are, one the obliteration of morality from the social sciences; the other is the evisceration of Hoarding from economic science. Adam Smith published *The Theory of Moral Sentiments* in 1759. Without the *Wealth of Nations*, the earlier work might have been classified as the work of a mad philosopher. That was no longer possible after the concreteness, the \\success of the *Wealth of Nations*. Who could ever pay much attention any longer to a set of moral *sentiments*? Who would pay any attention any longer to such fickle entities as our brittle movements of the heart? Adam Smith must have been aware of the ancient wisdom of Jeremiah (17:9), who said: "More tortuous than all else is the human heart, / beyond remedy; who can understand it?" Adam Smith obtained an audience in high places because he invoked "a higher" authority as the arbiter of our actions; he invoked the power of an "impartial spectator." Impressive. But to the knowledge of this writer, no one has ever asked who the impartial spectator is. The answer is lui-même. No matter. The influence of *The Theory of Moral Sentiments* has been decisive in expelling morality from the social sciences, especially from economics; who would ever want to lose the purity, the precision, and the sanctity of science by mixing it with such fickle entities as moral sentiments? The trouble is that the lack of moral judgment has been the culprit in determining the inability of the social sciences to solve "the free rider problem," the problem of fringe operator\s who want to get something for nothing in this life; see Gorga (2019). The trouble is that the free rider problem could not be simply neglected. Someone had to solve it, and no better candidate was ever found than The State. It is thus that the State has assumed its overwhelming importance in our social, economic, and political life—the life of the extreme political right just as well as the life of the extreme political left. All for *our* benefit (While the center periodically oscillates between the two extremes).

Needless to say, the expulsion of morality from economics deeply affected not only the structure of economic theory, but even more its practice. Without hesitation, it can be said that the expulsion of morality from the social sciences and especially from economics is the root cause of the dissolution of the social bonds that hold a community together, the root cause of the disorder, and the confusion that dominates the modern world. The grab for wealth. The inability to discover the sources of inequality. The denigration of the poor.

Totally unaware at first, it seems that I have been deeply involved in the task of finding solutions to these predicaments. It has been a long trek. The end of the road is nowhere in sight.

3.8 Toward the Reconstruction of Society

The seed of the work of reconstruction was sown by this writer in the distant year 1965, during a summer of intense intellectual struggle with Keynes' *General Theory*. All of Keynes' difficulties in writing the General Theory, I gradually realized, were due to his mistaken impression that he was fighting the "jejune" economics of Marshall, while his enemy was actually Adam Smith's conception of Saving. Erase the word Saving, substitute it with the word Hoarding and you are put on a steady road to understand the economic process and reconstruct economics by building Concordian economics. This feat has been acknowledged by several sources, including the *Journal of Economic Literature* (JEL). In its second annotation of *The Economic Process* (2002, 2009, 2016), on page 1462 of its December 2017 issue, JEL recognizes that "Expanded third edition presents the transformation of economic theory into Concordian economics, shifting the understanding of the economic system from a mechanical, Newtonian entity to a more dynamic, relational process."

The Economic Process *goes through* three mental stages: 1. An analysis of the logical deficiencies of Keynes' Model of the economic system; 2. A construction of the Revised Keynes' Model; 3. A detailed description of the Production Process, the Distribution Process, and the Consumption Process.

The present two volumes contain a rather detailed explication of the transformation of economics from a rational to a relational discipline, synthetically called Concordian economics, and some of the applications of this new paradigm. Brief presentations of Concordian economics can be found in Gorga (2009b and 2017). There are many practical implications involved in the development of Concordian economics; chief among them is its potential ability to yield financial independence to everyone; see Gorga (2021b). Among the theoretical implications, the most important perhaps is likely to be its fostering of the transformation of the *doctrine* of economic justice into the *theory* of economic justice. Here briefly is how.

3.9 From Mainstream Economics to Concordian Economics

Mainstream economics is a sprawling set of theories primarily concerned with the existence and the effects of money in society. Keynes said that mainstream monetary theory is "a haze where nothing is clear and everything is possible (1936: 292)." If anything, the number of monetary theories has multiplied. No need to spend any thought on this condition of mainstream economics.

As soon as I realized that Saving had to be defined as *all nonproductive wealth*, everything became clear in mainstream economics. Mathematics helped. By inserting this definition in the second equation of Keynes' model of the economic system, I escaped from the equality of Saving to Investment and fell into the embrace of the relation of complementarity between Saving and Investment. This relation yielded the equality of Investment to Consumption. An easy, verbal step was to change Investment to Production. What is the aim of an investment if not to produce new wealth?

Logic helped. Once I learned that equality, to be a valid relationship, has to be an equivalence, I went in search of the third term. It did not take me long to decide on the third term which was Distribution (of wealth). I had found the fundamental equivalence of Concordian economics:

$$\text{Production} \equiv \text{Distribution} \equiv \text{Consumption}.$$

Geometry helped. For ease of presentation and analysis, I found it very helpful to transform this equivalence into the following geometric format:

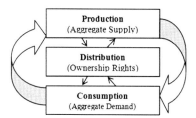

The economic process

The major interrelations among the key members of the economic process become quite visible and do not need to be repeated here. The core of the economic process is this: Only if we participate in the process of production of wealth, we are entitled to a fair distribution of the wealth we create. There is another major reason for the importance of this figure. Without it, I wonder whether the transition from the doctrine to the theory of economic justice might ever have happened and become so apparent.

Here is the geometric representation of the theory of economic justice:

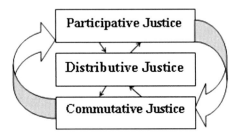

Theory of economic justice

Again, if we do not participate in the economic process, we are not entitled to share in the wealth we create. If this is the theory of economic justice, how did we get there?

3.10 From the Doctrine to the Theory of Economic Justice

Slavery, for many centuries, confined the Doctrine of Economic Justice to only two planks: Distributive Justice, and Commutative Justice. For all that many years the Doctrine of Economic Justice was forever without a visible head. Undoubtedly, this condition favored its disappearance from the social sciences as induced by John Locke. Relieved of the cultural burden of defending slavery and reassured by much economic theory, this writer has been able to add a third plank to the traditional two: thus, we now have Participative Justice, Distributive Justice, and Commutative Justice forming the *theory* of economic justice.

There is a one-to-one correspondence between the two figures: Participative Justice demands the participation of individual human beings in the Production Process; Distributive Justice demands the participation of individual human beings in the Distribution Process; Commutative Justice demands the participation of individual human beings in the Consumption Process.

The principle of equivalence is the principle of logic that holds the three planks of each figure together. Each of the three terms has to be constantly identical to itself; each has to be in a symmetric position with the other, each term can be exchanged with the other two and the results must be the same. One term transitions into the other, thus forming a trilogy. Mathematics and geometry confirm the validity of this organic arrangement of terms: *two terms* lead to the **circularity of argumentation**; science begins when a third point is found.

Much can be said about the Theory of Economic Justice. The briefest possible presentation is this: Without participating in the economic process, it is difficult to receive a fair share of the wealth produced; and without offering a fair share of wealth, it is difficult to obtain anything on this earth.

3.11 A New Transition: From an Abstract to a Concrete Theory of Economic Justice

As it can be seen, economic justice performs the function of a canopy protecting all segments of society. The detailed analysis of these protective functions forms the structure of the Theory of Justice. Indeed, in the general literature on the theory of justice, the functions of this canopy are analyzed in detail. Yet, the canopy itself remains suspended in the air—a true theory, a comprehensive theory, but an abstract theory.

It is in Concordian economics that the canopy is anchored to the ground through the recognition of the existence and functions of four economic rights and responsibilities.

For a full understanding of economic rights and responsibilities, however, we need an additional ingredient: we need to realize that scarcity, a conception that suffuses the entire structure of economic theory, is an unfounded **paralyzing conception.** Later in the book, we will look at some of the concrete evidence. Right now, let us look at the reality unadorned by theory. If we do that, we recognize that the resources of a nation are potentially infinite.

3.12 The Resources of the Nation Are Potentially Infinite

The resources of the nation are potentially infinite. The evidence that this statement is true is overwhelming. Physics tells us that the energy present in a grain of sand is potentially infinite.[3]

The issue concerning many problems in our world is not scarcity, but greed justified by social disorganization. No one knows today what is enough. Consequently, one is compelled to accumulate more than one needs. When one does that, one deprives other people of their due because at any one moment resources are finite.

---

[3] Not only is Einstein's formula for the conversion of mass into energy assuring us that a grain of sand does indeed contain all the energy that we will ever need. Not only is the sun's energy falling on a small patch of the Sahara desert capable of producing all the energy that we will ever need. Both Israel and Saudi Arabia, as the few positive headlines of our exasperating times shout, are making the desert bloom. Saudi Arabia has become a net exporter of wheat!

If the social organization is right, everyone knows what is enough. What is enough is what one needs today. If the social organization is right, one can assuredly implement the Gospel's injunction: "Look at the birds of the air... Consider the lilies of the field... O men of little faith..." The issue then is one of social organization.

Let us give a quick look at how the resources of a nation can best be put to use for the benefit of all members of the nation. This expression is too broad. Let us circumscribe the discussion by relating it to the four factors of modern production.

3.13 Four Economic Rights

As there are four (modern) factors of production, namely land, financial capital, labor, and physical capital, there must be four specific rights of access to those factors otherwise, instead of being productive, as Pope John Paul II points out, we will be marginalized.[4] Rooted in the natural law, these rights can be formulated as follows:

1. the right to share in the bounties of nature;
2. the right to share in the bounties of national credit;
3. the right to own the fruits of one's creation;
4. the right to protect the fruits of one's creation.

These four rights, once exercised in full, will renew the very roots of our culture and our civilization. They will work from within existing structures and might allow us to transform the provision of goods and services from the brutal exercise it has lately become into a very spiritual enterprise, as it inherently is.[5]

3.13.1 *The Right of Access to Land and Natural Resources*

If the resources of the nation are potentially infinite, everyone has the right to access them. They are a common good.

But how can society enforce such a right? The issue is not only one of will, but also one of reality. Some solutions work, some do not. Some solutions work in one

---

[4] See, e.g., Pope John Paul II, Encyclical *Centesimus Annus* (1991) #33. The Welfare State is blind to this reality. Hence, it goes after the symptoms of poverty and compounds the difficulties by trying to establish rights via entitlements. All that is wrong with this shortcut becomes evident only if it is realized that entitlements are not rights. They are privileges masquerading under the cloak of rights.

[5] Is not growing wheat a glorious spiritual exercise? Is not making bread a glorious spiritual exercise? Is not sharing information a glorious spiritual exercise? No. Michelangelo, Rembrandt, and Van Gough were not the only human beings blessed with the ability to give so much to all of us. The old lady who sweeps the floor gives us just as much every day. Without her services we would either be compelled to sweep the floor ourselves—God forbid—and deprive ourselves of the enjoyment of Michelangelo, Rembrandt, and Van Gough. Or we would be living in a pile of dirt.

society, at one time; some do not.[6] The solution that seems to be best applicable to the needs of the modern world lies in the use of taxes on the value of land and natural resources. They have to be generally higher than they are today and taxes on buildings and other human activities have to be correspondingly lower.

Owners who do not want to, or think they cannot afford to pay justly and fairly apportioned taxes on land and natural resources will not be dispossessed; they will simply sell their property and enjoy the fruits of interest on the money obtained in exchange for the transfer of their right of ownership to more capable hands who will make, for instance, the weeds and rubbish filled lots, in too many downtown areas today, bloom. These taxes are effective because they tend to eliminate hoarding, thus opening access to unused resources that ought to be used.

Let us briefly put the issue another way. We all have a duty to pay taxes on our property of land and natural resources. We all have this duty because most of the value of our land and natural resources comes first from God or Nature, if you will, and from the community thereafter. A rock in Arizona is worth a pittance; a rock in Manhattan is worth a lot. The difference lies in what the community brings to the rock: sewer lines, telephone lines, and on and on.

Correspondingly, we all have a right in this matter. We all have the right to enforce the payment by all of a fair assessment of taxes on land and natural resources because, if one does not pay his fair share of such taxes, all others will have to make up the balance.

3.13.2 *The Right of Access to National Credit*

Either in a positive or negative way, we all contribute to the value of our national credit. Therefore, national credit is a common good par excellence. It belongs to all of us.

National credit is a precious resource. From certain points of view, it is more precious than natural resources: misuse of natural resources reduces their availability and increases *their* price. Misuse of national credit reduces the availability and increases the price of all goods and services. National credit is mostly an untapped resource: what Central Banks tap is mostly *bank* credit. Bank credit is created by the savings of a limited number of people (however these "savings" are created);

---

[6] In ancient Israel, the solutions that gave access to natural resources to all were essentially two. In the short run, all the uncollected staples belonged to the poor. They had free access to them. In the long run, the institution of the Jubilee was supposed to take care of the fundamental issues: Uncollectible loans were to be forgiven every seven years. Stewardship of the land was to be relinquished every (7 × 7) 49 years and returned to the original steward. During the Middle Ages, the Catholic Church mostly enforced the rule that all "surplus" wealth legally belonged to the poor. Islamic banking institutions are still fighting against usury, in the face of enervating snickering from the international financial community. Modernity, the Age of Entitlements, has desperately and disastrously tried to enforce a different rule: redistribution of wealth. Some applications of this rule have assumed the form of "land reform"; as if that policy were not unfortunate enough, most have assumed the myriad forms of forced transfers.

national credit is created by us all. (Even when the Fed sell bonds, they absorb the "savings" of the people.)

The use of national credit constitutes one last frontier. We must not mishandle it as we have mishandled so many other frontiers in the past. Properly managed, the use of national credit will function like manna from heaven. It will fuel our creative engines to make us satisfy our immediate as well as our future needs. Properly used, it will be just sufficient for our needs. We will always have enough of it

In-depth consideration of the potential use of national credit leads to the formulation of Three essential Rules for its proper use: (1) national credit must be used only to issue loans that are necessary for the creation of new real wealth; (2) it must be issued to the benefit of us all; (3) it must be issued at cost.

The rationale for the first Rule is best seen in the negative. National credit cannot be used to finance the purchase of financial assets because these assets do not directly create real wealth that benefits the entire nation. For the same reason, national credit cannot be used to finance the purchase of goods that are to be hoarded. National credit cannot be used to finance the purchase of consumer goods because the consumption of these goods does not generate the income necessary to repay the loan.

The rationale for the second Rule is more complex. Some people are inept at creating wealth; some do not care about it. We must all pursue our destinies. And we must not become slaves to the creators of wealth in the process. The application of this criterion, rather than a limitation, presents us with a tremendous opportunity. It means that entrepreneurs have to share the ownership of the wealth they create with all those who help them create it: Employee Stock Ownership Plans (ESOPs) and co-operatives are some of the ideal legal instruments that serve to achieve this aim.

The number of people covered by ESOPs is now larger than the number of people covered by the union label. The ESOPs Movement will grow at a faster clip yet, if its leaders adopt the way of rights, the right of access to national credit, rather than the way of privilege, the privilege of tax favors as an inducement for corporations to adopt an ESOP. The right of access to national credit is for all citizens, whether they are within or outside corporations.

For those who are outside the workforce and are not yet independently wealthy, traditional and nontraditional channels of charity must be used to achieve the substance—although not the form—of economic justice. This is not to say that the form and substance of economic justice cannot eventually be united in nontraditional policies that will eliminate the need for charity altogether.

The rationale for the third Rule is easily specified. Interest rates for credit to create new wealth must cover only the cost of administration of the loan instruments and insurance of default risks.

3.13.3 The Right to Own the Wealth One Creates

If men and women have an indisputable right to own common goods such as land and national credit, how much stronger is the right to own the wealth they create?

That is the fundamental premise on which ESOPs and co-operatives rest. They are legal instruments that allow a fair apportionment of the right of ownership over the wealth that employees create in cooperation, of course, with the owners of capital.

Today, workers and employees are outside contractors. They offer their labor and receive wages. They have no right to the wealth created by the corporation, wealth which includes consumer goods, goods to be hoarded, and capital goods. ESOPs change all that. Following an established set of rules and regulations, they transform employees from contractors into stockholders. From outsiders, employees become insiders. Employees then become much more efficient workers. Provided ESOPs are not simply window dressing, legal arrangements to cajole the taxman, but in fact, do respect the whole person of the employee, they are mostly successful. ESOPs multiplied during the Eighties, and their growth continues.

The question is how can ESOPs be made tools of national policy? The answer lies in seeing them not as concessions from existing owners and managers to employees, but as means to give life to universal rights.

When the use of national credit is called upon to assist in the creation of new wealth, the use of ESOPs must be made mandatory. There will still be no compulsion in this practice because those who do not want to extend the right of ownership to their workers and employees would be free to recur to existing, although more expensive, credit channels.

3.13.4 The Right to Protect What One Owns

Included in the right of ownership of wealth is the right to protect it from outside incursions into its uses and enjoyment. As Pope Leo XIII maintained, the right of property is "sacred and inviolable" (*RN*: 35). Under the specter of Jefferson, the consequences of this right have been mostly feared and resented by governments and reformers alike. But it is proper and unavoidable. All justification for that fear and resentment will be annihilated once the *ownership of wealth* becomes not a privilege reserved for the few but a common right for all. To this right corresponds a duty, the duty to respect other people's property. This set of rights and duties can assume a hundred different manifestations, from trivial to momentous. Perhaps the application that is of utmost importance today regards the buying corporations as if they were "things" and not *organisms* deeply affecting the lives of the people within and without their direct area of influence. This practice produces uncountable horrors.

The practice of corporate aggrandizement has deep roots in human nature. An old example is how hermits became monks and monks created institutions too large for their own good. So new religious orders were created. And the process started anew again and again. We have had more than a century of intense experience to prove that this practice, the trustification process, creates havoc in the economic realm. It must be stopped.

Only if we put a stop to this practice will we protect our civilization from the quick and the cunning. Thousands of years ago, we made a huge stride forward when we decided that the murder of another person was not a private affair. We will make a huge stride forward when we realize that the buying and selling of corporations is akin to industrial murder. This practice cannot be tolerated. Captains of industry should not operate in a business environment in which the fruits of the labor of many can be gobbled up at the whim of any operator who, with the promise of quick results, gains command of untold financial resources. Our time horizon has to widen beyond the next accounting period; our horizon of concerns has to expand beyond the production of goods and services. What we affect, in the final analysis, is always the life of particular men and women. Since the practice of buying and selling corporations is so ingrained, we cannot hope to put an abrupt stop to it just as we cannot abruptly increase taxes on land and natural resources to the desired level.[7] We must start by imposing this prohibition on a limited number of the largest corporations and gradually extend it to the smaller ones until we reach a level of reasonableness that is satisfactory to everyone, including lawyers and investment bankers. But industrial murder must be stopped.

Lately, in deference to the genius of Luis D. Brandeis, I have named this policy the Brandeis Rule.

3.14 Who Are the Opponents?

Who are the powerful people who would object to this program of action? As pointed out on another occasion, Gorga (2017), four presumed antagonists are supposed to be:

(1) landowners who do not want to pay a fair share of taxes on the value of their land;
(2) central bankers who do not want to serve the public interest;
(3) entrepreneurs who do not want to offer full compensation for services received; and
(4) business people who want to gobble up the fruit of other people's efforts.

Where are they? Apart from their miniscule apparitions, when measured against the billions of entrepreneurs who behave morally, they are four phantoms—but more dangerous for being ingrained in the imagination of people who, blinded by their institutional power, see neither economics nor morality in daily vents. READ: tax assessors, politicians, and academicians who, unable to speak truth to power, make themselves powerless and paralyze entire nations in the process.

---

[7] The use of national credit and the expansion of ESOPs and cooperatives are inherently gradual processes, simply because the creation of new real wealth is unavoidably a gradual process.

3.15 An Organic Policy

These four rights form the backbone of an organic economic policy that will gradually produce self-reinforcing benefits. The dissolution of the power of privilege that ensues will, of course, require constant vigilance, but it will proceed by its own internal dynamics and thus will direct the whole gamut of problems affecting our world today on the way to a proper resolution. There are many ways of demonstrating the validity of these propositions. The simplest is to expand upon the set of distinctions between rights and privileges outlined at the outset of this discussion.

3.16 The Larger Context

In the beginning, an attempt was made to place this discussion within the historical-political context. These issues can also be studied from the sociological, teleological, and theological viewpoint. It is on this vast ground that we will find the ultimate justification for the suggested policy.

Privileges are based on envy, use greed as the engine to set the social dynamics in motion, are extracted through violence or the threat of violence, and foster sloth.

Rights are based on self-sufficiency, use self-reliance as the engine to set the social dynamics in motion, are exercised through mutual respect, and foster the dignity of the person. What did God—or Nature, or at the limit, our own will—put us on this earth for?

3.17 Toward a Grand New World

The availability of economic rights and responsibilities grants us the opportunity to create a Grand New World. Will we grab this opportunity?

3.18 Conclusion

These four rights are our own personal rights. They are ours, not because someone else is giving them to us, but because we earn them by performing our responsibilities. By exercising these rights, we do not take anything away from anyone else. On the contrary, by performing our responsibilities, we allow others to acquire and exercise their rights.

Once proclaimed, society does not have any role in the performance of these rights. That is up to an individual decision. The essential characteristic of these rights is that all the members of society have the same identical rights.

As for responsibilities, society, of course, can change the tax rate on land values at any time; society might intervene in determining relative percentages in the distribution of ownership rights over the wealth produced; society might exercise a final supervisory role in avoiding national credit levels that should cause inflation. Finally, society will determine the number of corporations that are subjected to the Brandeis Rule. Yet, all of these societal interventions will be general; they will cover the entire population; so the possibilities of abuse will be reduced to a minimum.

The application of these rules will render our particular society just. Who would not like to live in it? Is not the creation of a just society an age-old aspiration of human beings?

Appendix: Some Nuances of Land Tax Values

There are so many nuances to a program of land tax values, the policy advocated most warmly by our lovely Henry Gorge. They are all lovely. They are all important. An excellent report with a rather silly title to the business section of the *New York Times,* Dougherty (2023) presents quite a few of them.[8]

Mayor Mike Duggan of Detroit puts it starkly, in the absence of taxes on land "Blight is rewarded, building is punished." He explains that after the Great Recession, tens of thousands of Detroit properties were bought by absentee landlords and faceless LLCs. The owners are so negligent and hard to find as to let weeds and rubbish grow on their lots. [How much of this money was public money? Remember, in Concordian monetary policy public money is not allocated for such ventures.]

Daryl Fairweather, chief economist at the real-estate brokerage Redfin and one of the most widely quoted voices on the housing market, extols the land-value taxation as "the tax policy that can fix housing." Taxes on land values encourage housing development instead of discouraging it, she notes. They don't discourage work or investment, like taxes on income and capital gains. They're also hard to dodge since land is hard to move. "It's like there's this tool in our toolbox that could help solve a lot of our problems, and we refuse to pick it up," Ms. Fairweather said in an interview. "If more people understood how useful this was, they would advocate it."

Dougherty goes to the core of the argument, he points out that "George's argument was that since land derives most of its worth from its location and the surrounding community, that community, and not the owner, should realize most of the benefits when values rise. His fix might sound wonky—tax the value of land but not improvements atop it—but it made him a celebrity in the 1890s." In fact, he ran twice as a Mayor of New York City. Further, "There used to be Georgist newspapers. There are still Georgist foundations, Georgist conferences, and Georgist schools. If you've

---

[8] A special note of heartfelt thanks to Professor Raymond G. Torto is appropriate here. As I showed him my Revised Keynes' Model, he noted: "There is lots of Henry George there!" Is there joy greater than deep human communication? He also sponsored me for induction in the American Economic Association.

ever played Monopoly, you have been unwittingly George-pilled: A Henry George fan invented the board game, in hopes of spreading his teachings."

For a complex number of reasons linked by Dougherty to access to cheaper lands thanks to the automobile, there has been a lull of interest in land-value taxation since the 1920s. The interest is reviving now since, if we were to tax the land its price would fall and an overall positive result would affect the cost of living. Hence, many "who are angry about the cost of living have discovered Georgism. Suddenly there are organizations like Young Georgists of America, modern-day pamphlets like the Henry George podcast and the Progress and Poverty Substack, and an agreement that the shoshinsha emoji (which looks like a shield) is how Georgists will identify themselves online."

What, on the whole, tends to hold land-value taxation down, Dougherty points out, are two factors: the insistence by some pure Georgists on the conception of the single tax and the other is the permission by state legislation.

References

Dougherty, C. (2023). The 'Georgists' are out there, and they want to tax your land—Amid a crisis in affordable housing, the century-old ideas of Henry George have gained a new currency. New York Times, November 12, Section BU, Page 6. Available at https://www.nytimes.com/2023/11/12/business/georgism-land-tax-housing.html. Accessed on 12 November 2023.

Edmondson, A. (2017). "How to turn a group of strangers into a team." *Ted Salon: Brightline Initiative*, October. Available at https://www.ted.com/talks/amy_edmondson_how_to_turn_a_group_of_strangers_into_a_team/transcript?user_email_address=6f9d4528721d3cce57519d57f5f2d37d&lctg=62d1b4ae1c794c328c10d8f9. Assessed 12 October 2023.

Gorga, C. (2002, 2009a). The Economic Process: An Instantaneous Non-Newtonian Picture. Lanham, MD. and Oxford: University Press of America. Third edition by The Somist Institute, 2016.

Gorga, C. (2009b). Concordian Economics: Tools to Return Relevance to Economics. *Forum for Social Economics, 38*(1), 53–69.

Gorga, C. (2011). Some Shortcomings of the Social Contract. Available at SSRN: http://dx.doi.org/10.2139/ssrn.3143002.

Gorga. C. (2017). Concordian Economics: An Overall View. *Econintersect*, January 2.

Gorga, C. (2019). "The Free Rider Problem," Mother Pelican. *A Journal of Solidarity and Sustainability, 15*(2).

Tierney, B. (1959). *Medieval poor law: A sketch of canonical theory and its application in England*. Berkeley: University of California Press.

Wood, D. (2002). *Medieval economic thought*. Cambridge, UK: Cambridge University Press.

Chapter 4
A Peaceful March Toward Concordianism

Abstract A peaceful march toward Concordianism will accelerate its pace if we go beyond the intellectual strictures of two "defunct economists": Keynes and Hayek. Preeminent leaders of two schools of thought, although long gone, both still dominate and divide the economic discourse of the world. In a thorough treatment of the many interlocked questions, I have explored the issues at some considerable depth. I found solid barriers that made Keynes and Hayek unable to listen to and talk to each other. Beyond the analysis of those barriers, we shall find what **ideally** unifies them: the need to accept the presence of the Government and the presence of the Market as both necessary—as complementary positions. Has the time come for respective entrenched opponents to lower their barriers? Concordian economics is poised to resolve the ancient, perennial issue of what is the best form of government. The short answer is the government that governs on the basis of **self-imposed** (hence democratic) **rules of economic justice**. In this system, The Government—after much vetting—*declare*s a set of economic rights and responsibilities to be shared by the entire nation and leaves the Market free to *execute* them. Ideally, the vetting will converge on the creation of the set of economic rights and responsibilities enunciated throughout the work on Concordian economics. Once these issues are settled in Sect. 4.1, we can briefly address in Sect. 4.2 what we are leaving behind: a gentle walk-away from both 1% Capitalism and Marxism. In Sect. 4.3, we take a stride toward Concordianism.

4.1 Adieu Keynes, Adieu Hayek

4.1.1 Introduction

The obstacles that both Keynes and Hayek faced, obstacles that prevented an understanding of each other's positions are too numerous, too interlocked, and too intricate to be repeated; see Gorga (2012a, 2012b). Interspersed here I will mention only three of the most important flashpoints: (1) the methodology, (2) the culture, and (3) the categories of economic thought processed by Keynesians and Austrians.[1] These were the barriers that made Hayek and Keynes unable to listen to and talk to each other. These were unbridgeable differences. Rather than repeating all of those intricate issues, here we will concentrate on the beginning and the conclusion reached by the respective positions of these two giants.

4.1.2 The Beginning

Both Keynes and Hayek shared the belief that there existed a need to revisit the economic discourse that began in the 1930s, which involved their respective analyses of growth and the business cycle. Both Keynes and Hayek expressed the need to go beyond the terms of their respective positions. A few months after the publication of the *General Theory* (1936), Keynes issued this warning in the *Quarterly Journal of Economics*, February 1937: "I am more attached to the comparatively simple fundamental ideas which underlie my theory than to the *particular forms* in which I have embodied them, and I have no desire that the latter should be crystallized at the present stage of the debate" (emphasis added).

Following that invitation, during a summer of intense intellectual struggle with the *General Theory* in 1965, I changed Saving to Hoarding and Consumption of *consumer goods* to an exchange of money for *all products* produced by the production process. The investment came to be understood as all productive wealth. This is a new world, the world of Concordian economics.

By the same token, Hayek (1994: 145) confessed: "…one of the things I most regret is not having returned to a criticism of Keynes's treatise."

And in ([1995] 1963: 49), he more fully explained:

> When I look back to the early 1930s, they appear to me much the most exciting period in the development of economic theory during this century…. [T]he years about 1931,… and say 1936 or 1937, seem to me to mark a high point and the end of one period in the history of economic theory and the beginning of a new and very different one. And I will add at once that I am not at all sure that the change in approach which took place at the end of that period was all a gain and that we may not some day have to take up where we left off then.

---

[1] As an example, here are some basic differences concerning the complex issue concerning the measurability of economic affairs. Private, personal values, as Mises (1933: 216 and 217), forcefully insisted, are graded, not measured. And that is sufficient as a starting point to build a subjective micro theory of the market. However, public or social values of real wealth are different. They need to be measured if we want to know where the macro economy stands. Problems of measurement of values of real wealth, ancient problems of imputation, were recognized by Keynes as well as by Hayek; but their suggested solutions (*wage* units and *amount* of input) were admittedly unsatisfactory, cf. Keynes (1936: 37–45); Hayek (1941: 202–215). These practical problems are finally resolved in Concordian economics. They are identified and suggestions for solutions are offered; notorious problems of measurement are intellectually solved in Concordian economics, Gorga, (2012a, 2012b).

4.1 Adieu Keynes, Adieu Hayek

Mario Rizzo (2010) singularly put it in a straightforward way: "… the issues (treated by Keynes and Hayek in the 1930s) are basically the same today. The positions of the opposing sides are also the same. As I have said many times before, the great debate is still Keynes versus Hayek. All else is a footnote."

The delayed expressions by both Keynes and Hayek of willingness to accept criticism, whether from one another or others, are taken at face value. We will not use them to highlight their relative weaknesses. Here we will concentrate our attention on the end point of both their respective positions.

4.1.3 End Points

Clearly, Keynes did not communicate with Hayek and Hayek did not communicate with Keynes. Could the fact that Hayek belonged to Nobility and Keynes to high bourgeoisie have any effect on their communications? It might hardly have been different.

It is worse with the followers of either thinker. For them, both sets of thought ended in an antithetical position. For more than a century, the political discourse has been polarized between those who believe in the infallibility of The Market and those who believe in the perfectibility of The Government. *The economics of both, together or separately, impressive as they are from the inside, are clearly not capable of solving the ills of the world.* Yet, **combined,** they must form the foundation on which we can build a vigorous economic system. Is Concordiian economics such a system?

Making things worse, Institutions endorsing either discussant are wrapped in ideology; they interpret things through the lenses of Individualism[2] vs. Collectivism and Socialism vs. Capitalism. No variation on either theme is going to be satisfactory.

The current economic crisis has not been resolved—and cannot be resolved—without reconciling these two divergent viewpoints. The persistent hope for the resolution of this disjunction from reality is due to one fundamental technical reason: the two sets of economics do not and cannot stand by themselves. They are both *necessary*; they are complementary. Put together, they offer powerful tools of analysis and are likely the most useful tools of reasonable living.

---

[2] In a detailed essay titled "Individualism: True and False," as the first essay of a book titled *Individualism and Economic Order,* Hayek (1948) took great pains to distinguish between two antipodal strains that exist in this tradition.

4.1.4 Concordian Economics as the Bridge to Reality

Concordian economics offers a clear bridge to reality. Its fundamental position is that *The Government must promulgate the right policies and The Market must be free to execute them.*

Looking at these issues in slightly different terms, Concordian economics might be interpreted as the reconciliation of the macroeconomics of Keynes with the microeconomics of Hayek.[3] Intellectually, Concordian economics suggests that if the right economic policies are implemented, dynamic equilibrium in the macro economy is achieved, as Keynes desired. Societal equilibrium in the micro economy is obtained, not through bureaucratic planning, but in an organic fashion through the day-to-day, voluntary implementation of the Concordian economic rights and economic responsibilities (once the corresponding macro policies are understood and, whenever and wherever necessary, put in place), as Hayek desired.

The full reconciliation between the thoughts of Keynes and of Hayek occurs by realizing that the engine of the economic structure is not the government, but the private Schumpeterian entrepreneur.

The program of action recommended by Concordian economics, as we will see in some detail later on, is clearly advocated by no less notable a person than Carlos Slim, the (then) richest man in the world. Here are his terse sentences, as quoted by the noted economist Robert Frank (2011):

One: "The monetary and the fiscal policies, which are very aggressive, should go more to the real economy."

Two: "The structural change will come from more investment in the private sector."

Three: "Instead of stopping the investment in the public sector and creating austerity programs, which creates unemployment, it's better to rely on a development program financed by the private sector."

Evidently, there is much work to be done.

The aim of our work is not so much to verify whether, with the analytical engine of Concordian economics "put through its paces," it will be objectively demonstrated that a just economic system is a dynamically stable system. The aim of this investigation is especially to speed up the desire and the pace and the development of expertise necessary for the implementation and expansion of the overall program of action of Concordian economics.

---

[3] Concordian analysis becomes more complex than either the Austrian or the mainstream analysis, first, because categories of wealth are more detailed and are taken into account from the point of view of supply as well as demand, and, second, because once stocks are seen in action they transform themselves into flows of values that interact among themselves to produce, over time, economic growth and business cycles. The analysis is further refined by noticing that economic categories (not only markets) behave differently at different stages of the business cycle and that such stages often overlap. Finally, all these analyses have to be integrated into one comprehensive understanding of the economic system as a whole in which all agents with their property, controlling or being controlled by all these categories of thought, are not presented as lifeless lists but are put in functional relations with each other.

4.1 Adieu Keynes, Adieu Hayek 55

The road to travel, in other words, is broader than the one we have been able to follow up to now. Here we have tried to confine our observation to the relationships between Keynes and Hayek. The full task is much broader than that. The task is to evaluate what is living and vital in the enormous economic literature that has been accumulated over the centuries. in many cultures, and then determine whether it can indeed be poured into any structure of economics that is capable of solving the ills of this world.

4.1.5 Toward the Resolution of the Crisis

As observed in many quarters, modern economic theory is in a state of crisis. Long story cut very short, in Concordian economics, we find the resolution of the crisis. The resolution is this: Concordian economics assigns to The Government the function of deliberating and announcing adequate policies; Concordian economics leaves The Market free to execute the policies. Concordian economics does not start from scratch. It avails itself of the guidance offered by many sources preeminent in the past.

4.1.6 There Is Nothing New

Incredibly, perhaps, this resolution is indeed the position of none other than the First President of the United States, George Washington. In his first *Inaugural address* (1789), this is what George Washington said: "[T]he foundations of our National policy will be laid in the pure and immutable principles of private morality; and the pre-eminence of a free Government [will] be exemplified by all the attributes which can win the affections of its Citizens, and command the respect of the world."

Is this not a Market based *on morality* and a Government that *serves the needs of all* the people?

Well, it is. But how to apply these firm principles to the complexities of the modern world?

First, notice that our First President called on the forces of *both* the Market and the Government. Then, let us remember why the War of Independence was fought and won. Contrary to common wisdom that stops at the fig leaf of "no taxation without representation," it was to preserve the right of access to national credit, our commonwealth, upon which the American Colonists had fortuitously stumbled, that the war was waged and won.

4.1.7 From Two European to Four American Economists

Yes, much of the extraordinary fortune of the American Colonists was indubitably due to Benjamin Franklin.

It was Benjamin Franklin, a lad barely 23-year-old, who wrote that extraordinary essay titled "A Modest Enquiry into the Nature and Necessity of a Paper-Currency" (1729), which in no uncertain terms proclaimed for the Colonists the right of access to national credit that was first exercised in the Western world by the freemen of the Massachusetts Bay Colony in 1690, a corporation that was formed in my new hometown, Gloucester, Massachusetts, in 1623.

It was Benjamin Franklin, with his "disaffection" toward England, who contributed to powerfully coalesce the spirit of the colonists in favor of the War of Independence.

It was Benjamin Franklin, with his deep understanding of money and constant reliance on the will of the people, who caused the right of access to national credit (the financial capital of each nation) to be written in the first (!) Article of the US Constitution.

Egregious dignitaries who drafted and passed this article of the US Constitution were guests of Franklin the evening before.

These are the key recommendations of Concordian economics:

Let us exercise our right to national credit wisely, namely. let us use our national credit to increase our real wealth only, and not the"fake" value of financial assets.

Let us use our national credit to refurbish our public infrastructure and to repay these loans by increasing taxes on land values—and in parallel gradually reduce all other taxes, especially taxes on labor and corporate taxes (as recommended by Henry George—and quite a few other economists who have consistently been advocating for Land Tax Values (LTV).

Let us gradually make workers the owners of the corporations that benefit from the use of our national credit (thus incorporating the work of Luis O. Kelso into our politics).

Let us *not* use our national credit to keep zombie corporations alive; let the Market determine their fate (thus incorporating the work of Luis D. Brandeis in our politics).

If we do put these just policies in place, as William Jennings Bryan (1896) exhorted us long ago, "all other necessary reforms will be possible." Do not set monetary policy aright, and all our efforts at social, economic, and political improvement come to naught.

As seen in Chap. 2, I put all these recommendations together in a paper that I sent to Dr. Janet L. Yellen, Chair of the Board of Governors of the Federal Reserve System (the Fed); the Fed graciously examined the work, granted it the status of a "proposal ("for creating a new monetary system"), and wisely recommended that the proposal be presented to our "state and federal representatives."

This is a two-pronged proposal on how to stabilize the monetary system, first, to prevent a widely expected financial crisis and, then, whether the crisis occurs or not,

4.1 Adieu Keynes, Adieu Hayek

to shift our 5000-year-old paradigm from one that lets money control people to a new, Concordian paradigm, in which people control money.

4.1.8 We Have Met Our Four American Economists

We have thus met our four powerful American thinkers: Benjamin Franklin (1729), Henry George (1879), Brandeis (1913, 1914, 1934), and Kelso (1957, 1958, and 1967). They never met personally nor did they seem to know of each other's thoughts in-depth, but as in serendipity, each seemed to pick up the discourse where the other had left off. What the jealous guardians of each thinker do not seem to realize is that, individually, they do not stand. Individually, they are open to too many debilitating attacks. United they stand as an impregnable fortress.

Putting the thoughts of the four great American thinkers together—on the theoretical foundation of Keynes and Hayek **combined**—we will have the grace to stir our minds away from gossip and impossible political dreams. Putting their thoughts together, we will have the grace to concentrate our minds on a set of stable and just economic policies. We have to focus our minds on acquiring a brilliant future *for all*.

The chance is ours to lose. The chance is within our grasp. How?

Let us forget the *hard positions* of Keynes; let us forget the *hard positions* of Hayek. **In the end, let us forget Adam Smith as well.** He expelled Hoarding; he expelled morality[4] from the social sciences.

Let us give our undivided attention to our four great American thinkers. We can cobble out of their thought an All-American Policy. Four coordinated marginal changes in existing practices are all that it takes to strike an All-American economic policy. These changes can be expressed as follows:

1. Increase taxes on land and natural resources (while gradually reducing taxes on buildings and income);
2. Restrict access to national credit, the credit of a nation, solely for the creation of new real wealth—rather than using it to buy consumer goods, goods to be hoarded, or paper instruments; and coordinate credit creation with the expansion of ownership through individual proprietorships, Employee Stock Ownership Plans (ESOPs), and co-operatives; extend this opportunity to governing bodies with taxing powers for the purpose of creating real wealth in the form of public infrastructure—and not for covering administrative expenses that ought to be subjected to the stricter oversight of public taxation; issue credit at cost;
3. Own what you create; and
4. Respect other people's wealth.

These four economic policies are made concrete and specified in Concordian economics. Their reasonably gradual translation into practice is entrusted

---
[4] See, Lux (1990).

to the transmission belt of the four corresponding economic rights and responsibilities mentioned throughout this work. These economic rights and economic responsibilities are the conditions for economic freedom for all. Time should not wait.

The sooner they are *implemented*, the better.

4.1.9 Basic Rationale for the Four Macro Policies

This looks like an opportune moment to **briefly** give our undivided attention to the basic rationale for all four Concordian economics policies.

4.1.9.1 A Fiscal Policy

In Concordian economics, the responsibility of the landlord is to pay taxes on land and natural resources; only then does the owner/entrepreneur acquire the right to use that land in a legitimate way. Taxes on land ought to be established, not through whim, but through economic reasoning, which has this to suggest: The value of any land is created both by nature and by human improvements. These improvements can then be recognized as values brought about by private personal improvements from the landowner or by community improvements such as a road, a museum, and varied public investments. It is a portion of the value of the latter improvements that is proper to tax and return to the community.

4.1.9.2 A Labor Policy

The case is straightforward. The owner of labor has the responsibility to work—and the right to receive full compensation for the value s/he has contributed to the enterprise.

A Few Specifications

The term "owner of labor" means precisely what it says; a person is an owner, not a worker. To recognize this existential reality on a national scale, workers have to be brought into the legal structure of the corporation through co-operatives and ESOPs. Individual entrepreneurship accomplishes the same goal. The speediest way to reach this goal is for unions to struggle, not for a living wage—an indefinable goal that might result in self-defeating "cost-push" inflation—but for **equity sharing**. Once this is done, the issue is no longer the granting of a just wage, a millenarian dream that has proved to be impossible to fulfill, but the right to apportionment of profits—a right exercised on the basis of the right of ownership in relation to the fruits of the operation as well as the growth of the value of the enterprise over time: net capital appreciation (or capital depreciation, if that is the case).

4.1.9.3 A Bottom-up Monetary Policy

The right of access to financial capital is best gained through access to national credit, which is the power of a nation to create money.

(Bankers have arrogated to themselves the privilege to create money as debt.) At its origin, at the level of national credit, money is a pool of common resources, *owned by the nation as a whole*, because the value of money is created by the sweat and tears of all the people in a nation. Once "earned," through loans that have been repaid, money becomes a private good. Thus, as Steve Kurtz, an investment banker, recognized long ago in a personal communication, money is created as an asset—not as debt.

One day Professor John Kenneth Galbraith coiled down to graciously sit next to me in his studio and in his gravelly voice asked: "What do you mean by national credit?" Nearly terrified, I whispered: "But professor, national credit is the power to create money." Without missing a beat, he boomed back: "I like the direction of your thrust."

A Few Specifications

Does this policy politicize the process of capital formation? In Concordian economics, it is suggested that access to national credit be granted to an entrepreneur as a right, which means that the state and the political process will *not* have the right—and therefore the power—to interfere with the distribution of credit. The Federal Reserve System will reserve to itself only the right of refusal if and when the economy should become so heated that an addition to the money supply will create the near certainty of inflation. Access to national credit is granted as a loan, therefore, there has to be reasonable reassurance of repayment of the debt, and thus the pool of commonwealth will be constantly, consistently replenished. The repayment of the debt has the implicit advantage of *destroying* the money supply that remains in circulation; hence the danger of inflation is significantly reduced.

The loan has to be issued at a cost: it would be opprobrious for any public agency administering national credit to make a profit on such a basic operation, which is vital to the welfare of the nation. The loan has to be issued for the benefit of all: hence, the loan is issued to single entrepreneurs, co-operatives, and corporations that use ESOPs.

Government entities with taxing powers—through which they can repay the loans—should also have such access, only for wealth-creating projects, not to cover administrative expenses. As David Goran Shedlack puts it, don't give money to the bankers: give money to the entrepreneur, with conditions. There is no compulsion in this policy of Concordian economics: those who do not want to accept such restrictions are free to access the private financial market.

4.1.9.4 An Industrial Policy

A general observation. The fundamental difference that results from the Concordian conception of economic rights and economic responsibilities is that human beings are not commodities subject to the blind rules of the laws of supply and demand but are the owners of the wealth they produce. And since their wealth is acquired through the exercise of rights and responsibilities, they can rest assured in the enjoyment of the wealth they create. Neither Socialism nor Capitalism is capable of extending this assurance to every citizen of a nation; thus, neither is capable of recognizing and respecting the dignity of each and every human being—which does not mean that, especially due to the influence of the ideals of the free enterprise system, one cannot find sporadic examples of extraordinary respect for human beings, within and without the corporation.

4.1.10 Conclusion

Both Keynes and Hayek were dissatisfied with how they left things. Should we not feel free to heed their warnings? If we do, we will get rid of the strictures in which the economic discourse is constrained today—throughout the world. A Brave New World is indeed ahead of us. Four giant American thinkers will guide our steps.

Keynes and Hayek left the world in intellectual disarray; Concordian economics, guided by the serial thought of four American giants, is putting things harmoniously together again. We are left with only one alternative: we must operate the economic system under the guidance of four economic rights and responsibilities.

Through economic justice, Concordian economics neglects Adam Smith and recovers the wisdom of Aristotle, Aquinas, and the Doctors of Salamanca. Adam Smith's rationalizations are a case of their own. After giving **almost** free rein, to capitalists, he warned us in this way: "All for ourselves, and nothing for other people, seems, in every age of the world, to have been the vile maxim of the masters of mankind."

If we do all that, if we forget Keynes, Hayek, (even) Adam Smith, and most other modern economists in between, we are ready to step into the New/Old World of economics.

Or better, once purified, we must remember Keynes and Hayek **together**. Their positions are complementary. And thus they open the door to Concordian economics to build the best possible form of government. This is the short-form answer: The best form of government is the one that governs on the basis of **self-imposed** (hence democratic) **rules of economic justice**. In this system, The Government—after much vetting—*declare*s a set of economic rights and responsibilities to be shared by the entire nation and leaves the Market free to *execute* them. Ideally, the vetting will converge on the creation of the set of economic rights and responsibilities enunciated throughout the work on Concordian economics.

Economic rights and responsibilities are exactly the entities Hayek was looking for to rule the ship of state, namely "general abstract rules" to perform this function (1960, p. 153). The only difference is that ERs&ERs are very concrete rules. And that difference has too many advantages that cannot be singled out here. They must be left to the imagination and the savoir faire of the Reader.

But wait. To be firm in our path forward, we must be aware of what we leave behind. What do we leave behind? We leave behind two powerful intellectual movements. One is, not Capitalism, but 1% Capitalism; the other is Marxism. Good riddance to both.

4.2 A Gentle Walk Away from 1% Capitalism and Marxism. Adieu Locke, Adieu Marx

4.2.1 Introduction

History will find a hard time identifying even one soul who has given his or her life on the altar of Capitalism and even more difficult to identify people who have sacrificed their lives on the altar of 1% Capitalism. So, we will not add a word about abandoning 1% Capitalism to its fate.

Not so for Marxism. Millions of people have eagerly, hopefully, sacrificed their lives on the hot flames of Marxism all over the world. This characteristic alone calls for an extended tribute to Marxism. We will try to do so, but in an impossibly compressed form here.

4.2.2 History, Oh History: The History of Economic Justice

The *cri* of Rationalism and the Enlightenment for "clear and distinct ideas" caused a series of major unintended consequences from which we have not yet recovered. We abandoned; correction: We believed we could abandon abstract ideas in the pursuit of concrete ideals. There are many cases in point; see, for example, Gorga (2016a and 2017a). Here we shall be solely concerned with the effect of the overarching culture of Rationalism on the theory of economic justice. The Aristotelian distinction between *political* justice and *economic* justice, whose sum creates a full theory of justice, is passed under silence here.

With John Locke, we lost the "abstract" conception of economic justice. Strictly speaking, what we lost was the *doctrine* of economic justice. The shift was subtle. So subtle that, perhaps, not even John Locke was aware of it. Certain it is that, without mentioning the deed, he discarded the *economic content* of the Doctrine of Economic of Justice and replaced it with an approximation that might be called "business," "personal relations," "private affairs," and "private or personal justice."

John Locke abandoned the world of *economic justice* that ruled our daily actions from Aristotle, through Aquinas, to the Doctors of Salamanca, see, for example, Wood (2002), and abruptly started the pursuit of a similar looking, but completely different ideal: the pursuit of the *justice of property rights;* accordingly, he specified the well-known conditions for the "proper" acquisition of property rights: Locke (1689, Bk. II, Ch. v, paras 25–27). The conditions are: "The labour of his body, and the work of his hands, we may say, are properly his. Whatsoever then he removes out of the state that nature hath provided… makes it his property… for this labour being the unquestionable property of the labourer, no man but he can have a right to what that is once joined to, at least where there is enough, and as good, left in common for others." All extant theories of justice suffer from this shift. Coase (1937 and 1960), Rawls (1971), Nozick (1974), Gewirth (1985), and Sen, with his Theory of Social Choice as an aspect of the theory of justice (1998) as well as Pazzanese (2021) are all concerned with the many facets of the justice of property rights. Utilitarianism, with Jeremy Bentham at its head and its myriad applications, is mercifully passed over in silence. The practical implications of Utilitarianism are despicable. The intellectual roots of Utilitarianism have deep cultural flaws; see, e.g., Brady (2013). (Individual writers—see, especially, Monsignor Ryan (1906; 1916)—have dealt with one aspect of that doctrine, Distributive Justice. But they never formed a school, unless when they misapplied it as a requirement for *re*-distribution of wealth. An intellectual and practical impossibility: from whom, to whom, how much, how often? These are all arbitrary decisions that leave everyone disappointed.)

These are theories that are an implicit or explicit condemnation of the positions of Karl Marx and the Socialists. This is the pivotal historical event: To the proclamation of John Locke about the justice of property rights, many people retorted: Let us rather concentrate our attention on the *injustice* of property rights; let us concentrate our attention on the way they were mostly acquired, on the way they are exercised.

This is the chasm in which the social, legal, economic, political, and cultural discourse has been toiling during the last few centuries.

This chasm might be systematically and harmoniously bridged, if we take three steps: 1. We convincingly show the fundamental mistakes of Karl Marx; 2. We convincingly show the relation that exists between property rights and economic rights; and 3. We complete the Aristotelian/Aquinian *Doctrine* of Economic Justice and thus transform it into the Theory of Economic Justice.

The theory of economic rights *does not supplant* the jurisprudence of property rights; on the contrary, by unveiling the roots of property rights, the theory of economic rights puts the exercise of property rights on a more just and firm basis; see, Gorga (2010a, 2010b).

To put it pithily, economic rights are the fathers and mothers of property rights.

4.2.3 Three Fundamental Mistakes in Marx's Analysis

Karl Marx's positions have been rebutted in a thousand ways; when put to the test, his expectations have consistently resulted in disastrous practices. And yet, in high places, we are currently faced with yet another robust revival of his theories. Wrong ideals never die because it would be splendid were they to succeed. It is worth to go once more to the roots of the many failures of Marxism.

Karl Marx made three strategic mistakes. It is these mistakes that doomed his high expectations about an eventual elimination of the faults, the injustices really, associated with the exercise of property rights.

The ultimate justification for the perennial revival of Marxism is that we are *all* indeed mightily suffering from these injustices. Although not widely acknowledged, is not financial insecurity a general condition of the modern world? Well, it is.

First, Marx believed that his analysis was so convincing as to induce people to change their minds. This is the common, congenital belief of the Enlightenment in *the power of individual words*—as distinguished from systems of thought—*to change the world.* The reality is that the *analysis* of the faults of property rights can be extended from here to infinity; it is not going to redress any of those faults. The sum total of wrongs does not give any inkling as to possible needed solutions. Intemperate belief in the power of words is a common mistake of Enlightenment thinkers, which in its worst forms leads to bloviation, an explosion of words directed by muddy thinking, a form of intellectual bullyism; see, Gorga (2018). The shortest proof that Marx, the author of *Das Kapital,* fell into this trap can be found in the fact that today there is still deep uncertainty about the meaning of "capital." See disquisitions about Piketty's (2014) work.

Second, Marx believed that his analysis was so convincing as to induce people to change their ways. He relied mostly on the power of his words to incite people to action. But what action? Ideas have no legs. They acquire their legs when they enter the hearts of people who will then *change* **their** *practices.* And here Marx made his second strategic mistake. The *few suggestions* he offered about the need for Marxist *practices* to be implemented were largely without content. To see how weak the Marxist analysis is, we have to conceive of society as a box. Marx simply turned the social structure upside down: What was private, he suggested should be made public; strangely for a sociologist, he was not at all concerned with what happens within the box; he thought that social relationships would change *automati*cally. (This is mostly a repetition of the first mistake *enlarged* from economics to sociology, essentially meaning "culture" as a whole: a phantasmagoric change.) To see the weakness of this assumption, we need to ask, "Does it really matter whether the dominant factor in the making of cars is called The Department of Transportation or Ford Motor Company?" Karl Marx did not even consider the consequences of *joining* political power with economic power.

The third strategic mistake of Karl Marx is the most serious. He did not realize, and apparently, his disciples and followers have not yet realized, that he gave up the fight before entering the ring. Once he conceded that labor or, euphemistically, the "services of labor" can be—as indeed are—treated as *merchandise to be bought and sold on the market*, the fight for justice was over. Compensation for those services is determined within the governance of property rights—a sphere that is not encumbered with too many objective limits enforceable in a court of law.

The purpose of this analysis is clear. Only if we stop pursuing misguided programs of action, we might concentrate our efforts on what is feasible and just. A few consequences of these observations for Marxism are highlighted in the Appendix.

The right way *is* to consider labor as the **owner** of the wealth it produces.

This statement is Lapalissian. There is no question as to its truth, its validity, its tremendous implications for our social, economic, and political relations. It is nearly universally and consistently accepted in theory. As we have seen in the relative extended quotation above, even John Locke reaffirmed and emphasized it. Yet, it is often neglected in practice, where it counts most. Fortunately, the world is so constructed that the validity of this fundamental statement can be ascertained through the proper set of economic, let alone moral, theories. (Facts are infinite; therefore, theories are indispensable.) That the product of work rightfully belongs to the person who creates it, as we shall see, can be definitely ascertained through the analysis of economic rights. This writer has long advocated for union membership dues to be tied, not to wages, but to **equity sharing**—and for cash-back programs.

Many authors might have generally *stated* it, but neither Locke, nor Adam Smith, nor Marx, nor Keynes, nor Hayek, nor any of their disciples have yet made an analysis of economic rights (unless, through the doctrine of *social* justice in which rights are confused with the—ever growing—*list* of entitlements, namely entitlements or moral claims to the wealth of others). The fault belongs to none other than Kant (and his predecessors and followers). Immanuel Kant left undefined the category of public rights. *Economic rights belong to the category of public rights.* Economic rights are public, natural, universal rights, essential to the realization of economic justice; they alone foster conditions that lead to the promise of a full "Life, Liberty and the pursuit of Happiness." See, e.g., Gorga (1999).

Such an epistemological lacuna left even a concerned legislator and jurist of the caliber of Emanuele Gianturco with the only alternative to conceive of a "diritto privato sociale" (social private jurisprudence). Notwithstanding his excellent intentions, this was an unfortunate oxymoron that left Gianturco open to scorn.

4.2.4 The Emptiness of Property Rights

Property rights, in their character as legal documents, are inert; they literally are *pieces of paper*. They do not produce real wealth. [They can produce financial wealth; but this is a socio-legal-political attribute that is not pertinent to our discussion. Briefly put, financial wealth is not real wealth; for some clarification, see Gorga (2017c)]. A recent book by Michael Heller and James Salzman (2021) details how intrusive and pervasive property rights are; but property rights do not produce real wealth. Were the production process to stop tomorrow—even with a superabundance of property rights and no matter how well distributed should they be—life would soon come to a screeching halt.

It is the exercise of economic rights—today manifested and exercised as economic privileges; see, Gorga (1994)—that generates new real wealth. To understand how this is true is to understand *the operations* of the economic system. Economic rights are rights of access to and control over real wealth. Through economic rights, we pass from control over *paper documents* to control **over real wealth.** It is real wealth—again not a paper document—that produces real wealth.

The transition from a regimen of property rights to a regimen of economic rights does not abrogate property rights. On the contrary. Since the law abhors a vacuum, the right of ownership over new wealth is automatically and immediately extended to the *owners* of the real wealth engaged in the production of new wealth. It is thus essential that those who want to exercise their economic rights first acquire the legal ownership of property engaged in the production process—if they do not already have such rights. Economic rights do not confer ownership of property rights; they provide legal and moral *justification* for property rights, but do not create property rights. *They create property.*

It is, then, that, since the law abhors a vacuum, society will apportion ownership rights—or should apportion—ownership rights to those who have created that property as soon as wealth is created.

It is at this juncture that—often, way too often—power and privilege prevail. The law is overruled, and the rights of property are apportioned among those who are overbearing (i prepotenti); the bullies. Overbearing people do not come alone; they mostly are a product of the laws and those who make the laws. It is at this juncture that stealing (from the rightful owners of property) becomes legal.

Some laws *are* "illegal"—and immoral—since they sanction the apportionment of property among those who have **not** created property.

These are the hard legal rules that make abrupt changes in the social, economic, and political reality hard to obtain. Yet, this is the way to preserve order and avoid chaos. We all need that.

4.2.5 How to Eliminate Blatant Injustices from Many Existing Property Rights?

As usual, there are three ways.

THE FIRST SOLUTION. Marx and the Socialists and the Communists advocate the outside/short-term solution: Revolution. An abrupt and violent turn of events. This is the short-term approach, the human understanding approach to set things right.

THE SECOND SOLUTION. Then there is the inside/long-term approach. This might be called the Divine approach. The Gospel tells us that God does not punish the wicked personally; He/She/It allows the wicked to build traps into which they eventually fall. What an elegant solution. What is the trap that the wicked Capitalist builds? The trap is the weak market, and the unsustainable growth pattern. Most economic growth is widely recognized to be a "bubble." There is no real wealth inside the bubble, so at the least provocation, the bubble bursts.

THE THIRD SOLUTION. Then there is the patient way, the long-term non-violent way, the interdependent way, the Concordian way.

How do we eliminate the blatant injustices of many existing property rights? *We can obtain this aim through the exercise of economic rights.* We will see that they are not very slow in their operation, either. In any case, wounds of injustices built up over at least five *thousand* years of history cannot be healed in one day.

This is the way. It is not the *legal* right of property that creates new wealth. Rather, it is the **economic** right of *access* to the factors of production that creates new wealth. Property rights, as legal rights, determine the rights of ownership over new wealth. Thus, again, economic rights do not replace property rights but put property rights on a solid and rightful base; the proviso is that property rights be acquired through economic rights and responsibilities.

It is, in other words, true that access to real property is legally granted by property rights; however, since property rights are not acquired—and indeed not even exercised—through strict legal **responsibilities**, their legitimacy will always be questioned, and their existence threatened. *It is through privilege, not through rights, that new wealth is owned today.* And yet, economic rights do not even destroy privileges: *they legally **turn** privileges into rights*—once rights are extended to everyone.

4.3 Welcome Concordianism

4.3.1 Introduction

After sweeping away the ideologies and confusions created by Keynes, Hayek, Locke, and Marx, the ground is open to a new world. Will this ground be occupied by Concordianism? Concordian economic theory is for specialists. Here the concern is for Concordian economic policy—or Concordianism. Will Concordianism implement the recommendations of economic justice? Will Concordianism carry into practice the theoretical structure of Economic Rights and Responsibilities? Let us see.

4.3.2 A Bit of Recent History

To gain a full appreciation of economic rights, rights existing within the alcove of economic justice, we have to anchor them within the context of recent history. Thus we get closer to ways and means to translate them into action. Until we place them in the context of hard day-to-day practices, the discussion might fall on deaf ears. Let us pick up the discussion from the middle of the current age. Why, for all its many virtues, did the Progressive Movement in the United States fail to even touch the hard issues of poverty amidst plenty? Well, there are at least three fundamental answers: Members of the Progressive Movement 1. Failed to develop the theoretical structure of Economic Justice; 2. They failed to develop a conveyor belt to translate theory into practice, such as provided by economic rights and responsibilities; 3. They did not face head-on their real intellectual enemy, social justice.

Even though I have already published much on it, and much ought to transpire through the present work, an entirely new book will be devoted to this topic. There it will become most evident why, to redress the horrible injustices that manifest themselves as poverty amidst plenty, the political and cultural structure of a modern country is left with only one tool: moral suasion. Impotent.

Social justice is a condition in which two abstract entities, the *Individual and Society* are pitted in a battle to the finish against each other. The two abstractions, as we have seen, are personified by the followers of John Locke and Karl Marx, neither one of them an economist. The trouble is that, while intellectuals of the Right and the Left of the political spectrum are having the time of their life (see, in more recent history, Hayek and Keynes), the majority of the people is being more and more squeezed out of the discussion, marginalized, or left in the gutter in which hunger and homelessness reign supreme.

If and when the political body wakes up to the absurdity of this condition, governments will awaken the soul of each citizen to consider the reality of the four economic rights and responsibilities (Ers&ERs) enunciated throughout Concordian economics. Then governments will discover that, if they really want to serve human needs, they will have to concentrate their efforts on the prevention of injustices—an operation that is best carried out by implementing the recommendation of economic justice. Once they do that, governments will only need to proclaim the rules of the road and prevent the infractions of those rules.

4.3.3 Role of Governments

Even though the following four economic rights and responsibilities have been discovered and analyzed within the framework of Concordian economics, it will eventually be realized that these ERs&ERs are universal, human rights. Governments have only to proclaim them and allow them to be inscribed in the heart and soul of every human being—and get out of the way of the operation of the market. (Is not such a policy anathema today to both the right and the left of the political spectrum?).

Passage of appropriate legislation will undoubtedly have to take place, and a panoply of proposals will undoubtedly have to be formulated to introduce these ERs&ERs into the legislative body of a nation, and a panoply of procedures will undoubtedly have to be pursued that will render this achievement possible. The major role of governments will be the recognition that these ERs&ERs form the core of the continuation of the economic justice project, a project that was developed over the course of millennia, from Aristotle, through St. Thomas Aquinas, to the Doctors of Salamanca. The project was rudely interrupted by John Locke and Adam Smith and has gradually been replaced by the inane project of social justice. Has not social justice have had more than enough time to pursue its mirage? The evident answer is that one major ingredient, the negative ingredient, the Invisible Elephant in the room, is missing from the analysis. Social justice has created the **State as distributor of entitlements,** distributor of wealth belonging to others. This is the function that many people, Hayek included, attack. They will not succeed unless they fight *for economic justice* in which The State discovers and proclaims the presence of natural economic rights and responsibilities—and leaves The Market free to test its mettle.

4.3.4 Hints About the Transition

If and when the four ERs&ERs of Concordian economics are proclaimed and their operation safeguarded by principles of economic justice, human beings will gradually and peacefully carry forward the work of transition from the current stage of the "mixed economy" to the future stage of the pure economy. While it is nearly impossible to prescribe or even to imagine all the measures to carry this transition forward, the main mechanism will certainly be this: As soon as human beings are able to obtain the income they need from the market, their innate dignity will let them refuse any government hand-out. (Some minor, but strong evidence of the validity of this position can be found in the behavior of the Amish in relation to health insurance.) Thus, will the role of the Government be deflated and that of the Market be brought up to full speed?

4.3.5 A General Comment

Here one sole point can be emphasized. Economic rights and economic responsibilities are our best hope to make the corporations—and governments— serve the needs of human beings. Operating as tipping points in our modus vivendi, ERs&ERs will set in motion a process of economic interdependence that respects the reality of business affairs and the reality of human relationships. Recognizing that most people and most businesses always act morally, the increasing number of "bad apples" that at times seem to receive all the attention (and envious support) of a superficial intellectual world will be recognized as dangerous exceptions, perhaps ostracized, but certainly no longer applauded. Once the tendencies of these people are kept in check, all wealth will be distributed, not equally—that is meaningless utopianism—but fairly. Hence, there will no longer be any need for redistributive programs, which are an expression of double utopianism: First, people as if living in la-la land are allowed to accumulate much, no matter how; and then they are expected to peacefully discharge their ill-gotten wealth. Preserving their current wealth, the rich will grow richer at a steady but slower pace; and the poor will no longer be poor because they will have all they need. Lacking fuel at both ends, violent oscillations in the business cycle will be abated.

We will thus recover the essential truth of economics. This is the truth that there are two conditions of growth: economic freedom and economic justice, as concrete expressions of freedom and morality. Both are essential. The relationship between the two is quite clear: While freedom does not necessarily bring justice with it, justice unavoidably brings freedom. One can abuse freedom by denying freedom to others, one can never abuse justice. Hence, the initial condition of freedom for all is proof positive of the existence of economic justice in the land. The import of economic justice and economic rights and responsibilities is simply stated: We must prevent injustices from occurring; once an injustice has occurred, there is nothing that can be done to undo the dastard deed. Justice delayed is justice denied. This is the bosom of realism.

4.3.6 *A Recap: Few Specifics About Economic Rights and Responsibilities*

It is essential to know economic rights. As there are four (modern) factors of production—land and natural resources, labor, financial capital, and physical capital—so there must exist four economic rights that give access to these factors, namely:

1. The right of access to land and natural resources;
2. The right of access to the fruits of one's labor;
3. The right of access to financial resources imbued in our national credit; and
4. The right of access to the fruits of one's property.

How are these rights acquired? To the best of this writer's understanding, economic rights are acquired through the exercise of corresponding economic responsibilities; namely:

1. The responsibility to pay taxes on land and natural resources under one's control;
2. The responsibility to perform tasks required in the process of wealth creation;
3. The responsibility to repay loans obtained through access to national credit; and
4. The responsibility to respect the property of others.

This is the chain then: Economic rights, acquired through the exercise of economic responsibilities, are rights of access to real wealth that allow for the creation of new real wealth. Ownership of the new wealth automatically belongs—ought to belong, must belong—to the creators of such wealth.

Some of these economic rights and responsibilities (ERs&ERs) need more explanations than others. The duty to pay taxes on land under one's control—emphasized not only by John Stuart Mill and Henry George but by eight Nobel Laureates in economics—is rooted in a simple reality: Most of the value of land is given, not by efforts of individual owners, but efforts of the community in which the land is located. A rock in Arizona is worth a pittance; a similar rock in New York City is worth gazillions. Figuratively speaking, we all want to stand on this rock to enjoy the benefits of the Metropolitan Museum, the Guggenheim, the New York Philharmonic, the many Museums of Science and Tech, the subway, and myriad other public—and private—facilities. Land taxes are primarily destined to destroy the latifundia (vast holdings generally set to inefficient uses); when owners of vast estates do not wish to pay such taxes, they will opt to sell the land. The market of the land is expanded; the price of the land will thus be reduced (economists know this mechanism all too well); hence, the opportunity to own land is extended to present property-less people.

The right of access to the fruits of one's labor (remember Marx) gives right, not only to wages, but to participation in the capital appreciation of the firm. This right is acquired, not by violent upheavals, but—thanks to the genius of Louis O. Kelso—through the legal transformation of workers, and (potentially) consumers, into stockholders, respectively through fabled ESOPs and CSOPs. ESOPs are Employee Stock Ownership Plans and CSOPs are Consumer Stock Ownership Plans.

The right of access to financial resources imbued in our national credit—thanks to the indefatigable efforts of Benjamin Franklin—is inscribed in Article 1, section 4.8 of the U.S. Constitution. The Federal Reserve System (the Fed), our central bank, creates (or ought to) and distributes money, not out of "thin air," but on the strength of our **national credit**. Since all residents of a nation contribute to the value of its national credit, all residents of a nation are rightfully eligible to receive loans, *at the cost of administration*, issued by the central bank—or a decentralized facility that can be adroitly operated by local banks. The responsibility, of course, is to repay the loan. Without such a reasonable assurance, there is no right of access to national credit, our last commonwealth. A paper outlining this proposal as well as the need for a systematic (Mosaic) Debt Jubilee every seven years was sent to the Fed, Gorga (2015), and the Fed gave a nod of approval to this policy; see, Durr (2016). The writer has had precious few resources of time and money to follow this directive of the Fed.

Notwithstanding the appearance, more difficult is the case of the right of access to the fruits of one's property, with the corresponding responsibility to respect the property of others. This right is respected everywhere, except—in an industrial society—where it counts most: in relation to the ownership of our large corporations. In this area, rather than "law and order," one observes the operations of the Pac Man Approach. In honor of the strenuous efforts of Louis D. Brandeis and the cohort that created the Progressive Movement with its *feeble* anti-trust laws in the United States, this writer has conceived of the Brandeis Rule as a substitute for the Pac Man Approach: Let the first 100 largest corporations grow internally as large as the market allows them to grow, but sternly prohibit them from engaging in buying or being bought by other entities. After analyzing the results, enlarge the number of corporations subject to the Brandeis Rule to the next 100 or the next 200 largest corporations, up to the level in which corporations operate only within a limited geographic area, such as any one state in the United States. The expectation is that the captains of our great industries will love being freed from looking sideways and over their shoulders. They will love to concentrate their attention on the internal needs of our wondrous corporations—with passionate relentless pursuit of the common good of stockholders and stakeholders.

A full understanding of these ERs&ERs is acquired, not through the reading of Keynes or Hayek, but through understanding the legacy of four giant American thinkers, in their order of appearance on earth: Benjamin Franklin (money), Henry George (land), Louis D. Brandeis (physical capital), and Luis O. Kelso (labor). As a unit, they form an unassailable fortress.

4.3.7 Economic Rights and the Theory of Justice

Briefly put, economic rights and economic responsibilities are especially important for the theory of justice; they give concrete answers to questions posited by the extant theory of justice, Gorga (2023); they perform functions required by the conception of "general abstract rules" by Hayek (1960, p. 153), the "original position" by Rawls (1971, pp. 12, 72, 136, 538), the "reverse theory" by Nozick (1974, p. 238), and the "Principle of Generic Consistency" by Gewirth (1985, p. 19). (The many unexamined questions in these theories can then be examined and become satisfactorily answerable.) Practically, they function as Gladwell's "tipping points" (2000). Ultimately, it was a poet, Vincent Ferrini (2002), who caught the essence of economic rights and responsibilities by identifying their ability to provide "the answers to universal poverty and the anxieties of the affluent."

Among other benefits, economic rights and responsibilities allow us to identify four privileges that make for much *inequality* in today's world.

4.3.8 Four Horses of Inequality

Control over the four factors of production, acquired today as a *privilege with no, or very limited, responsibilities,* gives rise to four horses of inequality: 1. Land and natural resources ownership *without* the payment of taxes (while extracting oil "depletion" allowances from the taxpayer); 2. *Legal* appropriation of the value of the work of others; 3. Gaining *control* over the process of creation and distribution of money, while saddling the majority of the population with exorbitant interest payments for consumer credit; see, Bhutta et al. (2016); and nearly shutting everyone else out of capital credit markets. Consumer credit, in any case, enslaves the borrower, while capital credit potentially liberates the borrower; and 4. *Gobbling up* friendly and potential enemy corporations to corner the market in order to pay low wages and exact high prices for consumer products. These are the abuses of market power that can be controlled only through a regimen of economic rights and responsibilities.

They are the only tools to reduce inequality and obtain—not equality—but economic justice.

There are many other ideological, sociological, and institutional factors that determine existing conditions of inequality. But they are contributing factors. The animating forces can be found only among the privileges enjoyed through control of the four factors of production.

4.3.9 Inequality Benefits no One

Inequality is certainly inimical to the poor and the propertyless. However, since inequality is the source of instability of the market, its ultimate effect is this: It is the wealthy who suffer most from periodic financial collapses of the economy.

Happy are the penniless. Happy are those who rely on more permanent values than those bestowed by money.

4.3.10 Conclusion

The existence of property rights has been in danger ever since the emphasis was placed on them by John Locke; the world has never witnessed such an ever-widening set of conflicts as those experienced during the last three centuries. The assault comes from many well-intentioned sources. The hidden power of these sources lies in the lack of existence of better solutions to the need to redress the injustices prevalent in society. The ultimate result of this course of action is this reality: By destroying property rights, we are gradually destroying the bonds that hold people together in society.

Opponents of property rights, of course, change the direction of the vectors. They theorize that property rights are destroying the bonds of society. (They could be given the benefit of the doubt, were they to offer realistic solutions.)

A better solution is the creation of a regimen of economic justice in which economic rights *extended to everyone* are the indisputable source of property rights. Ecologists fear not: the exercise of economic responsibilities will be the ultimate source of protection of Mother Earth; to say the least, ERs&ERs foster an automatic reduction of waste; see, for example, Gorga (2021a).

To install a regimen of economic rights society does not need the contribution of even one cent, let alone two cents of the wealth of the affluent. What society needs to do is to use all its powers to *transform the privileges* that the affluent enjoy *into rights—and responsibilities*—that **everyone** can exercise. This program of action can be presented as a Grand Compromise: the affluent release their privileges (but not their rights); the propertyless set their use—or threat of use—of pitchforks aside once and for all. Pitchforks is a metaphor that includes all fatuous attempts to re-distribute wealth, through taxation or forceful expropriation.

As Vincent Ferrini knew well, pitchforks are an essential ingredient of the anxieties of the affluent. A psychologist will add the pangs of conscience. I am far from rich, but those commercials calling for contributions to alleviate the pains of homeless children from all over the world make me squirm in the chair.

Pitchforks for **surplus** money, that is the Grand Bargain. Let us enter into this bargain en mass. Then what to expect?

Justice will reign. Peace will reign. Perhaps forever. We humans have better things to do with our lives.

Appendix: A Few More Observations on Marxism

The mistakes highlighted in the text do not stem from anything outside Marx's thinking but from the very core of that thinking. Apart from the unavoidable general influence of the culture of the age, there is no one else, no other entity to blame for those errors. This is the truth, which is hard to swallow for a faithful disciple: *Marx was not an economist:* **he was a very opinionated sociologist**. He did not do any field work; his brain sufficed for him.

As to economics, he knew not what is capital. Capital is a wondrous thing. Although not alone, he failed to distinguish financial capital from physical capital. Worse, he assumed that profit, interest, and rent are "surplus value" that is derived from "unpaid labor" (or stolen from workers.)

They are not that. They are the fruit of financial capital, an invaluable benefit to mankind. As my barber next door knew well, and Marxist ideologues still find it hard to recognize, money is the best labor-saving device. Yes, indeed, we have better things to do with our lives than spend our energies on manual labor. Robots can do that for us, but they have to be our robots.

In Marx's incomplete system of thought there is no room for Archimedes' conception of the world, a conception that was encapsulated in this statement: Give me a fulcrum, a lever long enough, and I will lift the world. A lever is an expression of physical capital. A lever is not a gift of Nature. A lever itself, or at least the *use* of the lever, is the creation of the human mind. The universal recommendation to mankind has traditionally been this: Do use the lever to transform the human condition. But not Marx. But not the Marxists.

Capital, in both its financial and physical incarnation, is a factor of production. It is an invaluable *factor* of production. Capital is not something to be erased from the face of the earth; capital is something to put to work *for* men and women. Men and women are not destined to **work** only; they are destined to think, to feel, and to love as well.

To reposition the statement in the text that "Wrong ideals (ideologies) never die because it would be splendid were they to succeed," one must courageously recognize that it is a divine gift that some ideologies are never materialized: What a horrible world is Marx's world; what a nightmare of the human mind; what *a slavery to the human hand*.

Yes, given the assumption that we are descendants of monkeys, our best hope would be to evolve into strong gorillas. This is the best that historical materialism can offer.

References

Bhutta, N., Goldin, J., & Homonoff, T. (2016). Consumer borrowing after payday loan bans. *Journal of Law and Economics, 59*, 225–259.

Brady, M. E. (2013). John Maynard Keynes's upper and lower valued probabilities: A study of how statisticians, philosophers, logicians, historians, and economists failed to comprehend keynes's breakthrough application of g. boole's interval approach to probability in the 20th century. *International Journal of Applied Economics and Econometrics, 21*, 254–272.

Brandeis, L. D. (1913). *Other People's money and how the bankers use it*. Frederick A. Stokes Company (1932).

Brandeis, L. D. (1914). *Business a profession*. Small, Maynard and Company.

Brandeis, L. D. (1934). *The curse of bigness*. The Viking Press.

Coase, R. H. (1937). The nature of the firm. *Economica, 4*, 386–405.

Coase, R. H. (1960). The problem of social cost. *Journal of Law and Economics, 3*, 1–44.

Durr, J. (2016). Personal communication, September 14. In *Public affairs office, board of governors of the federal reserve system*. Available at file:///C:/Users/cgorg/OneDrive/Attachments/ECONOMICS/Documents/2nd%20Jean%20Durr,%20FRS.pdf.

Ferrini, V. (2002). Gorga worthy of note. *Gloucester Daily Times*, December 11, p. A6.

Frank, R. (2011). World's Richest Man attacks wall street bailouts: carlos slim says the U.S. government should be spending more on main street and less on wall street. WSJ Blogs: *The Wealth Report* (October 25). http://blogs.wsj.com/.

Franklin, B. (1729). A modest enquiry into the nature and necessity of a paper-currency. In A. M. Davis (Ed.) *Colonial currency reprints* (Vol. II, pp. 336–57) 1910. Boston, MA: Prince Society Publications.

George, H. (1879). *Progress and poverty*. Robert Schalkenbach Foundation (1979).

Gladwell, M. (2002). *The tipping point*. Back Bay Books.

Gewirth, A. (1985). Economic justice: Concepts and Criteria. In K. Kipnis & D. T. Meyers, (Eds.), *Economic justice: Private rights and public responsibilities*. Totowa, N.J.: Rowman & Littlefield.

Gorga, C. (1994). Four economic rights: Social renewal through economic justice for all. *Social Justice Review, 85*(1–2), 3–6.

Gorga, C. (1999). Toward the definition of economic rights. *Journal of Markets & Morality, 2*, 88–101.

Gorga, C. (2002 and 2009). The economic process: An instantaneous non-newtonian picture. In M. D. Lanham (Ed.), *The somist institute,* 2016b (3rd edn.). Oxford: University Press of America.

Gorga, C. (2010a). Roots of property law: From the moral contract, and the doctrine of economic justice, to the social contract. Is the legal contract next? In *World Institute for Research and Publication (WIRP)*, June 4. Available at SSRN: https://doi.org/10.2139/ssrn.1600595.

Gorga, C. (2010b). The unconstitutionality of federal fishing law. In: *Gloucester daily times, my view*, January 10. Available at https://www.gloucestertimes.com/opinion/my-view-the-unconstitutionality-of-federal-fishing-law/article_d559164d-96f5-508e-a04c-8efccf842d44.html. Accessed 13 December 2023.

Gorga, C. (2011). *Some shortcomings of the social contract*. Available at SSRN.https://doi.org/10.2139/ssrn.3143002

Gorga, C. (2012a). Reconciling keynes and hayek through concordian economics. *International Journal of Applied Economics and Econometrics,* Part 5 of the Special Issue on J.M. Keynes,

References

20(3, July-Sep), 358–387. Available at https://econcurrents.com/2022/08/21/reconciling-keynes-and-hayek-through-concordian-economics. Assessed 29 September 2023.

Gorga, C. (2012b). Beyond keynes….. toward concordian econometrics. *International Journal of Applied Economics and Econometrics*, Part III of the Special Issue on J.M. Keynes, *20*(1), 248–277. Republished in *Econintersect*, May and June 2016.

Gorga, C. (2015). Two proposals in the form of two petitions designed to stabilize the monetary system. *The Somist Institute*, December 3. Available at Two Proposals.pdf.

Gorga, C. (2016a). Wake up America. Wake up from Your 250-Year-Old Slumber. *Mother Pelican, A Journal of Solidarity and Sustainability, 12*(6).

Gorga, C. (2016b). Two proposals to stabilize the monetary system. *Econintersect*

Gorga, C. (2017a). A cascade of errors (1517–2017). *OpEd News.*

Gorga, C. (2017b). Concordian economics: An overall view. *Econintersect.*

Gorga, C. (2017c). Money, banking, and the economic process. *Econintersect.*

Gorga, C. (2018). *The redemption of the bully: Through love toward the beloved community.* Scholars' Press.

Gorga, C. (2021a). Toward economic, ecological, and human interdependence. *Mother Pelican, A Journal of Solidarity and Sustainability, 17*(6).

Gorga, C. (2023). Finding economic justice. *EconCurrents.* November 12. Available at https://econcurrents.com/2023/11/12/finding-economic-justice. Accessed 7 December 2023.

Hayek, F. (1941 [2009]). *The pure theory of capital.* Auburn, Al: Ludwig von Mises Institute.

Hayek, F. (1948). *Individualism and economic order.* University of Chicago Press.

Hayek, F. ([1995] 1963). The Economics of the 1930s as Seen from London. In *Contra Keynes and Cambridge: Essays and Correspondence* (vol. 9 of *The Collected Works of F. A. Hayek*), Bruce Caldwell, ed. 49. Chicago: U. Chicago Press (1995).

Hayek, F. (1994). Hayek on hayek: An autobiographical dialogue. In S. Kresge & L. Wenar (Eds.), *Quoted in Bruce Caldwell, Hayek's Challenge: An intellectual biography of F. A. Hayek.* Chicago: U. Chicago Press, 2004, p. 401.

Heller, M., & Salzman, J. (2021). *Mine! how the hidden rules of ownership control our lives.* Doubleday.

Kelso, L. O. (1957). Karl marx: The almost capitalist. *American Bar Association Journal, 43*, 235–38, 275–79.

Kelso, L. O., & Adler, M. J. (1958). *The capitalist Manifesto.* Random House.

Kelso, L. O., & Hetter, P. (1967). *Two-Factor theory: The economics of reality.* Vintage Books.

Keynes, J. M. (1936). *The general theory of employment, interest, and money.* Harcourt.

Keynes, J. M. (1937). The general theory of employment. *Quarterly Journal of Economics, LI*(February), 211–12.

Locke, J. (1689 [1965]). Two treatises of government. In P. Laslett (Ed.), London: Awnsham and John Churchill, NY: A Mentor Book, Bk. II, Ch. v, paras 25–27.

Lux, K. (1990). *Adam Smith's Mistake: How a moral philosopher invented economics and ended morality.* Shambhala.

Mises, L. (1933 [2003]). *Epistemological problems of economics.* Auburn, Al: Ludwig von Mises Institute.

Neill, R. (2011). *Slavery in the writings of Thomas Aquinas*, Yumpu.com. Available at: https://www.yumpu.com/en/document/read/12426173/slavery-in-the-writings-of-thomas-aquinas

Rizzo, M. (2010). Keynes versus Hayek: Past is Prologue. *ThinkMarkets.com* (June 10).

Nozick, R. (1974). *Anarchy, state, and Utopia.* Basic Books.

Pazzanese, C. (2021). Amartya Sen's nine-decade journey from colonial India to Nobel Prize and beyond. *The Harvard Gazette*, June 3.

Piketty, T. (2014). *Capital in the twenty-first century.* Harvard University Press.

Rawls, J. (1971). *A theory of justice* (Vol. 12, No. 72, pp. 136–538). Cambridge, Mass.: Harvard University Press.

Ryan, J. A. (1906). *A living wage: Its ethical and economic aspects.* Macmillan.

Ryan, J. A. (1916). *Distributive justice: The right and wrong of our present distribution of wealth*. Macmillan.

Sen, A. K. (1998). The possibility of social choice. In T. Persson (Ed.), *Nobel lectures, economics 1996–2000*. Singapore: World Scientific Publishing Co., 2003.

Wood, D. (2002). *Medieval economic thought*. Cambridge University Press.

Part II
Financial Interdependence

Chapter 5
King Cash

Abstract A crude and crass expression of Concordian economics is its aspiration to see more cash in everybody's pockets. One might expect a unanimous agreement on this basic policy. But no. On the contrary, there is much opposition to it. Strange things we are being told of you these days. We used to call you, Cash, "King Cash" to signify our deep affection for you. No more. Ever since Jefferson deleted the word "property," the most direct manifestation of which is cash, from the Declaration of Independence, the word "property" has become a "political" word, a word not to be uttered in polite society.

5.1 Introduction

There is even a book out titled *The Curse of Cash* (2017). When one goes beyond the shock of the title, one can definitely accept all concerns expressed by the author, Professor Kenneth Rogoff, in the subtitle about the potentially nefarious uses of bills of large denomination. The need and the advantages of cash of small denomination are reaffirmed.

An even more drastic approach was advocated by Professor Joel Kurtzman in a book titled *The Death of Money* (1993). Actually, there are many books out by this title. The eulogy is often pronounced rather prematurely. But certainly the death of money is declared and plotted in a hundred different creations. The most devious are those mathematical constructions which are not understood by anyone, often authors included. The catafalque is solemnly built but does not contain the real thing, no author worth his salt would risk his own cash. A simple effigy suffices. The dollar sign is a universally recognized symbol of money. And that is what is used in these studies.

There are many proposals that call for the abolition of money—in one form or another. We shall see that there are even proposals to destroy the Federal Reserve System, our Central Bank. These proposals share a set of assumptions: that we can "operate" a society without the assistance of money; that we can "distribute" money as a grant; that we can develop an advanced societal "honor system," because people will be **trained** to create the common good.

In this chapter, we are going to look at the history of Cash and Money: how it was treated in the past; how it might be treated in the future; and how it being treated in the present—all this still within the realm of politics. In next chapter, we shall observe cash or more generally "money" in the context of Concordian economics.

5.2   The Importance of Cash

As an ingenious business coach, Grant Cardone (2023) says: "82% of Business Failure Are Due to Poor Cash Flow Management." *Cash is that important.* People without cash are poor, of course. *Cash is that important.* People who owe cash to other people, people in debt, are people in trouble. *Cash is that important.*

5.3   Past: The Old American Way

5.3.1   The Use of Cash

The use of cash was the outward manifestation of many virtues: the self-assured posture that one had to "save" money before spending it. Today most of us are in a hurry; we want what we want **now.** And we have found a way to gratify our urges: While we buy on credit, our lending institutions are more than happy to lend us money at interest. And what is interest if not *our* cask in **their** pockets?

One finds the use of cash payments is still prevalent among the Amish people and that used to be "The American Way," cash on the barrel (cash on the nail is the English way). See Gorga (2017a).

The political discourse, especially on how to pay for healthcare, is locked into an impossible vise. We think that there is either the Market Way or the Government Way. At most, we can conceive of the Mixed Economy Way.

Generally, this third way carries with it most of the disadvantages of the first two approaches: Freedom is restricted, and costs remain stubbornly high.

Let us explore the Amish Way.

The Amish pay cash, their own cash to purchase all the healthcare they need, wherever they want it, and receive it at up to 40% discount.

Not a bad solution at all.

(The sociology and the economics of it are intriguing, but will not be explored here.)

Once upon a time, this happened to be the way for all Americans and for all citizens of the world. This is still the rich man's way. How can we return to it—how can the poor gradually make themselves adequately rich?

5.3 Past: The Old American Way

The solution lies in looking into the operations of the Federal Reserve System (the Fed), our Central Bank. And adapting them to serve the needs of all the people. There has to be a two-pronged tack: Reduce costs of producers and increase income of consumers.

The Fed is the pivot in both approaches.

Let us start at the top.

Since money created by the Fed goes first to financial corporation—the so-called primary dealers—all industrial and commercial corporations pay high interest on their loans.

Why can't loans be issued directly to industrial and commercial corporations?

Why can't loans be issued directly by the Federal Reserve System to industrial and commercial corporations—still making use of local banks?

There is no reason, except custom.

Customs can be changed.

Indeed, the Fed has examined a proposal along these lines, and, provided it is adopted by Congress, the Fed seems to be ready to consider such a change of custom.

Indeed, the Fed is ready to go one step further. The Fed is ready to respond to the same questions about interest. There is no reason why the Fed is charging interest on capital expansion loans. Hence, the Fed is ready to consider the possibility of issuing such loans at cost. The cost of creating and servicing the loans.

The Fed is ready to consider such changes provided they become part and parcel of a uniform national policy. Three Rules need to govern such a policy: 1. Loans have to be issued only for the creation of real wealth; 2. Loans have to benefit as far as possible all citizens; 3. Loans have to be issued at coast.

All conditions are ultimately aimed at increasing the income of consumers.

Capital expansion loans, loans aimed at creating new real—as distinguished from financial—wealth, can be issued at cost by the Fed (*through the intermediation of local banks*) to all qualified entrepreneurs. This practice is most useful to unleash the creative and entrepreneurial juices of the people. The key qualification is a monstrance of the ability to repay the loans.

But not everyone has an entrepreneurial, a business spirit. How to help them?

The solution is ready-made; it is well known; and it is much used.

The solution is that public capital ought to be given to corporations as well as individual entrepreneurs and co-operatives. But corporations must have an Employee Stock Ownership Plan (ESOP) in their constitution. Through this ingenious legal instrument, created by an American lawyer and investment banker, Louis O. Kelso, workers are legally, peacefully, and justly transformed into co-owners of the corporations in which they work. The ownership base of the country is thus expanded. More money enters the pockets of consumers; more money is available to allow producers to keep up their creation of new useful wealth.

The Fed is ready to make these rules a condition of making loans at cost to American corporations. Indeed, with little prodding the Fed might be ready to add Consumer Ownership Plans (CSOPs) as a condition of federal loans.

Through CSOPs and ESOPs we can look forward to an equitable distribution of the income produced. The age of robots will be welcomed, rather than dreaded—provided their ownership is spread as widely as possible, rather than concentrated into a few hands.

Given these conditions created by Fed policy, pharmaceutical corporations as well as insurance corporations and hospitals can be expected to operate at lower costs.

By the same token, workers/consumers can be expected to have more income to spend on health services—or on any other type of product or service.

The Market and the Government will be there to create and enforce the rules of the road. But entrepreneurs as well as citizens will have to be ready to use the roads and should be free to use them when and how they please.

Cash in the pocket does wander.

5.4 Present: Cash-Back—A Silver Lining

5.4.1 Cash-Back

Are cash-back programs multiplying under our eyes? Is anyone keeping track of this progress systematically? The last report I saw was very encouraging. It seems that corporations are quietly joining the bandwagon, and that is a good thing. See Gorga (2017b).

Cash-back programs are a unique silver lining on an otherwise bleak horizon. Observed by just a few specialists, it seems that a financial crisis of unheard-of proportions is galloping toward us. You have to listen to them to see the inevitability of the crisis. The question is not if, but when.

Bill Bonner is one such specialist. His credentials are impeccable. He predicted the collapse of the Soviet Empire, the savings-and-loan debacle, the crash of the dot-coms, and the bursting of the housing bubble. He keeps a steady eye on the burgeoning debt of families, corporations, and governments, here and abroad. He has created a compact research organization that analyzes complex records with an open, unbiased mind.

In his latest private publication, *When the ATMS Go Dark* (2017), Bill Bonner offers not only a detailed chart of past financial crises world-wide. Most importantly, he offers a step-by-step analysis of the effects of the bursting of the debt bubble.

Bill Bonner also offers a detailed list of remedies for the individual person of means.

In certain circles, it is said, "Forget saving 'The System' - Save Yourself."

But there is no such thing as safety for the individual person. Even assuming that such a thing is possible, to which world will this person emerge when he finally gets out of the bunker?

Civilizations have died in the past.

* * *

5.4 Present: Cash-Back—A Silver Lining

Sixty years ago, in the context of intense conversations fostered by the Lisle Foundation, I was fingered as an "incorrigible optimist." I still am.

How can I not be?

How can I not be grateful for my life and grateful to the Lisle Foundation for having lived that marvelous experience twice—through instant recall?

Let us see whether we can prevent the dissolution of our present civilization. There are many wrongs in it—and those we should try to correct. But there are also many goods in it, they make the effort to save it worthwhile.

In the relatively recent past, I have proposed two systemic solutions, Gorga (2015a); accordingly, I have developed two Internet petitions—MEND THE FED[1] and DEFUSE THE BOMB[2]—to gain support for them; and I have—oh, so incredibly—obtained a letter of support for these remedies from the Federal Reserve System (!).

Here, however, I will not go over them. I would rather like to emphasize that cash-back programs can be another way of gently deflating the bubble from within so that we might end up escaping the impending catastrophic financial crisis with relative impunity.

Corporations have accumulated inordinate amounts of cash in the recent past. As I have pointed out elsewhere if these corporations were to spend these funds whether on capital or consumer goods, we would be engulfed in the traditional flames of inflation.

These hoards can, however, be put to good use by gradually transferring them into the hands of penniless consumers. Cash-backs are indeed a silver lining on our bleak horizon. But this transferal has to become general and systematic.

The legal vehicle is the Consumer Stock Ownership Plan (CSOP). It was conceived by Louis O. Kelso, the genial lawyer/financier who also designed the Employee Stock Ownership Plan (ESOP). While ESOPs have quietly assumed a major role in our economic life, CSOPs are still dormant.

The number of people covered by ESOPs is now larger than the number of people covered by labor unions. To recover their erstwhile, necessary, status, I have for long suggested that unions have to learn how to tie their dues, not to higher wages, but to a more even distribution of profits—a task achievable through ESOPs.

While ESOPs are on their unstoppable way to success, burgeoning cash-back programs might inject much-needed life into CSOPs. CSOPs might, after all, supply consumers with that amount of cash, which at the burst of the debt bubble cannot, at least temporarily, be received from ATMs any longer.

Checks sent by corporations (shh: out of their "savings"—or out of their creditworthiness) directly to their customers as cash-back for their year-to-date expenditures might provide sufficient money to prevent the collapse of our commercial and industrial organizations. In a pinch, grocery stores and department stores will surely accept these checks as money. The Harvard Coop has done this for quite a few years now.

---

[1] At https://sign.moveon.org/petitions/a-patriotic-petition-1?r_by=2016207&source=c.em.

[2] At https://sign.moveon.org/petitions/the-jubilee-solutio

If generalized, in the future, a CSOP civilization—born out of the self-interest of generating loyal consumers—will reveal that *cheating the consumer is cheating oneself*. Can we imagine the day in which McDonald's, Target, and Macy's adopt such a policy?

Let the financial behemoths of the world collapse—not too much damage will be done, provided Central Banks are no longer cajoled into providing them with financial artificial resuscitation at the expense of taxpayers and/or bank depositors.

Employees of financial behemoths have enough financial resources to retire to personal safety; on the other hand, if they so wish, their enormous technical know-how will make them invaluable employees elsewhere; they might even conceive of starting their own new ventures.

The silver lining in the incoming crisis is the possibility of a soft-landing due to consumer cash-backs.

5.5 Future: Those Lazy Workers—They Are Gaming the System

5.5.1 *Those Lazy Workers*

It was the worst of times. It was the best of times. And then there is the everlasting present of Lao Tzu in which: "*Those who speak do not know. Those who know do not speak.*" It takes a mountain of chutzpah for people to be railing against workers who prefer to "play for nothing than to work for nothing." Sorry, did I mix my metaphors? The thought is that of Adam Smith, the father of modern economics, who basically acknowledged that workers are "rational" human beings: If you don't pay them adequately, they will not work.

Coronavirus times have changed us, see Gorga (2021a). Some of us prefer to get $600 per week and stay home rather than $400 (?) per week and go to work.

It takes a mountain of chutzpah to begrudge $600 a week to a mother or a father who might prefer to stay home with their kids, rather than going to work in a dangerous environment.

It takes a mountain of chutzpah to begrudge $600 a week to a multitude of people while granting millions of dollars to the few who sit on top of the economic ladder.

What are the respective sum totals? In an age in which trillions are bandied around as if they were "real money," what difference does it make?

Perhaps, this is too rational a discourse—already made in many different shades of color by many sources—to impress anyone.

What I really want to do is to try to convey the idea that withdrawing such people from the workforce *adds to the efficiency* of the economic system as a whole.

I wish I had enough money at my command to run an in-depth long longitudinal study to prove my case.

5.5 Future: Those Lazy Workers—They Are Gaming the System

Barring this opportunity, and not having the hard data at my disposal, I will verify Lao Tzu's wisdom: I do not know, therefore I speak.

The population according to me is divided into two gross segments: those who love their work, and those who hate their work.

I let the Reader imagine the proportions of the two segments. But accurate numbers are, again, not necessary. To prove my case, I will repeat my most favorite joke about economists. Here it is. At the May Day Parade, squadron after squadron passed by the stand where Khrushchev was reviewing the state of alertness of his military apparatus. Armored tanks followed armored tanks. Missiles on flat trucks after missiles on flat trucks. You got the vision.

The parade was, unexpectedly, closed by two short men in dark suits.

Mr. Khrushchev turned to his secretary and asked: "Who are those two men?"

Sotto voce, the secretary answered: "Sir, they are economists. You do not know how much damage they can do."

There is much truth to this tale. In a more highfalutin environment, one of our brightest Nobel Laureates in economics, Professor Ester Duflo (2010), at a prestigious TED Talk, assessed the work of economists this way: "*[Without foreign aid, Africa might have turned out better, or worse, or the same.]* '*We have no idea. We're not any better than the medieval doctors and their leeches.*'"

To really impress you, I should now dredge the actual numbers involved in the foreign aid given to Africa, yearly, over the decades of its existence, not only by the United States, but also by each and every European country. That is not sufficient yet. I should also add the aid given by Saudi Arabia, by Russia, and, lately, by China.

Well my homework assignment for the day is to urge you, dear Reader, to consider how much damage can do the, admittedly, small fraction of workers who go to work and hate their job.

Their influence can start in small doses, when they detain workers at the water cooler who are anxious to go to work.

Their influence is more manifest at conference tables in which they advance preposterous ideas just to rile some of the more faithful workers.

Their influence explodes when they consciously put monkey wrenches in production lines which no longer run smoothly for a time.

Do we not all hear of spectacular recalls and mammoth class action suits? How many of them are due to actions of spite against a spiteful supervisor? Because of lawyerly sworn secrecy agreements, we will never know.

I can put all this in more technical terms: Unless we believe that the accounting of the Stock Market exhausts the economy, Capitalism works for the independence of the few, an independence acquired at great expense for the majority of the people. To achieve a full evaluation of the economic system, we ought to measure not only the wealth possessed by the few, but also the deprivation of health, food, and shelter experienced by the many.

As against these two evaluations, there ought to be a third evaluation: the evaluation of the results of interdependence.

Interdependence is the "normal" state of affairs in the economic system. That is true Capitalism (as opposed to Financialism). As Philip Pilkington (2021) has pointed out in a slightly different context: *"Whether in a football team or an army unit, every good manager or superior officer knows the importance of having people work in sync. The same is true in a band or any other group formation. If people do not form into an aggregative unit with solid interconnections the group formation will breakdown - the team will lose the match; the army unit will lose the battle; the band will play terrible music."*

Do not begrudge the people who want to stay home on $600 per week. To keep them out of the workforce might actually immeasurably add to the efficiency of the system as a whole.

Will Coronavirus—and Concordian economics—eventually make room to work only for those who love their work?

5.6 An Innovative Program

5.6.1 All-Labor Reward Program

Boy, how deep is the Chinese wisdom?[3] They say that every crisis is an opportunity. How true. Our current deep financial crisis offers us the opportunity of resolving the horrors of labor exploitation once and for all. Let us explore the ways; see Gorga (2021b).

5.6.1.1 Money as a Common Good

Nothing is resolved in economics until we develop a thorough understanding of money. The source of much misunderstanding is the common expression that money is created out of "thin air." Thin air can be hot or cold, but it does not create money.

A relatively long story analyzed some time ago reveals that money, all money, is created on the strength of credit. National money is created on the strength of national credit. That explains why a US dollar is worth more in international trade than most other currencies. The US economy is still more valuable than most other economies.

5.6.1.2 Who Creates the Value of National Credit?

The answer is self-evident. All people of a nation create the value of their national credit. And if this is so, then all money created on the strength of national credit belongs to all people of the nation.

---

[3] Joan M. Gorga, my wife, has mightily contributed to this presentation.

Money, then, is a common good. It does not belong to the government; it belongs even less to the agency that is entrusted with the creation of the national currency, the Federal Reserve System (the Fed).

That is why, since 1981, I have been advocating that the creation of national money be accomplished as a loan—not a grant—following three firm rules:

- For the creation of real wealth alone, not to purchase financial assets;
- For the benefit of individual persons and, through ESOPs, all the people in the participant enterprises (no ESOPs, no access to national credit);
- At cost.

5.6.1.3 Why not Grants?

Two major reasons have so far prevented me from advocating the creation of money in the form of grants:

- First, because the government is not the owner of national credit;
- Second, because the creation of loans involves an automatic accounting destruction of money as the loan is repaid; thus, loans create an automatic insurance against inflation.

The ongoing financial crisis, with the immediate need to inject money into the system in order to sustain the economy, is opening up new vistas on the economic reality. The reality is this: Much wealth is being created by people who do not receive any monetary compensation for their contribution to the wealth of the nation.

5.6.1.4 The Value of Housework Appears in High Relief

If mentioned at all in the past, this condition has generally been swept under the rug for a great variety of reasons. Now we need to pay attention to it.

5.6.1.5 Necessity Is the Mother of All Invention

By bringing the value of this wealth to the forefront of our observation, and finding ways to reward it financially, we might be able to eliminate a flagrant crime so widely committed and overlooked up to this moment in history, the exploitation of work.

No, this call goes much beyond the cry about "equal pay for equal work."

This is a call to find a just compensation for housework.

Since slavery is no longer a legal institution in most of the world, this form of exploitation of work need not necessarily be considered retrospectively but prospectively; these considerations might indeed shed new light on the exploitation of so much labor that is forever being conducted under our very eyes. This is the work of love, love that involves housework.

Ways to calculate the value of housework have already been taken into consideration: Detailed invoices can easily be constructed by calculating the value of work that is being contracted out in commercial venues.

Averages and other more elaborate statistical indices can be rather quickly developed to eliminate the need to request specific vouchers from people who do not have adequate information.

Bills can be presented, not to a husband or a wife, but to the federal government.

An implicit benefit of inestimable value will then be automatically achieved: the value of men's work will be identical to the value of women's work. Parity will finally be achieved.

The presentation of these vouchers might offer many advantages. Rather than use helicopters to blindly distribute federal money from above, the request would come from below; thus, money would hit the pockets that most need to be reflated. Such an approach might also eliminate the need to provide adequate cut-off points, points that are always arbitrary and unfair. The hope is that families that do not need financial support will spontaneously avoid presenting such vouchers to the federal government.

Not only would unavoidable accusations of unfairness be overcome, but the political insidious work of this or that lobbyist to favor this or that class of people would also be dodged.

The novelty under consideration here, to repeat, is that the bill can be presented, not to a husband or a wife, but to the federal government. The Treasury can rather easily verify the validity of such bills, with penalties for fraud clearly written out in the appropriate legislation. The Treasury can rather easily pay for such bills. Depending on the accounting techniques used, the Treasury does not necessarily need to clear such operations with the Fed.

If national credit has a greater value because it automatically includes the value of housework, then it is entirely proper and economically justified to compensate the creators of this value for the work they do.

There is a present need to inject money into a tottering economy, to say the least to preserve it for available expansion when the dreadful current conditions pass us by. This present need can be reinforced by the requirement of stopping past and present injustices. Thus, the requirements of economics finally meet the requirements of morality.

5.6.1.6 The Value of Housework

There are many reasons why the value of housework is not taken into consideration yet. One is that this value appears to be ephemeral and transient. No so. Accurate accounting ought to give us a comprehensive view of such values. Two considerations might suffice. First, without daily maintenance, would not the value of houses be subject to rapid deterioration? Two, should not raising kids be considered an indispensable part of national capital investment? How much did raising Steve Jobs add to our national wealth?

5.6.1.7 How to Curb Inflationary Forces?

If housework is compensated in the form of grants, the money remains in the system forever and in the long run it is going to raise its ugly head in the form of inflation. How to avoid such a disruptive tendency of such a necessary and valuable action as fair compensation of housework performed?

Taxation is the answer. The Treasury can tax these funds and place them out of existence—as necessary, at least in part. (This requirement implies that the Treasury actually destroys, rather than spends, these funds once they have been collected.)

5.6.2 Conclusion

There are many ways to inject cash into the economy. The urgent satisfaction of this need is widely recognized today. Many such programs are being recommended and even new ones put in place these days. However, they all seem to be suggested on the basis of arbitrium and wishful thinking. They are all short-term programs with necessarily highly destructive long-term effects.

Rights are separated from responsibilities.

Needs are hardly individualized. Past injustices are hardly taken into account. And the money so indiscriminately being put into circulation today, unless inordinate hoarding of cash is foreseen, eventually will unavoidably destroy the overall economy in the flames of inflation.

Paying for housework out of the national treasury will solve many problems at once.

5.7 Appendix: Some Considerations About Men's and Women's Work

These are the major findings of a study published on April 8, 2020, by the Lund University School of Economics and Management: "Over the past decades, men's and women's time use has changed dramatically suggesting a gender revolution across industrialized nations. Women increased their time in paid work and reduced time in unpaid activities. Men increased their time in unpaid work, but not enough to compensate. Thus, women still perform more unpaid work irrespective of context."

(Ariane Pailhé, Anne Solaz, and Maria Stanfors, 2020, *"The Great Convergence? Gender and Unpaid Work in Europe and the United States."* Lund Papers in Economic Demography, n°2020–1, Lund University School of Economics and Management.)

5.8 Jobs—and Money—Through Financialization

5.8.1 About Financialization

Where is the real wealth created between November 1916 and March 1921? Where are the jobs? Where is the money? Quite apart from the issue of its concentration into relatively few hands, what is the value of the real wealth created by the Stock Market?

Apart from a bunch of zeros, what has ultimately been created by the Stock Market in this period of time? See Gorga (2017c).

Surely Presidents can be basking in their glow, but zeros are empty, hollow entities. The glow that they emanate can be as easily shut down.

And the glow will disappear as soon as a few individual or corporate stockholders and bondholders will cash in their stocks and bonds, as soon as they will transform their paper wealth into real wealth.

The trigger can be anything. A curb in greed: Some people might say, I got mine Jack—and it is enough for me; the need to repay an accumulating debt might be another trigger.

The few who will do it first will be the lucky ones. They will grab the little cash that lays around as pocket change of the many. As soon as a few others will attempt to carry out the same operation, they—and the rest of the nation—will discover that the pockets are empty. Even the banks do not have enough cash on hand to satisfy the demand. The supply becomes nil.

Personal credit and national credit have been stretched to their limit of credibility.

It is highly unlikely that the current U.S. Congress will ever again allow the Federal Reserve to bail the failing corporations out and the bail-ins will not last forever.

What can the US government do on its own? The national debt is already bursting at the seams. Few national and international creditors have much residue of trust in the creditworthiness of our government. The faith and credit of the U.S. government are already less than full.

The Federal Reserve System and the Treasury will also be hamstrung this time around: They cannot buy that many more government bonds; they cannot print that much more money. Their accounts are already bursting with unpayable debt. Although everyone knows it, this "secret" is heavily guarded.

The way out is bankruptcy.

The solution is to leave with zeros the many who are caught standing when the music stops.

Panic ensues. Deflated will be the values of stocks and bonds and derivatives and infinities (they do not exist yet, but they will certainly be created unless regulators become serious about prohibiting the issuance of shacky derivatives).

Deflated values for many assets will go way down, if not all the way down to zero.

Panic spreads in the markets of real wealth; real-estate values will crash; stores cannot sell their wares; food will disappear from supermarkets. Looting and mayhem will occur in the streets.

5.8 Jobs—and Money—Through Financialization

The government will be imposing martial law, but the soldiers will not be able to replenish the stores.

How can these frightening events be prevented?

A convincing solution can be found in the Mosaic laws concerning the seven-year jubilee: In the seventh year, all debts among Israelites were canceled; they were reduced to zero.

The rationale for this solution is without fault; it is unimpeachable. What can you do to a creditor who has exhausted his last resources—foolishly or not? Send this person to jail? That used to be the solution until it was discovered that it costs money to keep people in jail.

It is so much better to forget the debt and put this debtor in a position to be productive again.

Presumably, this person will have learned his lesson and never incur unpayable debts again.

Only the cancelation of debts clears the slate and makes things new again. Faith and credit are restored to its fullest extent.

What does it ultimately mean that—one way or another—debts are cancelled?

Zeros, zeros. This is the meaning of the cancellation of debts. Debts are reduced to zero.

We ought to concentrate our attention on this profound truth. Behind *a certain number* of zeros, there is no wealth. There is nothing but empty space.

Why not combine this reality of economics with the wisdom of ancient Israelites? Why not?

One has to be that brave. Of course, I hear the howls of those who will suffer psychologically from this willful destruction of zeros. But a sturdy statesman or stateswoman will stand up and make the suffering howlers realize that, if the reduction of zeros occurs systematically, people will be as rich at the end of the process as they were before the destruction of zeros.

This is why: I have one million dollars. Therefore, I am rich.

What does it mean?

The real meaning is that I am *richer* than you, because I have one million dollars and you have fewer dollars than I have.

If you were to accumulate one million dollars, what then? We would both be equally rich. Thus, if we **both** reduce our wealth by ten or more percent, we are still **both** equally rich!

Our nature and our intellectual education about things economic are such that too many of us would feel poor (!) and strive to accumulate more and more dollars.

The essential point is that if the zeros are reduced systematically and wisely, the *relative* position of the players will be preserved. All will be as rich as before the escalation of zeros in their accounts. All will be in the same relative position as before.

The authorities have to make sure that everyone is affected—not equally, but proportionately the same.

Above all, the authorities, national and international authorities, will have to burst the bubble in such a way that values of monetary wealth will now have a nearly one-to-one relationship with the values of real wealth.

This is ultimately the mechanism that Keynes tried to establish at Bretton Woods. Only, instead of advocating the destruction of zeros, he called for the **creation** of zeros, the creation of Special Drawing Rights eventually created by the International Monetary Fund. Eventually, the system became unsustainable.

Is not the organized destruction of *zeros* so much better than the unplanned destruction of *real wealth* that ultimately results from the sudden collapse of the financial system?

5.9 The Lender Is not a Hoarder. And What Is Interest?

5.9.1 The Lender Is not a Hoarder

I am not a Jew.

How to staunch the rivers of opprobrium poured over the head of the lender during the last 5000 years of recorded history? See Gorga (2019).

5.9.1.1 The Lender Is not a Hoarder

Even Shakespeare got into the act. Who can forget Shylock? To understand Shakespeare, we have to put him within two bookends: The near universal misquotation of the First Epistle of Paul to Timothy and the *culture* that eventually created the forgery of the Protocols of the Elders of Zion. The details are too well known and too painful to recite here.

The first obvious observation to make, and to stress, is that not all the lenders are Jews.

Period.

The second observation to stress is that neither Shakespeare nor those who misquote Paul are economists. They simply do not know what they are talking about. They know not what money *is*.

A silly point. I am not a Jew. I am not writing this long overdue re-evaluation of the lender because I am a Jew and somehow want desperately to put the record of antisemitism straight at least as the lending of money is concerned.

No. My evaluation of the lender is based on the study of Concordian economics. Through Concordian economics, it becomes exceedingly clear that the lender is not a hoarder.

The long bill of particulars against the hoarder is not of concern here.

5.9 The Lender Is not a Hoarder. And What Is Interest?

The long bill of particulars in favor of the lender can be shortened by asking: Would the world be better off if people with money, people with money who do not have an immediate use for it, were to hoard the money? The question answers itself.

5.9.1.2 What Can We Demand from the Lender?

No, I am not going to proffer an indiscriminate approval of the actions of the lender. Especially after witnessing the abuses of the lending power of large financial corporations committed before the last financial crash, when loans were approved for people who could clearly not sustain the load, but nonetheless offered a variety of immediate profits to the lender; it is evident that "society" must demand that the lender use judgment in the evaluation of the loan.

The lender has responsibilities.

Loans that have minimal chance of being repaid ought not to be issued at all. I wonder whether society will ever find adequate sanctions against irresponsible lending practices, but we can certainly summarily spotlight them and condemn them fully.

The framework of the second condition through which society must evaluate lending practices is the amount and form of interest to be applied to a loan. To answer these questions appropriately, we need to know what interest is.

5.9.2 What Is Interest?

Interest, Keynes said, is "the reward of not-hoarding" (1936: 166–167, 174, and 182). Keynes, of course, is the supreme economist of the last century. One of the two dead economists who control our lives. All mainstream economics is based on Keynes' fundamental book titled the General Theory; all heterodox economics, in its various shapes and forms of "post-Keynesian" economics, as well as Austrian economics, is all economics written "against Keynes." The other dead economist is Hayek.

In the meantime, no one has paid attention to Keynes' definition of interest, because no modern economist understands what hoarding is.

Rather than demanding an effort to understand hoarding, I will be satisfied if the Reader makes an effort to understand interest. Benjamin Franklin knew, he understood what interest is, and welcomed it. Did he not famously say something like: *"I'm glad to give the other fellow 5%, if I can earn 6%."*

But notice that our Beloved Benji, if my love for him gives me permission to be so disrespectful, was talking of capital credit—not the abyss of consumer credit into which we have lately plunged. Consumer credit is only fruitful for the lender. Yet, the loan agreement is entered voluntarily; apart from advocating for education about economic affairs, there is nothing that economics can do to save the borrower and make the consumer loan productive… unless one approaches the situation indirectly… unless the "cash-back" movement becomes truly widespread, unless capitalism becomes truly responsive to the needs of consumers—and its own survival—and so responsible as to elect, eventually, most likely, representatives of consumers on the Board of Directors of modern business corporations through the legal institution of Consumer Stock Ownership Plans (CSOPs).

That is it. With capital credit, interest is the fruit of the use of other peoples' money. With consumer credit, interest is giving to the lender the fruit of one's own future productivity: A totally destructive activity; how many enterprises are undertaken, and how many trees are felled to pay interest on consumer credit? The principal in consumer credit is never likely to be paid back. Two institutions will create some relief: cash-back and CSOPs.

And yet, does not the consumer derive the benefit of immediate use of real goods and services? Don't we live in the moment? It might be vain to ask: What's the rush?

To summarize, apart from the abyss of consumer credit, with a loan agreement voluntarily entered into by the majority of the population, would society be better off if money remained in the pocket of a person who does not know, or does not want to go through the pain of making money bear fruit?

Let the lender be finally praised.

5.9.2.1 Two Caveats

This is not an idiosyncratic blessing of interest. There are two important caveats that I would like to attach to the unjustly vituperated 5000-years-old practice of lending money at interest. The first caveat is that society should forever be on the alert against exorbitant interest. My brain is too small to define what an exorbitant rate of interest is. But my heart knows it when it sees it. The ancients, up to 1971 (!) in the United States, knew what usury is. Yes, my heart bleeds a bit at the sight of exorbitant interest.

Where blood gushes out of my heart is at the mention of compound interest. I cannot find any justification for compound interest, except in the power of the lender and the "beauty" of mathematics.[4] To elaborate on the power of the lender, especially the political power of the lender is fruitless. It will forever be exercised,

---

[4] Perhaps, I have discovered a way to undermine the construction of compound interest. On borrowed $100 at 5%, to ask for interest **on $105 next** year is not charitable at all to say the least. The $105 amount is NOT your money; the $5 belonged to the debtor a moment ago.

Next year, you should be entitled to receive another $5 as interest on YOUR $100, but not on $105 as in the practice of compound interest.

It is an abstract conception, the conception of ownership that determines the outcome favorable to compound interest.

If we focus our attention on the imprint of history, the $5 paid in interest remains what it WAS: an amount belonging to the debtor.

The transaction is voluntary; if debtors insist on it, creditors will no longer be entitled to interest on $105 next year. The lender will be entitled only to interest on the original loan of $100 until the capital is repaid.

whether openly or through the subterfuge of clever lawyers and accountants—and legislators, should I whisper?

What must be open for discussion is the justification of compound interest. I find none. Let us run a small thought experiment, an experiment whose conclusions can, eventually, be easily tested through the inordinate intellectual and financial power of the modern University. Let us pose this alternative to a "perfect" representative sample of lenders: "What is fairer, Simple Interest—with its linear growth pattern—or Compound Interest, with its exponential growth pattern?

My suspicion is that most people, to repeat, most lenders, will agree that the linear growth rate is fairer than the exponential growth rate.[5]

Will this exercise become the seed to set loan agreements on a just and sustainable basis? Let us find time to give some undivided attention to the issue. Let us not sheepishly accept diktats from the past.

If this solution is not chosen, especially because its implementation is surely going to be a slow process, rather than advocating a vainglorious attempt to curb the power of lenders, let us see what can be done, systematically—as a society.

5.9.3 *A Fruitful Curb of the Power of the Lender*

Yes, the modern world—ah, Progress, Enlightenment, Reason, and all that—is bereft of defenses against the power of the lender. We have no intellectually solid, no morally valid defense against the power of the lender.

It is scouring the past that I have unearthed "the" solution: The Jubilee Solution. The Jubilee Solution is a systematic cancelation of all debts on the eve of the Jubilee Year. The Jubilee Year starts at the end of the seventh year.

There were various forms of jubilee. There was the Seven-Day Jubilee regarding Time; the Seven-Year Jubilee regarding the tillage of the Land; and the end of the $7 \times 7 = 49$th Year Jubilee regarding stewardship of the Land. These are all extremely important manifestations of Jubilee, jubilation of the heart. This encompassing vision is too much for one lazy afternoon. Let us concentrate more of our attention on the Seven-Year Jubilee regarding debt.

Much to say. Compressed, it is this: It is only money, people; it is only money that, remaining in the pocket of the lender, would most likely be hoarded; it is only money that keeps the debtor in knots; it is only a set of zeros that, once canceled from the accounting books, make everyone free to start a new life as a productive agent again. (Have not modern venture capitalists learned not to shy away from first,

---

[5] These observations might be corroborated by the results of empirical studies to determine whether a) borrowers are aware of the mechanics of compound interest; b) whether bankers explain these mechanics to borrowers; c) whether lenders might not be more at peace with themselves if loans were issued at simple rather than compound interest.

A final consideration. If money is the legal representation of real wealth, where is the real wealth created by the accumulation of compound interest charges?

second, and even third failure? If the borrower has used the painful experience to learn how to succeed, why waste all that learning?).

It was Moses who legislated the Debt Jubilee. It was the Jewish society that had the intellectual talent to see the wisdom of the Debt Jubilee and the moral stamina to practice it every seven years. Cynics doubt the debt Jubilee was ever practiced. I personally do not care whether it was practiced even once and Michael Hudson (e.g., 2015, 2018) has provided an unobjectionable wealth of evidence of the soundness of this solution in the number and quality of copycats: Every Emperor, every King—well, most Emperors, most Kings; many Emperors, many Kings?—upon installation has declared a Debt Jubilee.

Moses was a Jew. And Jesus did not ever contradict Moses, but he asserted his readiness to fulfill the mission of Moses and the Prophets. In the words of Paul, Jesus did not say that money is the root of all evil. The correct quotation is: *"Love of money is the root of all evil." Not money, but love of money.*

Love of money is the root of hoarding and, in the Parable of the Talents, Jesus, uncharacteristically, sends the hoarder straight to Hell: No trial; no appeal.

Yes, I am not a Jew, but I am very proud to acknowledge my intellectual debt to Moses, and to Jesus.

5.9.4 Conclusion

The lender is not a hoarder.

References

Bonner, B. (2017). *When the ATMs go darik.* Bonner and Partners.
Cardone, G. (2023). 10 X Finance Essentials. In *10 X World* (p. 24). Grant Cardone Enterprises.
Gorga, C. (2017a). To pay for health care there is also the amish way, the American way. *TalkMarkets,* January 14. Available at https://talkmarkets.com/content/to-pay-for-health-care-there-is-also-the-amish-way-the-american-way?post=118766. Accessed on 14 October 2023.
Gorga, C. (2017b). Cash-back: A silver lining.' *TalkMarkets,* September 18. Available at https://talkmarkets.com/content/economics--politics/cash-back-a-silver-lining?post=149602. Accessed on 14 October 2023.
Gorga, C. (2017c). Three trillion worth of zeros. *TalkMarkets,* March 2. Available at https://talkmarkets.com/content/us-markets/three-trillion-worth-of-zeros?post=124215. Accessed on 14 October 2023.
Gorga, C.(2019). The lender is not a hoarder. And what is interest? *Mother Pelican. A Journal of Solidarity and Sustainability,* 15(12). December. Available at http://www.pelicanweb.org/solisustv15n12page8.html. Accessed on 14 October 2023
Gorga, C. (2021a). Those lazy workers who are gaming the system. *Mother Pelican A Journal of Solidarity and Sustainability.* 17(10). October. Available at http://www.pelicanweb.org/solisustv17n10page5.html. Accessed on 14 October 2023.

References

Gorga, C. (2021b). All-labor reward program. *EconIntersect*. September 6. Available at All-Labor Reward Program - Global Economic Intersection (econintersect.com). Accesssed on 6 November 2023.

Hudson, M. (2015). *Killing the host: How financial parasites and debt bondage destroy the global economy.* Islet Press.

Hudson, M. (2018). *...and forgive them their debts: lending, foreclosure and redemption from bronze age finance to the jubilee year (1) (Tyranny of debt).* Islet Press.

Keynes, J. M. (1936). *The general theory of employment, interest, and money.* Harcourt.

Kurtzman, J. (1993). *The death of money: How the electronic economy has destabilized the world's markets and created financial chaos.* Simon & Schuster.

Pilkington, P. (2021). Keynes on parts and wholes. *EconIntersect,* September 6. Available at https://econintersect.com/pages/analysis/analysis.php/post/202008060120. Accessed on 19 October 2023.

Rogoff, K. S. (2017). *The curse of cash: How large-denomination bills aid crime and tax evasion and constrain monetary policy.* Princeton University Press.

Chapter 6
Whence Money

Abstract In this chapter, we will attempt to give an answer to a perennial question. Professor Melissa Lane (2016), the director of Princeton's University Center for Human Values, is right (of course): "Rising levels of economic inequality and social immobility raise a challenge faced continually in antiquity, with fresh force: how, and in what circumstances, if at all, can the rich and the poor be enabled to act as political equals?" Perhaps not even for the first time, this is precisely the thrust of the dialogue between Alcibiades and Pericles reported by Xenophon. Analyzing the essential elements of a long sweep of history, it becomes evident that Concordian economics offers a clear-cut set of answers. This chapter is divided into two parts: The first part offers a broad review of how major thinkers of the past have dealt with "money"; the second part presents a practical and intellectual understanding of money within the context of Concordian economics. Both parts analytically deny any validity to the "fractional reserve" theory of money, the assumption that money is created by bankers on the strength of money saved by depositors.

6.1 How to Use Public Policy to Guide Accumulation Toward Virtuous Ends

6.1.1 Summary of Section 6.1

Within the context of the history of philosophy, we can say that most economic analysis has been pursued as a development of Plato's positions; see Brady and Gorga (2019). Plato's *Republic* was the result of his reaction to the death of Socrates. Socrates's conviction and death sentence resulted from actions carried out at the hands of a democracy, which took over from a plutocracy. Plato did not see any way of reconstituting the Athenian republic as it had once existed. Plato despaired of any public measures that might reinstitute in Athens the dominance of private virtue constraining or minimizing public corruption.

Therefore, he sought to create a NEW REPUBLIC, dominated by his virtuous philosopher-kings and warriors, who would be prevented from ever choosing to become corrupt because they would not be able to ever make decisions that lead to the accumulation of money, wealth, and riches. The new government would create a virtuous city state by walling off the rulers from any access to financial temptations at accumulation. There would be a large middle class, which he called a "Lower" class because he was concerned with the division of political power. In terms of the distribution of political power, they would be the lower class.

However, in terms of economic wealth, they would be middle class from an economic point of view, since they would be able to accumulate property, wealth, money, and riches. But they were forever cut off from using such wealth and power to dominate the state; they were banned from doing so because they could never attain any office. Plato solves the potential problem of political and economic corruption by preventing those who have wealth from ever ruling. They are cut off from the political life of the state.

Aristotle, followed by Augustine, Aquinas, Oresme, and Adam Smith, recognized, to a lesser or greater degree, that the ownership and control of private property (wealth, money, riches) is an initial, necessary condition to be able to put one's self in a position to help others in need. A person is or has been corrupted by the process of wealth creation if that person decides that he/she will not help others in need.

Smith attempted to *move beyond* the political analysis of Aristotle, Augustine, and Aquinas on the question of whether economic growth (accumulation of wealth) would or would not promote Virtue (giving) or Vice (greed). Smith believed that the effective control of money and loans by an independent Central Bank would create an institution that could promote the fortunes of those who were charitable (the sober people) while penalizing/neutralizing those who were greedy (the prodigals, projectors, and imprudent risk takers). This would prevent a state from degenerating into the type of state epitomized by Athens in 400 BC.

The Central Bank would maintain the dominant economic position of a very large, prudent, circumspect, judicious, careful, frugal, thriving middle class by skewing credit and loans toward them and away from the prodigals, projectors, and imprudent risk takers, who made up the rich, upper income class.

History did not bless Adam Smith with the achievement of his ideals, ideals that were a distillation of the wisdom of the ages. Another chance is given to us by the development of Concordian monetary policy. Will we avail ourselves of this opportunity? Intellectually, this chapter serves to reinforce the *negation* of the central core of mainstream economics that started with Keynes—or at most with Adam Smith.

6.1.2 The Core of the Issues

Plato's works—and Aristotle's works, like the *Politics* and *Nicomachean Ethics*—are centered on political and economic positions that Plato thought Socrates would support, based on his familiarity with the growing corruption that became endemic over time in Athens. Economic growth in Athens led to a decline of what had been a stable state. This stability was based on a large middle class. The goal of the citizen in such a state was to live a virtuous life.[1] The virtuous life was not about the collection of money, wealth, and power. The optimal state was one based on the existence and continuity of a large, thriving middle class. Economic growth created changing conditions that could lead to the rise of either a dictatorship of the poor (democracy) or the dictatorship of the rich (oligarchy). The best form of government was the polity. This required, as a necessary condition, a very large middle class with a small lower class and a small upper class.

Economic growth would, however, upset the balance that resulted from the large middle class as the beneficiaries of economic growth once they would find themselves to have more in common with the rich. Thus, both Plato and Aristotle had rather jaundiced views of economic growth as it relates to the stability of a state over time.

Aristotle's "Golden Mean" can thus be seen to have applications to both economics and politics that go far beyond personal, individual applications. Aristotle argues that the necessary condition for a stable state is that the state must have a very large middle class, a small lower class, and a small upper class. This has to apply both economically and politically. The middle class must control the majority of the economic resources and the majority of the economic power, as well as the majority of the political power.

This position is actually quite close to the viewpoint of the Ancient, Hebrew prophets of the Old Testament. The whole purpose of the concept of the seven-year jubilee and fifty-year jubilee is to redress and correct imbalances that start to diminish the middle class. Augustine and Aquinas heed quite closely to these positions; for a more detailed discussion of these relationships, see Gorga (2009a, 2009b).

6.1.3 Structure of Section 6.1

The chapter is structured in the following manner. Section 6.1.4 will cover Aristotle's critique of Plato's "division of labor" that ruled out the accumulation of property by the warriors and the philosopher-kings. However, this would also rule out any virtuous actions on their part at charity or what Adam Smith called beneficence. Section 6.1.5. will review and slightly amend Aristotle's analysis of the role of money in society. Section 6.1.6 will cover Adam Smith's realization that (disputing Aristotle, Augustine, and Aquinas) an independent Central Bank could be used to mitigate and control the corruption problem by essentially making loans **only** to the middle class (Smith's "sober people") and not to the upper class (prodigals, projectors, and imprudent risk takers). A properly functioning Central Bank could serve to show how Aristotle's jaundiced view of economic growth could be remedied so that the accumulation of wealth brought on by economic growth would benefit

---

[1] Both Aristotle and Aquinas (!) committed the grievous error of justifying the institution of slavery. It is also surprising that Aristotle overlooked that physical or wage slavery is an institution that will undermine the middle class, both politically and economically.

the lower and middle classes by being channeled into productive results, as opposed to the speculative outcomes (so prevalent in our world since the late 1970s).

Since Adam Smith's recommendations have *never* been applied in an integrated fashion, in Sects. 6.1.7 through 6.1.12, we call upon the recommendations of Concordian monetary policy to give greater specificity, generality, and rationality to the positions outlined by Adam Smith.

Concordian monetary policy is not only rooted in a detailed, comprehensive analysis of the economic process. Concordian monetary policy brings to completion the structure of the millenarian tradition of economic justice. Concordian monetary policy is also rooted in the practice of the American Colonists. Theoretically, Concordian monetary policy is not only rooted in a major pronouncement of the U.S. Constitution at Article 1, Section 8; theoretically, Concordian monetary policy responds to a conclusion drawn by Oresme, the XIV century author of the first monetary treatise in the West. "*Oresme argued that coinage belongs to the public, not to the prince, who has no right to vary arbitrarily the content or weight.*"

6.1.4 Aristotle's Criticism of Plato's Position

We can better understand Aristotle's criticism of Plato's position, if we use the overall conception of life later adopted by Augustine, Aquinas, and Adam Smith: If you want to do good, then you must be successful, but must not be corrupted by the process of the accumulation of wealth. If you are successful, then you will have the resources with which to help others.

This perspective led Aristotle to criticize Plato's position where the warriors and philosopher-kings would have no property (wealth, money). This condition would prevent them from engaging in virtuous acts of giving to the needy; see Simpson (1998:1263b5): "*The first argument rested on love of self. The second one rested on love of others, which must be natural and good as love of self if human beings are naturally political. Hence, the pleasure associated with doing favors for others, and the private property this requires, must be natural and good too.*"

This policy would place constraints on the ability of the warriors and philosopher-kings to do virtuous acts while the "Lower Class" would be able to perform such virtuous acts, assuming that they had not allowed themselves to become corrupted during the process of generating their wealth, income, and money.

Augustine does not differentiate between hoping to do good, but not being able to follow through due to a lack of the means to do so, as opposed to being able to actually do good (Augustine *Enarrationes in Psalmos* 131.19): "*God doth not heed the means a man hath, but the wish he hath, and judgeth him according to his wish for temporal blessings, not according to the means which it is not his lot to have.*"

The problem here, from Smith's point of view, is that Augustine is overlooking the virtue of prudence. Frugality and patience, over time, can help create the conditions that will result in the attainment of the means that will allow one to not only wish to do good, but to actually do good.

6.1.5 Aristotle's Analysis of the Use of Money in Virtue Ethics

Aristotle's analysis is based on the assumption that the proper use of money is to be evaluated within a context of virtue ethics and not utilitarian ethics, especially the type of ethics promulgated by Jeremy Bentham (Benthamite Utilitarianism) which is the system of ethics and philosophy that has dominated the economics profession since Smith's death in 1790. If the use of money does not promote ethical behavior, conduct, and outcomes, then its use must be heavily circumscribed and heavily regulated by the state or independent Central Bank.

Aristotle's four categories used to describe the different uses of money are well known. We will make a small adjustment in one of them.

The first category is barter:

$$C - C' \tag{6.1}$$

The second category is money used as a medium of exchange to facilitate the production and trade of consumption and production goods and activities:

$$C - M - C' \tag{6.2}$$

The third category is money used for commodity speculation:

$$M - C - M' \tag{6.3a}$$

We will modify this to incorporate genuine shifts in the demand curve for a quality product resulting in increased desires by consumers for such a good as opposed to (6.3a), which deals with the deliberate attempt to manipulate the price of hoarded goods through the use of artificial supply restrictions, innuendo, half-truths, false information, etc. We will denote this case as

$$M - C^* - M' \tag{6.3b}$$

The fourth category is

$$M - M' \tag{6.4}$$

No actual goods or services are created in category (6.4). The goal is monetary profit without the actual production of any good or service. Stock market speculation and currency speculation would be good examples of this, as well as the use of financial derivatives. Aristotle, Augustine, Aquinas, Adam Smith, and J. M. Keynes condemned these specific misuses of money because they created speculative bubbles that would inevitably crash. The rich speculators, like the British East India Company and Goldman Sachs, used their political connections in order to be bailed out while the middle and lower classes were forced to absorb the social and economic costs.

Smith was, in the *Wealth of Nations*, specifically concerned with the Mississippi Bubble that was manipulated by John Law and Richard Cantillon early in the eighteenth century in France.

This activity represents financial speculation or financialization. Categories 3 and 4 comprise uses of money that Smith identified with the pejorative terms projectors, prodigals, and imprudent risk takers.

Unfortunately, neither Aristotle nor Augustine nor Aquinas had concrete suggestions on how to prevent such behavior other than suggesting that men should turn from their evil purposes in order to be good. However, this will require some sort of "stick" to enforce.

6.1.6 *Adam Smith and the Institution of Central Banking*

Adam Smith saw that society could prevent and constrain the misuse of money that took place in categories (6.3a) and (6.4), while promoting categories (6.2) and (6.3b), through the institution of Central Banking. The Central Bank would be able to control credit and loan arrangements so that the loans are made to those segments of society that actually produce real goods and services. Smith termed these citizens the "sober people." He contrasted the "sober people" with the "projectors, prodigals, and imprudent risk takers" like Cantillon and Law.

Smith's goal is to use the Central Bank to maintain a thriving, dominant middle class. He calls the middle class the "sober people." His first requirement is that the long run rate of interest must be permanently fixed and maintained a little bit above the prime rate of interest that the banks' best customers were charged to take out loans. His second requirement is that projectors, prodigals, and imprudent risk takers must be prevented from obtaining bank loans. Otherwise, the saving and demand deposit accounts of the bank's depositors will be "wasted and destroyed." Smith's third requirement is that money and banking policy must concentrate on determining who is getting the bank loans and what purpose are the bank loans being used for.

Smith would view current American monetary policy as fatally flawed, since Geithner's, Bernanke's, Rubin's, Summer's, Paulsen's, and Lew's would be judged to be the twentieth and twenty-first-century equivalents of Cantillon's, Law's, and Andrew Dexter, Jr.'s.

Thus, the Central Bank can guide economic growth into areas involved in the production of consumption and investment goods where (6.2) is the general case. Of course, if the Cantillons and Laws are able to get control of the Central Bank, catastrophic depressions will be the result.

Note that the Central Bank can prevent the hoarding of money by simply keeping it out of the hands of the potential hoarders and speculators, like the British East India Company, Cantillons, and Laws.

Smith's approach would reward the prudence and patience of the middle class by granting them access to sufficient credit and bank loans to expand their productive businesses, thereby expanding employment for the lower class.

Smith would argue that no other economic controls are necessary except for the provision of education, which he viewed as a necessity and not a luxury.

Concordian monetary policy, Gorga (2015a), attempts to reach the same three goals that Adam Smith proposed and adds greater specificity, generality, and rationality to the discussion of the problem at hand.

6.1.7 The Pessimistic Interlude

The period between Adam Smith's analysis and Concordian economics might be denoted as the Pessimistic Interlude. It was filled by Hegel's analysis. Hegel was concerned that Individualism was in a collision course with a stable "social" life. He called this course the "knot."[2] The question is still open. Will the knot get so tight as to strangle us? Concordian economics suggests how to untangle the knot.

6.1.8 The Greater Specificity of Concordian Monetary Policy

First Goal. Adam Smith suggested that the Central Bank should be able to control credit and loan arrangements so that the loans are made to those segments of society that actually produce real goods and services. Concordian monetary policy suggests that this goal can be reached directly by providing credit, *not to a specific class* of people, but to specific business operations: those operations that create real wealth—as distinguished from financial operations and hoarding that operate in a vacuum and at worst shuffle ownership rights.[3] This is a major implicit requirement for making loans that follow from the public policies based on Concordian economics. Purchasing land and letting it lay fallow beyond the rotation need of the crops is hoarding. Capping oil wells is hoarding. Purchasing gold and other minerals can be hoarding. Hoarding of cash is, of course, hoarding, see Gorga (2013).

Second Goal. Adam Smith suggested that banking policy must be concentrated on determining who is getting the bank loans. Concordian monetary policy suggests that Central Bank loans be made available to all qualified citizens of the country; the main qualification is reasonable assurance of repayment of the loan. Since financiers do not

---

[2] Thanks to Soini (2023). Interestingly, ever since the election of Pope Francis I have placed my pleas at the feet of Mary, Untier of Knots. See *Wikipedia* (n.d.). I do that whenever I pass under the statue of Joan of Arc, in Gloucester, with her unsheathed sword in the air.

[3] Behind acts of financialization there are few responsibilities and much sheer power.

produce real wealth, in a Concordian monetary policy regime, they are automatically excluded from accessing national credit.

Third Goal. Adam Smith suggested that the long run rate of interest must be permanently fixed. Concordian monetary policy suggests that Central Bank loans be issued at cost.

6.1.9 The Greater Generality of Concordian Monetary Policy

First Goal. That the Central Bank should make loans to those segments of society that actually produce real goods and services, as suggested by Adam Smith, is not a general requirement as indicated by the possibility of those segments of society changing their minds and mores over time. The requirement of Concordian economics that business operations create real wealth is a general and constant classification.

Second Goal. Calling for "who" is getting a loan is inherently discriminatory; this is a condition that cannot be determined ahead of time. Besides, a loan is always issued to a person. What guidance does this requirement offer to the authorities? That loans for capital expansion—not for purchasing financial assets or goods to be hoarded or consumer goods—should be issued to all qualified citizens or better, inhabitants, as required by Concordian monetary policy is a most general principle.

Third Goal. Adam Smith suggested that the long run rate of interest must be permanently fixed. But at what level? And is the permanence of the level something that is supposed to last forever, even when conditions arise that call for a determinate change in that rate? Concordian monetary policy suggests that Central Bank loans be issued at cost: This is a general principle that never changes; yet it is imbued with an inherent flexibility, because the cost of the loan will change when specific costs of bank operations should change.

6.1.10 The Greater Rationality of Concordian Economics

Adam Smith's conditions for issuing Central Bank loans are open to attack because he does not offer any rational justification for his recommendations. His recommendation seems to be based on little more than a personal preference, which cannot be thoroughly justified; and indeed, no serious effort has ever been made to implement those recommendations during the 240 years since their enunciation.

The recommendations offered by Concordian economics are based on the following:

- A rational restructuring of mainstream economics, Gorga (2002, 2009a, 2009b, 2016);
- A completion of the millennial structure of economic justice, Gorga (1999);

6.1 How to Use Public Policy to Guide Accumulation Toward Virtuous Ends

- An application of the most important economic right and responsibility that serves to implement the urgings of economic justice, Gorga (2009a, 2009b).

1. *Rational Re-Structure of Mainstream Economics*

Adam Smith is considered the father of mainstream economics; yet a brief recourse to history shows that economic theory has been in a state of crisis since the publication of his *Wealth of Nations* in 1776. Classical economics was soon followed by neo-classical economics and the marginalist revolution and the economics of Keynes and Keynesian economics and post-Keynesian economics and monetarism and neo-neo-classical economics and real business cycle theory and behaviorism—let alone Marxist economics or Austrian economics or Georgist economics or Kelsonian economics; indeed, let alone the splinter programs of research within each major school of economic thought.

These efforts are not accretions to basic scientific knowledge; they are revolutionary attempts to start the economic discourse anew again and again. They are failed attempts to describe the mechanics of the economic process. As Pilkington (2014) has pointed out: "*Mainstream economics moves forward not through logical development and integration, but through forgetting.*"

The fundamental reason for this continuing state of crisis can be found through an in-depth analysis of the structure of mainstream economics. The structure disobeys all principles of logic; the structure is based on a set of "balancing contradictions," Gorga (2002: 49–50).

The structure of Concordian economics, instead, is built on "relentless," Davidson (2003) respect for the principles of logic and rationally integrates the three levels of economics—theory, policy, and practice—into one organized unit.

Figure 6.1 presents the main elements of the economic process and how they relate to each other:

Two observations should suffice. A cycle of the economic process is completed when all the production of the accounting period passes from producers to consumers and money passes from consumers to producers. For the exchange to occur, both sets of agents must be legal owners of what they exchange. In the economic process, there are always three elements: real goods, money, and ownership rights, which, for instance, in the case of a purchase and sale of a chocolate bar, are indicated by the sales slip.

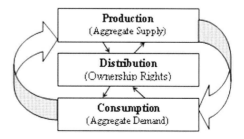

Fig. 6.1 The economic process

And there is another major implicit logical benefit at the core of Concordian economics. The quagmire represented by the assumed "equality of saving to investment" is transformed into the wholly logical, understandable, and explainable relation of complementarity between hoarding and investment. This relationship, and some of the consequences that flow from it, are made clear when cast into a Lorenz diagram. In this fashion, with more hoarding, there is clearly less growth and more poverty. More inflation results from more money put in circulation by hoarding wealth. And then no correspondent increase in real wealth takes place (Fig. 6.2).

2. *Completion of the Millennial Structure of Economic Justice*

There are various uses to which a theory can be put; one immediate use of Concordian economics has been the formulation of an appropriate economic policy. As it can be seen from the following Fig. 6.3, this search has led to a near-automatic completion of the millennial structure of economic justice:

Figure 6.3 offers a one-to-one correspondence between economic theory and policy. In short form, this figure can be read as follows: The right to participate in the process of production of wealth (Participative Justice) is essential, because it alone offers a reasonable assurance to receive a fair share of the wealth created (Distributive

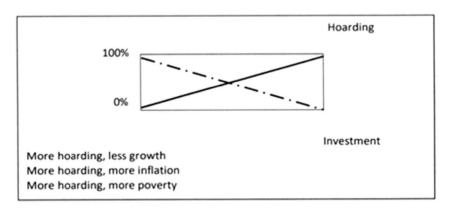

Fig. 6.2 Hoarding-investment nexus

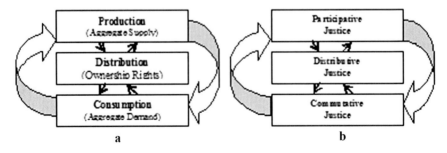

Fig. 6.3 a Economic theory. **b** Economic policy/economic justice

6.1 How to Use Public Policy to Guide Accumulation Toward Virtuous Ends

Justice); only then can one also have the means to assure a relation of equivalence between what one gives and receives (Commutative Justice).

3. *Implementation of One Important Set of Economic Rights and Responsibilities*

Concordian monetary policy stems directly from the application of an important economic right and responsibility; the right of access to national credit, with the responsibility to repay the loan thus obtained. (In correspondence with each factor of production, with capital distinguished between financial capital and real capital, there are four such economic rights and responsibilities in Concordian economics.) In a monetary system, access to national credit is not only essential to participate in the economic life; it is a natural right, because the value of money is not created by bankers, but by the blood, sweat, and tears of all inhabitants—and the person without money is thrown into the gutter.

In the United States, this right belongs to the people in a very particular way: The American Colonists established it in a very natural and organic way in the Massachusetts Bay Colony in 1690.[4] When the British Crown, acting at the behest of the British East India Company, tried to deprive them of this right, they waged a War of Independence and won it. Thanks to the efforts and understanding of Benjamin Franklin, this right is inscribed in the very first article of the United States Constitution.

To gather the full importance of this right, it might be useful to enter into a brief digression concerning culture and history. Why did not any one of the great thinkers of the past that we have examined so far, and these are the major thinkers of all ages, unearth such an important right as the right of access to national credit? Why did Adam Smith not enunciate it clearly?

6.1.11 Some Cultural Consequences of Slavery

Since it was part of the common background of all our authors,[5] we would like to emphasize two cultural consequences of slavery. There were two heavy penalties that cultures that tolerated slavery suffered from. While all our writers shared an understanding of economic justice, and, with greater or lesser enthusiasm, they tried to follow its dictates, none of them could bring the structure of economic justice to its logical conclusion. Because of slavery, none of them could see the need for the addition of participative justice to complete the structure of economic justice, which remained forever focused on distributive and commutative justice. Since slaves were the workers, slaves could not be conceived as having any right to participate in the economic process. That was a heavy loss to each one of our authors personally

---

[4] As the Tablet at Stage Forth Park in Gloucester, Massachusetts, records, "On this site in 1623, a company of fishermen and farmers from Dorchester, England, under the direction of Rev. John White, founded THE MASSACHUSETTS BAY COLONY".

[5] The most interesting case to study, of course, is that of Aquinas. See, Neil (2011)

(not unjustly, one can attribute to them a lack of moral integrity) and to society as well, because as Gissy (2013) has pointed out, one can use participative justice to build a strong anti-trust policy. We have briefly seen that participative justice is also essential for a thorough application of economic justice—and we should never forget that justice is the harbinger of peace.

Slavery also had another subtle, deleterious effect on the mind. Even though our thinkers undoubtedly were the most accomplished human beings of their respective ages, they were automatically compelled to split society into classes. This misconception was not only the seed of everlasting social strife. It was also the source of a faulty sociological construction. Human beings were encased into castes; they could not be autonomous human beings. Slavery prevented each one of our giant thinkers from seeing that people do not act as a (social) class. Mimicry might not grant us absolute freedom, but we certainly act as individual human beings. We have also implicitly seen that the tripartite division of society into the higher, middle, and lower class did much damage to their clarity of mind.

6.1.12 *A Discontinuity in the Conception of the Creation of Money*

Oresme has been neglected; the experience of the American colonists has not been clearly identified. Thus, we see a continuous link between our ancient thinkers to the modern European conception *as well as* current American practice concerning the creation of money: the Sovereign has the right to create money—and the Sovereign can pass it along to the Bankers.

Yet, in addition to Oresme's position, there is a blip in history in which such a conception was challenged. The American Colonists believed that they, as sovereign human beings, had such a right. They asserted this right at first in 1690, under the aegis of the Massachusetts Bay Colony. They so believed in the importance of this right that they, together with all other Colonists—under the subtle guidance of Benjamin Franklin—ultimately fought a war, the American War of Independence, to preserve such a right. Benjamin Franklin, as a merely 23-year-old lad, put it in writing—first in his magisterial essay of 1729 titled "*The Nature and Necessity of a Paper-Currency*." Then he fomented the American Revolution as no other person did—or could. And then he was so influential that such a right was inscribed in the First Article of the US Constitution, Section 8 (The evening before the adoption of the Constitution in Philadelphia, in 1787, delegates from various colonies spent time in company of Franklin.)

Stated otherwise, the focus of attention should fall especially on this type of statement: The American Revolution was fought, not so much to gain "No Taxation Without Representation," as to preserve the right of our Colonial Governments to coin our own currency. We won the war; thus, we preserved this right; but the day

6.1 How to Use Public Policy to Guide Accumulation Toward Virtuous Ends   111

after we lost it—when Hamilton, perhaps unaware, patterned the Bank of America after the Bank of England. For nuances, see Brown (2023).

That is where we stand today: As William Jennings Bryan warned us, we either regain our right to coin our own money (and to distribute it fairly), or we only make the rich richer, until they collapse, for lack of sufficient "effective" demand. In the process, no other reform no matter its promises will have any lasting and meaningful effect. As Benjamin Franklin (!) and Baron Rothschild (nd) well put it, "Allow me to control the currency of a nation and I care not who makes its laws."

6.1.13 Oresme: The Lost Link

Even though it is unlikely that the American Colonists ever heard of Oresme, the Bishop of Lisieux, he is the lost link between Concordian monetary policy and the monetary policy practiced by the American Colonists.

He is remembered today for writing the first modern treatise in monetary theory and especially for being the first formulator of Gresham's Law, bad money casts good money out of circulation. Good money is hoarded. Yet, as a symptomatic treatment of the most important issue in the whole monetary universe, not even Irving Fisher[6] reported what Oresme stated: "... *coinage belongs to the public, not to the prince, who has no right to vary arbitrarily the content or weight.*"

This principle is the central tenet of Concordian monetary policy.

6.1.14 Conclusion

Aristotle, Augustine, and Aquinas took a jaundiced view toward accumulation and economic growth because the dynamics involved in the process of economic growth quickly led to speculative practices that severely damaged the social fabric of society. The result was a severe decrease in the size of the middle class and an abrupt rise in ranks of the lower class. This is, of course, a recipe for civil war and revolution.

Aristotle, Augustine, and Aquinas advised that the maintenance of a stationary, static state would maintain the relative balance of political and economic power so that the middle class would continue to prosper.

Adam Smith believed that there was another path that would maintain the dominance of the "sober" people while allowing for the accumulation of wealth through economic growth. Adam Smith thought that there was a way of using economic growth to maintain a large, dominant middle class. Macroscopically, the lower and middle classes would be benefited by a Central Bank, whose guiding principle was that economic growth had to be targeted to avoid the inherent dangers of bank financed

---

[6] Irving Fisher (1911: Chap. 7, paras 2 and 3).

speculation, which benefited only the upper class and hurt the lower and middle classes.

The virtue of prudence would manifest itself and allow many citizens to go beyond wishing to help other citizens. They would be able to actually become virtuous because they would be able to actually help.

The moral and economic enemy of Aristotle, Augustine, and Aquinas was the greed, selfishness, and exploitation wrought by what later was formalized by Jeremy Bentham as Benthamite Utilitarianism. Adam Smith completely rejected any role for utilitarianism in both the *Wealth of Nations* and *The Theory of Moral Sentiments*. The severe confusion concerning Smith's statement about the brewer, baker, and blacksmith being patient, careful, and prudent, in the manner in which they ran their businesses so that they accumulated surplus funds to safeguard their own families, has been confused with utilitarian greed and selfish egoism. Smith completely rejected any type or sort of Utilitarianism in his life.

Unawares, Concordian economics picks up the same concerns and aspirations as those of Adam Smith and, through an integration of economic theory, policy, and practice, offers a detailed, comprehensive program of action—only in part observed above—to translate those ideals from the abstract realm of thought into living and vital everyday life.

Perhaps, the greatest import of Concordian economic policy is that, if set in place in time, the consequences of a crash in the financial sector over the real sector of the economy will be mitigated to an enormous extent.

Intellectually, this chapter negates the validity of the central structure of mainstream economics, its atomism and determinism. To accomplish this aim is a need emphasized by many writers, but most consistently and effectively by Edward Fallbrook and the World Economic Association.

But perhaps the most important benefit of Concordian economics will be gathered in the associated field of Political Science, a field that can only lightly be touched here. Concordian economics resolves the ancient, perennial issue, in the words of Melissa Lane, of how "can the rich and the poor be enabled to act as political equals." This is the short-form answer: The best form of government is the one that governs on the basis of **self-imposed** (hence democratic) **rules of economic justice**. In this system, the Government—after much vetting—*declares* a set of economic rights and responsibilities to be shared by the entire nation and leaves the Market free to *execute* them. Ideally, the vetting will converge on the creation of the set of economic rights and responsibilities enunciated throughout the work on Concordian economics.

6.2 Money, Banking, and the Economic Process

6.2.1 Introduction

Surely, there is a reason why in writing the *General Theory* Keynes was in search of "a theory of output as a whole."[7] Without it, one cannot understand money, banking, and the economic process.

Surely, there is strong evidence that he thought he had accomplished this task. The inner conversation of the General Theory revolves around the interrelationships between the interest rate and the marginal efficiency of capital (mec).[8] And he distinguished between the two by recourse to the use of "labor units" as tools to measure capital in real terms.[9]

To understand the status of economic theory today one has to realize that the definition of real wealth is "monetary wealth minus inflation"; hence, the existence of the marginal efficiency of capital has disappeared from the literature; hence, there is confusion about what is "capital"[10]; hence, there is no clear understanding of money.[11] This is such a striking feature of mainstream economics that it has given rise to much opposition from economists who, just for that reason, call themselves New Monetary Theorists.

One cannot fill these fundamental gaps in our understanding of the economic system without jettisoning the extant structure of macroeconomics; see Gorga (2023). This feat is accomplished in Concordian economics. The fundamental book of Concordian economics is titled The Economic Process.[12] The two books in the present set cover the interstices between the detailed analysis of both the original and revised Keynes' model as well as a thorough analysis of the Production Process, the Distribution Process, and the Consumption Process. In the present set, we are mostly

---

[7] Keynes (1936, Preface). From the full quotation of this sentence, it becomes clear that Keynes did not set his target quite right. His search was for a "*monetary*" theory "of output as a whole." And that is what he got; he did not create an "*economic*" theory of output as a whole.

[8] Keynes (1936: esp. Chaps. 11–13).

[9] *Ibid.*, see esp. Chap. 4. For a definitive solution to the problem of measurement of real wealth, see Gorga (2017).

[10] For a measure of this problem, it might be sufficient to follow the discussion related to the publication of Piketty's *Capital in the Twenty First Century* (2017).

[11] There is no definition of money in economics; there is only a detailed description of the *functions* of money.

[12] Gorga (2002, 2009a, 2009b, 2016). Full disclosure: *The Economic Process presents* a full length treatment of the logical deficiencies of the General Theory and the outline of the structure of Concordian economics. Quite apart from numerous positive reviews, the book is hobbled by two negative reviews, one because the reviewer (Davidson, 2003) openly admitted he was unable to accept the logic of the exposition of the book; he also reasoned in terms of two propositions, one that does not exist in the General Theory—I = S—and another that does not exist in EP—H = I; the other because the reviewer (Broski, 2003) could not find hoarding in the economic system. All reviews can be found at http://www.a-new-economic-atlas.com/p/review-of-ep.html.

analyzing some of the dynamics of the economic process and some applications of the resultant Concordian economics.

6.3 Concordian Economics

Concordian economics is all based on the fundamental proposition that Investment equals Consumption ($I = C$). A correspondent who wishes to remain anonymous has written: "*$I = C$, I love it! In fact, I think Keynes's General Theory is incoherent without it… Someday, $I = C$ will shift from radically ridiculous to patently obvious.*"

$I = C$ is "scaffolding" which disappears at construction's end.

In Concordian economics, Investment (I) is understood as the Production of real wealth like tables and chairs and dentist's services (is there any rational reason why "investment" occurs other than to create real wealth…?); in Concordian economics, Consumption is understood as expenditure of any monetary instrument to purchase real wealth (the arbitrary[13] decision of Keynes to cut the meaning of expenditure to the purchase of "consumer goods" was determined by mathematical constraints of his model of the economic system. This constriction removes economics from reality. Is an expenditure to purchase capital goods not "consumption" of money also?).[14]

Finally, since an equality to be logically valid must be an equivalence,[15] Concordian economics makes visible the otherwise invisible factor of Distribution (D) of ownership rights that, since the law abhors a vacuum, occurs automatically at the moment wealth is created. The $I = C$ scaffolding is therefore ultimately transformed in the equivalence of Production to Distribution and to Consumption ($P \leftrightarrow D \leftrightarrow C$). These interrelationships are best captured in the given geometric construction: see, Fig. 6.1.

This figure allows us to observe the economic process as a whole; the economic process describes the dynamics of the economic system. Even in the purchase of a chocolate bar, these three elements of the economic process are present: 1. real wealth (Production), 2. money (Consumption), and 3. ownership rights (Distribution). Real wealth is exchanged for money and money is exchanged for real wealth; in a civilized society, both transactors have to be legal owners of the wealth they exchange. The sales slip is the visible proof of ownership.

---

[13] At page 61 of *GT*, Keynes writes: "Any reasonable definition of the line between consumer-purchasers and investment-purchasers…".

[14] Gorga 2002, 2009a, 2009b, 2016: Chap. XIV, esp. pp. 141–42.

[15] See, e.g., Suppes (1957: 213–220) and esp. Allen (1970, 435–47, 748–52).

6.3.1 A Review of the Economic Process in the History of Economics

For the Classics, as well as Neoclassics and Marginalists, money was a "veil" that obscured the vision of the "real" economy. Thus, they neglected money and, therefore, they never acquired a view of the economic process as a whole.

Keynes was fierce to fight against that—as fiercely as he later on had to fight against econometrics; see, e.g., Syll (2017). The General Theory integrated the real and the monetary economy; yet it left the task of analyzing issues of distribution of income and wealth to future generations. Thus, Keynes never acquired a view of the economic process as a whole.

Post-Keynesians and Monetarists, in this view, differ from Keynes mainly in their understanding of interest rates and relative functions. For them, real wealth disappears. Thus, they never acquired a view of the economic process as a whole.

The Austrians, fixing their attention on capital, which is never definitely specified as physical capital or financial capital, and neglecting issues of justice that are inextricably related to the distribution of money and wealth, also lose the vision of the economy as a whole.

American Monetarists and New Monetarists focus indeed on money and banking. But they mostly neglect issues of the creation of real wealth. Consequently, issues of distribution of money and wealth become singularly ideological utterances. They also lack the vision of the economy as a whole.

6.4 Money

As it can be seen from Fig. 6.1, money is anything that allows us to purchase real wealth. In barter, real wealth is exchanged for real wealth; thus, real wealth transitorily performs the *function* of money in that type of social organization of the economic system, but real wealth is not money; real wealth remains real wealth—even when it performs the real function of money as in the case of sea shells, feathers, and glass beads. In a monetary economy, one finds a wealth of financial instruments that perform the function of money, including gold. But gold is not money. Currency is money. And money is not exclusively currency. *Money is a legal representation of real wealth.*

Gold is real wealth, just as a table, a chair, a house, or land—or the dentist's services—are real wealth. Gold functions as money only in a barter system. In a non-barter system, gold is "cashed" in, it is generally exchanged for money, before it will be accepted in any trade. Otherwise, how to determine the "value" of gold?

The list of financial instruments that enter the broad category of money starts with coins (whose content is real wealth of little current value) and evolves into all forms of currency and bank deposits. The list does not stop there. Surely, since stocks and bonds are accepted in the purchase of entire firms, stocks and bonds have to be listed as money. (To the knowledge of this writer, only Murray Rothbard advanced this proposition (2010: 259–265).) And then, of course, there are all sorts of other financial instruments from mortgages to insurance policies to derivatives that function as money.

Cash is a synonym for currency. But cash is always coins and paper money in the form of banknotes, while currency can be anything. Currency is anything that is accepted in the exchange of wealth, and legal currency is anything that is accepted by the government in payment of taxes.

Money is a legal representation of real wealth. To repeat, money is a legal representation of real wealth. This means that money serves to purchase real wealth that is located anywhere in the world.

This reality also means that the creation of financial instruments without the corresponding creation of real wealth is a counterfeit operation.

6.4.1 The Creation of Money

We achieve a clearer understanding of money through an understanding of the process of the creation of money. There are three creators of money: individual human beings, business corporations, and financial corporations. The State creates money through such a financial institution as the Central Bank.

Individual human beings create money. The operation is so simple—and so complex at the same time—that two modes must be distinguished from each other. One mode is the creation of money on the basis of real wealth; the other occurs on the basis of credit—or creditworthiness.

In the exchange of fish for berries, both fish and berries are money.

You give me a pen; *we* agree that the value of the pen is one dollar and we write this value down on a piece of paper; if a third person accepts this piece of paper in exchange for a basket of berries, this piece of paper has automatically become money.

The creation of money might occur without the presence of any real wealth at all. If you give me a piece of paper, placing a certain currency value on it, for the promise of the delivery of a pen *tomorrow* and I exchange that piece of paper for a basket of berries today, we have created money, not on the basis of real wealth but on the basis of "credit," your credit—and mine—to deliver to me or to a third party the corresponding value in real wealth tomorrow.

It is on the basis of this simple reality that local currencies are created. Today there are about 6000 local currencies circulating in the world. More ought to be created, and more will be created. But local currencies, just because of their intrinsic nature of being local, will never be a substitute for national currencies. National currencies are, by definition, accepted throughout a country and, under certain conditions, abroad as well.

Business corporations undoubtedly create money. Money is created directly by corporations as discount *coupons* on their merchandise; discount coupons are money.

6.4 Money

And are not *sales* discounts a form of *negative* money? Corporations create much more money than that: They create stocks and bonds. Stocks and bonds are used to buy entire physical plants and corporate entities. Are they not to be counted as money?

Financial corporations create money. There is a great variety of financial corporations: credit institutions, credit unions, mutual banks, cooperative banks, savings-and-loan associations, industrial loan companies, mortgage loan brokers, thrift institutions, savings banks, commercial banks, investment banks, money market institutions, insurance agencies, mutual funds, state banks, national banks, international banks, private banks, and public banks.

Indeed, the whole array of (their own) stocks and bonds, insurance policies, and even derivatives offers evidence that financial corporations create money. If not used directly to buy real wealth, these instruments can be exchanged for cash. Corporations buy and sell their own stocks.

These financial instruments are not currency, because the government does not accept them in payment of taxes. But all these financial instruments are money.

They *represent* real wealth; they can be exchanged for real wealth and for cash.

The banks that are of special interest here are those that issue loans beyond the amount of their own "capital" and borrower's deposits. These are banks that create money.

On what basis do these banks create money? They create money on the basis of credit, but not necessarily the bank's credit, unless money is raised to increase the capital stock of the bank, and this capital is lent out. The major part of the money created by banks is created on the basis of the *borrower's credit*, namely a promise to repay interest and capital in time and on time.

Professor Galbraith (2001) was absolutely right, "The process by which banks create money is so simple that the mind is repelled."

Institutional constraints determine limits to the amount of money that banks can create. In the United States and in the rest of the world, these rules are dictated by economic theory, which has currency world-wide. Specific rules change from country to country and from time to time. The system itself is called the "fractional reserve" system. Generally, for every dollar in capital deposited in the accounts that banks keep with the Federal Reserve System, the bank can create ten dollars of credit and, therefore, make ten dollars' worth of loans.

A most important distinction is the difference between public and private banks. Public banks are the only institutions that can legally create cash, or dollars in the United States. The United States public bank is the Federal Reserve System (the Fed). The second important distinction is that public banks have no limit to the creation of money; it is only in Concordian economics that the limit is determined by the value of real wealth in existence and promised to be created. As seen in Fig. 6.1 for the economic system to work properly, monetary wealth has to be equivalent to the value of real wealth.

The Fed creates money in three different ways. A small part of cash is in the form of dollar bills, namely banknotes (which are printed by an arm of the Treasury, the Bureau of Engraving and Printing); a much larger amount is in the form of checks and digital bank accounts. The Fed creates money by purchasing (a wealth of different) bonds either from the government or private primary dealers; proceeds go to the government to serve its various purposes. The Fed finally creates money by (overnight) lending money primarily to banks through federal funds as well as the discount window. (Financial platforms seem to multiply these days.) The New York Fed is engaged in dealing with national and international operations.

The Fed restricts the money supply by selling bonds to the public.

6.4.2 The Government Keeps a Monopoly on the Creation of Cash

The reasons for this monopoly condition are many: First, because one unit of cash is exchanged for one unit of cash throughout the entire nation. (For the exchange of one local currency for another, it is first necessary to ascertain the exchange "value" of each currency.) In the United States, this historic reason is determined by the fact that one unit of cash could at one time be legally converted into one unit of gold (or silver). This uniformity of value is of extreme importance in the field of commerce. It is its extrinsic value; it is its face value. (The intrinsic value of cash is a different entity; it is derived from the local price of goods and services; and since the local price of goods and services varies from place to place, the intrinsic value of cash also changes from place to place. This is true as to place. Ditto for the difference in the value of cash over time.)

One more reason for the necessity of the government monopoly over the creation of cash can be found in the mechanisms of exchanges of cash for cash not only internally within a nation but abroad, in exchange for or conversion into foreign currencies.

Another major reason why the government has, and must have, a monopoly over the creation of cash is to limit to the maximum extent possible the counterfeiting of the currency. This function is performed at an extremely high cost: Measures to prevent counterfeiting are highly complex and need to be changed from time to time. An addition to this cost is the expenditure to disseminate, and equally from time to time change, methods and procedures for the *detection* of counterfeit activity. Were each citizen, each city, or each bank to incur this cost, the benefits from the creation of cash might be highly diminished.

It is due to these inner characteristics that cash is distinguished from all other financial instruments.

6.4.3 Origin of Cash in the United States

Up until 1971, one deposited gold with the Treasury of the United States and received a Federal Note, which was legal tender for any purchase and for the payment of taxes as well. In this transaction, gold acquired by the Treasury was an asset; and, following the requirements of the double-entry bookkeeping system, the currency was accounted for as a liability. It is due to this historical connection that cash created by the Treasury, kept there, and/or transferred to the books of the Fed is accounted as a liability. This is an accounting fallacy.

Cash created by the Treasury and transferred to the Fed is not owed to anyone; it is an asset of the government, or, better, the nation and ought to be accounted for as such.

6.5 Rules for the Creation of Money

Today, the Federal Reserve System creates money following two directives dictated by the Congress of the United States: the Fed is obliged to keep the price level in check and to create conditions that favor full employment of the working force. History proves that it is very difficult to put these two directives into practice. Indeed, the whole array of monetary theories proves how elastic those two rules are.

The framework of analysis of Concordian economics allows us to reach two firm points:

First: The Fed, like all banks, creates money, not out of thin air, but on the basis of the credit, the creditworthiness, of the people in our nation, specifically, on the basis of our *national credit*.

Second: The creator of the value of national credit is not the banking system, but the public as a whole. Hence, national credit is owned by the people of a nation. Hence, We the People have the right to access national credit.

Thus, the framework of analysis carried out by Concordian economics suggests that the Fed has to follow Three firm Rules for the creation and distribution of money. The Fed has to issue:

1. Loans only for the creation of real wealth, not for the purchase of financial assets;
2. Loans to benefit all members of the community, which implies that loans ought to be issued only to individual entrepreneurs, co-operatives, corporations with Employee Stock Ownership Plans (ESOPs), and public agencies with taxing powers, so the loans can be repaid;
3. Loans at cost, not at variable interest rates.

In a society thus gradually made securely and justly rich, love/charity will easily take care, with great dignity, of the few who for any reason do not want to or cannot participate in the economic process. In a healthy society, those who do not want or cannot participate in the economic process are naturally few. What is generally not recognized is that most people love to work; indeed, they need to work to earn self-respect—from themselves and from others. The essential proviso is that they should be free to, and have the opportunity to do what they love. Most people with "free" time on their hands do works of love: they do not ask for any monetary compensation.

The transition to a Concordian paradigm ought to be voluntary and gradual. Three provisos can be outlined here:

1. Corporations that dislike ESOPs remain free to access the private market for their financial needs;
2. Given the long-term stability of the monetary system, investors who tolerate a high degree of uncertainty and risk regarding the use of their privately earned resources ought to be free to earn correspondingly handsome rewards;
3. Apart from rules of common justice, the government ought to gradually dismantle all those rules and regulations that have accrued over the centuries in the vain hope to curb the "animal spirits" of the people.

6.6 Pricing Policy

Monetary policy will forever remain, as Keynes puts it "a haze where nothing is clear and everything is possible" (1936: 292). Monetary policy will forever remain in such a haze, unless it is treated as part and parcel of pricing policy. Unless, in other words, monetary policy is studied and applied in the context of the supply and demand of real goods and services. The importance of the apparatus of demand and supply emphasized by the Marginalists comes into full bloom. This apparatus is presented in the following classic figure (courtesy of http://www.producingohio.org/lesson/draw.html) (Fig. 6.4).

Long story that must be cut to its bare bones. Monetary policy becomes clear and firm once a set of obvious observations is brought to the fore. The function of money is not to grow money, but to serve the economic system. The purpose of monetary policy ought to be to foster real wealth—and to keep the values of monetary wealth within a safe proportion to the values of real wealth. This means that the laws of supply and demand ought to function as ascertained in theory. For these rules to govern, the Market must be free. In turn, the market will be free if it operates within a balanced set of economic rights and responsibilities. No responsibilities, no rights. No rights, no free market.

6.7 Concluding Comments

A monetary policy rooted in rights and responsibilities is an entirely new construct in the long history of monetary analysis.

6.7 Concluding Comments

Fig. 6.4 Supply (S) and Demand (D) relationships

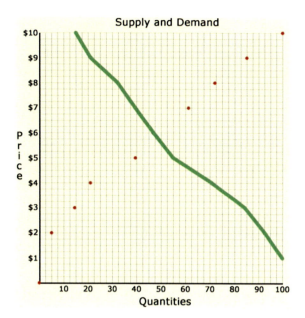

Some Readers might be tempted to say: This policy will never be implemented; the powers-that-be will never allow it to be implemented. This response might cover deep fears. Indeed, Concordian monetary policy, if not Concordian economics as a whole, is bound to raise anxiety and even anger in the soul of Readers who have devoted their lives to mending the many widely acknowledged shortcomings of mainstream theory.

Clearly, to anger the Reader is definitely not the intention of the writer. For these Readers, I can only recommend traditional remedies. They have to undergo the rigors of self-analysis and self-control emphasized by well-known treatises penned by Stoics, Buddhists, and modern Phycologists; see., e.g., Golden (2020).

More generally, my answer to skepticism is this: If We the People do not exercise our right of access to national credit, *our* common wealth, Concordian monetary policy will certainly not be implemented. But the cause for its lack of implementation is not *the* opposition of the powers-that-be; it is *our* unwillingness to exercise this right.

The Fed has clearly indicated its willingness to consider the Three Rules of Concordian monetary policy; but, equally clearly, the Fed has indicated that these rules cannot be adopted if presented by a solo researcher. The Fed wisely suggests that the request should come from our "state and national representatives" (Durr, 2016).

And when do state and federal representatives intervene? Well, when it is politically safe to do so. It is for economists and social scientists to say that Concordian monetary policy is safe.

That is a one-prong answer. The other prong is this: People who want to see Concordian economics implemented should not feel isolated. I know from ResearchGate, I know from SSRN, I know from EconCurrents, I know from Academia.edu, I know from OpEdNews, I know from TalkMarkets, I know from Ethical Spectacle, I know from LinkedIn, I know from Facebook, I know from Google, I know that my readers are scattered all over the planet. From now on there is finally an organization that welcomes you all. Search for it. This is your organization: Friends of Concordian economics (FoCe). This is your organization. Make it do your will. Make it thrive; make it successful; make it powerful. You will feel proud. You will feel virtuous. St. Thomas Aquinas said that "Virtue is the peak of power."

My thought is scattered all over the Internet and in eight books, one of them translated into eight foreign languages. With the present set on Concordian economics, two more books are added to the chain.

Read my work. It is not written for my aggrandizement but for your empowerment. Perhaps you have read some of it in the past. Read a new piece. Perhaps you'll like it. And remember my motto: If you like what you read, tell your friends; if you do not like what you read, tell me—but tell me why.

Within the context of the evaluation of Concordian economics vs. current disheartening events, I was happily quoting Edmund Burke, "Evil triumphs when good men do nothing," when I stopped in my trucks and asked, is that true? Am I accusing economists of committing evil acts? Most certainly not. I know better than that. It is modern economics that creates conditions in which evil thrives. Modern economists are impotent onlookers.

Up to now, economists have had no choice. As Jefferson pointed out, "I believe that banking institutions are more dangerous to our liberties than standing armies." Now Concordian economics is offering economists a choice. For how long will they—and other social scientists—neglect Concordian economics? Concordian economics is a new paradigm that reconnects us with a more just world, the millennial world of economic justice of Aristotle and Aquinas.

New paradigms always prevail; it is only the timing of their acceptance that is uncertain.

Jefferson (1774) also said: "When the representative body have lost the confidence of their constituents, when they have notoriously made sale of their most valuable rights, when they have assumed to themselves powers which the people never put into their hands, then indeed their continuing in office becomes dangerous to the state, and calls for an exercise of the power of dissolution." Mainstream economics has done enough damage. The Invisible Government of the World, ruled by an unwritten Economic Constitution, has reached such a stage.

It is high time for We the People to exercise the power of dissolution of such a state.

All this might ultimately be granted. But do we ultimately have a complete understanding of what money does? We will find out that we do not.

On to the understanding of the uses and abuses of money, then.

References

Allen, R. G. D. (1970). *Mathematical Economics* (2nd ed.). London and New York: Macmillan, St. Martin's.

Aquinas, T. (2010). *Summa Theologica (Complete and Unabridged)*. Coyote Canyon Press.

Aristotle. (1999). *Nicomachean ethics (Introduction and Translation by Terence Irwin)* (2nd ed.). Hackett Publishing Company.

Aristotle. (1998). *Politics (Introduction and translation by C. D. C. Reeve)*. Hackett Publishing Company.

Brady, E. M., & Gorga, C. (2019). How to use public policy to guide accumulation toward virtuous ends. *Mother Pelican, A Journal of Solidarity and Sustainability, 15*(5). Available at http://www.pelicanweb.org/solisustv15n05page4.html

Broski, M. (2003). Review of "The economic process: An instantaneous non-Newtonian picture. Carmine Gorga". *Journal of Markets and Morality, 6*(1), 297–298.

Brown, E. (2023). Three Presidents Who Made Thanksgiving a National Holiday—And What They Were Celebrating. ScheerPost, November 23. Available at https://scheerpost.com/2023/11/23/ellen-brown-threepresidents-who-made-thanksgiving-a-national-holiday-and-what-they-were-celebrating/. Accessed 23 November 2023.

Davidson, P. (2003). In C. Gorga (Ed.), *A review of the economic process: An instantaneous non-Newtonian picture* (Vol. XLI, pp. 1284–1285). University Press of America.

Deane, H. A. (1963). *The social and political ideas of saint Augustine*. Columbia University Press.

Durr, J. (2016). *Personal communication to Carmine Gorga, September 14*. Public Affairs Office of Board of Governors of the Federal Reserve System. https://1drv.ms/w/s!AgFxYQBpjmMFj06wiz_G_fkJWeWO

Fisher, I. (1911). *The purchasing power of money*. Macmillan.

Galbraith, J. K. (2001). *Money: Whence it came, where it went*. Houghton Mifflin Harcourt.

Gissy, W. (2013). Do merger restrictions promote social development? *International Journal of Humanities and Social Science, 3*(19), 150–159.

Golden, B. (2020). How do anger and anxiety interact? *Psychology Today*, April 11. Available at https://www.psychologytoday.com/us/blog/overcoming-destructive-anger/202004/how-do-anger-and-anxiety-interact. Accessed on October 19, 2023.

Gorga, C. (1999). Toward the definition of economic rights. *The Journal of Markets and Morality, II*(1) 88–101. Reprinted with a new introduction and postscript at Pelican, M. (2014). *A Journal of Solidarity and Sustainability, 10*(12).

Gorga, C. (2002, 2009, 2016). *The economic process: An instantaneous non-Newtonian picture*. University Press of America. 2009, expanded softcover edition. The Somist Institute, 2016 edition.

Gorga, C. (2009a). The economics of Jubilation—Blinking adam's fallacy away. In *Social Science Research Network (SSRN)*, October 15, SSRN.

Gorga, C. (2009b). Concordian economics: Tools to return relevance to economics. *Forum for Social Economics, 38*(1), 53–69.

Gorga, C. (2013). A three-part proposal for investing hoarded cash. *The Catholic Social Science Review, 18*, 261–263.

Gorga, C. (2015a). Economics of morality: Economics of Moses, economics of Jesus. *Mother Pelican, 11*(4).

Gorga, C. (2015b). The world of economics since 2008. *Mother Pelican, 11*(9).

Gorga, C. (2017). The economic bubble and its measurement. *Theoretical and Practical Research in the Economic Fields, 8*(1), 19–23. Available at: https://journals.aserspublishing.eu/tpref/article/view/1286

Gorga, C. (2023). Money, banking, and the economic process. *Econcurrents*, May 13. Available at https://econcurrents.com/2023/05/13/money-banking-and-the-economic-process/. Accessed October 18, 2023.

Jefferson, T. (1774). *A summary view of the rights of British America.* Available at https://www.revolutionary-war-and-beyond.com/a-summary-view-of-the-rights-of-british-america.html. Accessed December 2, 2023.

Keynes, J. M. (1936). *The general theory of employment, interest, and money.* Harcourt.

Macqueen, D. J. (1972). Saint Augustine's concept of property ownership. *Recherches Augustiniennes, VIII.*

Mary, Untier of Knots. (n.d.) Wikipedia. Available at https://en.wikipedia.org/wiki/mary_untier_of_knots. Accessed December 1, 2023.

Neill, R. (2011). Slavery in the writings of Thomas Aquinas, Yumpu.com. Available at: https://www.yumpu.com/en/document/read/12426173/slavery-in-the-writings-of-thomas-aquinas

Oresme, N. (2017). *Quoted in Stanford encyclopedia of philosophy.*

Piketty, T. (2017). *Capital in the twenty-first century* (A. Goldhammer, Trans.). Belknap Press.

Pilkington, P. (2014). Authoritative arguments in economics. *Econintersect Blog*, November 9, 2014.

Rothbard, M. N. (2010). *Strictly confidential: The private Volker fund of Murray N. Rothbard, and David Gordon.* Ludwig von Mises Institute.

Simpson, P. (1997). *The politics of Aristotle* (P. Simpson, Trans.). The University of North Carolina Press.

Simpson, P. (1998). *A philosophical commentary on the "politics" of Aristotle.* University of North Carolina Press.

Smith, A. (1759). *The theory of moral sentiments* (6th ed., 1790). Forgotten Books.

Smith, A. (1776). *The wealth of nations. Modern (Cannan) library edition with the fore ward by Max Lerner.*

Soini, W. S. (2023). RFK Jr. and Hegel's knot. *Gloucester Daily Times*, August 31. Available at https://www.gloucestertimes.com/opinion/letters_to_the_editor/letter-rfk-jr-and-hegels-knot/article_20ecec90-2a51-11ee-a4fc-e3647f7bdfe1.html. Accessed October 14, 2023.

Syll, L. P. (2017). Keynes' devastating critique of econometrics. *Statistics & Econometrics*, February 24 at https://larspsyll.wordpress.com/category/statistics-econometrics/page/3/

Tkacz, M., & Kries, D. (1994). *Augustine: Political writings.* Hackett Publishing Company, Inc.

Wikipedia. (n.d.) *Mary, Untier of knots.*

Chapter 7
Where-To Money

Abstract These are indeed perilous times. The worst can happen. In this chapter, we shall observe (i) where does money go in a Stock Market Crash, (ii) the state of unpreparedness of the economics profession and how to be ready for the next crash by (iii) "defusing the bomb" and (iv) "mending the Fed." We shall also examine (v) the rationale for our proposals, and (vi) expected effects of these proposals. The chapter is divided into three parts: Sect. 1 deals with the current state of affairs; Sect. 2 deals with what can the private sector do; Sect. 3 deals with what can a Central Bank do.

7.1 The Current State of Affairs

7.1.1 Where Does Money Go in a Stock Market Crash?

A loss of twenty/thirty percent in the value of stocks and bonds during a Stock Market crash is a normal occurrence. Greater loss of values is not an uncommon occurrence. Where do these values go?

They go puff, dispersed in the ether world. Values lose some zeros.

The most important question is: What to do then? What does the economics profession tell us to do?

7.1.2 The State of Unpreparedness of the Economics Profession

Unless they are keeping it a secret, or the economics journals are not publishing it, or the press is not reporting it, nothing has changed in academia since 2008; see Gorga (2015). The world of economic theory is still where the renowned Nobel Prize Laureate and New York Times columnist, Paul Krugman, found it in 2014: "The economics profession has not, to say the least, covered itself in glory these past six years. Hardly any economists predicted the 2008 crisis—and the handful who did tend to be people who also predicted crises that didn't happen. More significant, many and arguably most economists were claiming, right up to the moment of collapse, that nothing like this could even happen." Paul Krugman added: "Furthermore, once crisis struck economists seemed unable to agree on a response. They'd had 75 years since the Great Depression to figure out what to do if something similar happened again, but the profession was utterly divided when the moment of truth arrived."

This is not an idiosyncratic position. More surprisingly perhaps, due to his voluminous investigations, and perhaps just because of them, Piketty (2014) has forcefully made the utter truth explicit: "There is no such thing as an economic science."

What is indeed the status of economic theory? Too many discussions of public affairs are driven by the assumption that grave economic decisions are taken on the basis of sound economic theory—certainly, overpowering economic theory and overwhelming mathematical reasoning—as opposed to pure ideology. This is an assumption as widespread in secular as in religious corridors.

It is a fundamental misconception.

7.1.3 A Continuing State of Crisis

The naked truth is that economic theory has been in a state of crisis ever since the publication of Adam Smith's *Wealth of Nations* in 1776. What else do major upheavals in the history of economic analysis since then signify? Why did we pass from classical economics to neo-classical economics to the marginalist revolution to the economics of Keynes to Keynesian economics to post-Keynesian economics to monetarism to neo-neo-classical economics to real business cycle theory to behaviorism—let alone Marxist economics or Austrian economics or Georgist economics or Kelsonian economics; indeed, let alone the splinter programs of research within each major school of economic thought?

These efforts are not accretions to basic scientific knowledge; they are revolutionary attempts to start the economic discourse anew ever and again. They are failed attempts to describe the mechanics of the economic process. Pilkington (2014) has nailed this complex issue down: "Mainstream economics moves forward not through logical development and integration, but through forgetting."

These quotations confirm the validity of steady accusations of irrelevance launched at mainstream economic theory from within and from without the economics profession.

Intellectual irrelevance has not yet translated into political irrelevance. Quite the contrary. If so many economic doctrines come and go, it is because—in accordance with the winds of the moment—they tend to justify the status quo from the right or the left or even the center of the political spectrum. They invariably seem to rationalize the economic behavior and policies of the "powers-that-be."

7.1 The Current State of Affairs

The sad part, the maddening part, the hopeful part is that the powers-that-be do not know what they are doing. They work at cross-purposes with their own best interests.

We are at a breaking point.

Indeed, we have now reached a point in which the system is not working for the powers-that-be either. No one is benefiting from the workings of the system in which we are entrapped. Certainly, the system is not serving the poor; and it has undoubtedly caused a collapse of the middle classes. It is hard to conceive of the case, but we have reached a point at which the rich, perhaps, suffer most from the breakdown of the system—at least from a purely psychological and arithmetical point of view, the rich undoubtedly suffer most.

The rich deserve more attention than they have been given during the last couple of hundred years.

Against the general scapegoating of the rich, there is the Biblical assertion that the creators of poverty are, not the rich, but the "wicked." What a politically liberating verity. From a practical point of view, here is a little parable to unpack. You go to bed with the assurance that your portfolio is worth $3.0 million—not too much money, by today's standards. You wake up in the morning to discover that, because of shenanigans in a far away land, your portfolio is now worth $1.5 million. How will you feel?

And what if, as the rich frequently do, you had borrowed $1.5 million yesterday? That is the condition that pushes some rich through glass windows. Isn't that true?

Wait. Do the poor, do members of the middle class, ever lose $1.5 million overnight? They—we—are blessed with not having that much "capital" to start with. We are not in such danger. Our hearts tremble less at the gyrations of the Stock Market.

There must be a better way to run the country. And, in fact, there is. But alternative ways to run the country cannot be discovered from within the strictures of mainstream economics. One must abandon that paradigm; we must abandon the Austrian as well as the Keynesian paradigm.

Mainstream economics has repeatedly been proved to be a faulty system by the very academic profession that tries to sustain it. Why wallow in error? Einstein might have put it straight: To expect different results from repeatedly taking the same steps is not rational; actually, he said, it is "insanity." (This is a misattribution, but too good to waste.)

The difficulty, of course, resides in choosing the alternative to mainstream economics.

The difficulty is that there is a **wealth of alternatives**, some more serious than others; some better grounded in reality than others; some experientially proven to produce more positive results than others, even though necessarily piecemeal results, for not being thoroughly and consistently applied. And we are all biased toward our own personal preferences.

We confuse ourselves and, what is worse, we misdirect our representative politicians by sending them in a hundred different directions. We are clearly at an impasse. To say the least, the impasse is created by analysis paralysis.

7.1.4 How Can We Ever Get Out of the Current Spectrum of Opinion?

Among the many, the most dangerous opinions are these two, and unfortunately, they occupy a large spot at the center of the political spectrum of opinion: 1. Most people are somehow satisfied with the status quo; 2. With much overlap, most other people, while spending huge amounts of energy, seek tiny changes to the system. They do not yet see the wisdom of Bryan (1896), whose words resonate even more strongly today: "When we have restored the money of the Constitution, all other necessary reforms will be possible, but until this is done there is no other reform that can be accomplished." Then, of course, there are the realists who believe it is a waste of time talking truth to power. The subset is composed of people who are afraid of talking truth to power.

A special niche is occupied by the small subset of fanatics who will not lift a finger to avoid the impending disaster because they believe that, amidst the eventual rubble, they stand a better chance to concentrate the people's attention on their pre-selected solution.

Two subsets which, whether consciously or not, want to destroy the existing monetary system need to be specified. One uses mathematical reasoning; the other, whether consciously or not, uses money itself by indiscriminately distributing (or suggesting to distribute) public money—even by helicopters.

When granted by the relatively few that we must concentrate our efforts on the weaknesses of the monetary system, efforts are still splintered around this inner circle of ideas: some want "to end" the Federal Reserve System (the Fed), the Central Bank of the United States, as well as any other Central Bank presumably; many others—intentionally or not—want to subvert its might by creating competitive, local currencies. There are about 6000 local currencies in the world, at last count. Many want to add one more currency, the one on which they have spent months if not years of effort.

Those who want to create a new local currency ought to consider whether any local group has the intellectual and financial resources to create, administer, and safeguard a better physical currency than the state's currency. And yet, the growing call for the creation of local currencies must be encouraged, not only because of the incomparable ability of local currencies to teach the "nature" of money, but especially because—if and when the financial collapse of national currencies occurs— our lives will rely on barter and local currencies.

7.1.5 What Is Amiss with All Current National Monetary Systems?

In the previous chapter, we have seen what is amiss with the theoretical understanding of "money." No need to repeat that. Here we will concentrate our attention on what is amiss in the *administration* of whatever ruling monetary system that exists in a country.

If there are real resources—human and physical resources—available, if there are real needs to be met, why are resources not utilized? Why are real needs not met? The common explanation is "For lack of money." Well, no. The real explanation is, "For lack of a well-functioning monetary system." The money supply is capable of expanding to meet the availability of real resources. Indeed, in a well-functioning monetary system, the money supply is always sufficient to meet the real resources of a country.

That said, we must be certain about what is amiss with all current national monetary systems. The answer lies, not in the administration of monetary policy, but in the inner conception of monetary policy.

The two key questions concern the **creation** and **distribution** of the money supply. This is an area in which two diametrically opposed conceptions prevail: one is the European conception in which money is assumed to be created and hence to be controlled by bankers; the other is the American conception which assumes that, since the value of money is created by the blood, sweat, and tears of all the people in a nation, the process of creation of money ought to be controlled by the people, and its distribution ought to benefit all the people. New money created on the basis of national credit ought to benefit the **common good**. New money created by Central Bankers is not their money; it is not my money either: it is **our** money. Within duly specified conditions, We the People, as sovereign citizens—on a decentralized, democratic basis—have the right of access to national credit on the basis of a loan and the responsibility toward the community at large to repay the loan.

With the broad background assistance of Concordian economics, we are able to reach an overarching conclusion. To build a well-functioning monetary system, we need to go through three sizeable hurdles: we need to concentrate our mind on 1. the creation, 2. destruction, and 3. distribution of the money supply. In non-technical language, we need to "defuse the bomb" and "mend the Fed."

The fundamental background reality at certain periods of time like ours is the existence of an inordinate amount of money in circulation and its distribution among the wrong hands. We have observed earlier some of the dangers of "financialization." No need here to specify the degree of inequality existing in our world; no need to insist that the system is not stable. We have an urgent task.

7.2 What Can the Private Sector Do

7.2.1 Operation "Defuse the Bomb"

We have a choice. We either allow for a periodic catastrophic collapse of our financial structures of debt or accept the reality of the impossibility of repaying the debt. If we make peace with reality, a new/old world opens up to our investigation. We can opt for an organized voluntary reduction of debt in a systematic, rational, purposeful way, rather than through a catastrophic financial collapse of the monetary system as a whole; thereafter we can create and distribute money in a rational democratic way.

The next financial collapse is going to be dreadful. Knowledgeable people are talking of the collapse in terms of trillions. It is the monetary system of the world, not the financial system involving a few corporations, which will collapse.

The modern, prevalent solution of letting the taxpayer come in and save the "too-big-to-fail" corporations might not be available at the next meltdown. Sequestering the deposits of individuals and perhaps even corporations in banking institutions will not be sufficient for the creation of money to run apace with the growth of interest.

General knowledge is gradually growing that charging compound interest on a loan sets up an impossible race between growth of real wealth and growth of financial wealth. No matter how much new money is ever created, it is never enough because interest—especially in the form of compound interest—grows inexorably at a faster rate. Money can never keep up. Interest always wins. But its victory is ephemeral. Bankruptcies result.

Next time around, not even the Fed might have enough latitude to fill the gap. Rather than accepting a financial collapse, why not adopt a rational solution: the Jubilee Solution.

7.2.1.1 The Jubilee Solution: A Systematic Reduction of Zeros

Reduce all debt to zero in seven years.

Start with a 30% reduction in the first year and reduce all debt by 10% per year for seven years.

At the end of the seventh year, start the process anew.

This Proposal Truly Calls for a Systematic Reduction of Zeros.

Wealthy people will remain wealthy, as at the beginning of the escalating creation of ZEROS in their accounts—because wealth is a RELATIVE thing.

Just be alert: Find ways to isolate the smart ones, who might not join you at first.

7.2.1.2 A Bit on the Rationale

Debt that benefits both creditors and borrowers is a wondrous thing. The assumption here is that the debt is created for capital expansion, not for the purchase of consumer

7.2 What Can the Private Sector Do

goods or goods to be hoarded. This practice has perhaps been engaged in ever since the dawn of civilization, and it is not going to be extirpated from society any time soon. Nor ought it to be extirpated. Why? Why should it be?

As soon as debt crushes the productive ability of the debtor, that debt changes its nature from a beneficent to a maleficent reality that benefits neither the borrower nor the lender—and rational people ought to be able to identify that difference and take appropriate action to ameliorate the ensuing harmful conditions from which nobody gains and everyone suffers to one degree or another.

If zeros are systematically destroyed in financial accounts in a way to preserve relative relations among lenders, no harm is done to anyone; indeed, much good is done to everyone.

This proposal attempts to adjust the ingenious Mosaic invention of the Jubilee Solution to the complexities of the modern world. In addition to the restitution of the land to the original steward at the end of $7 \times 7 = 49$ years, namely the beginning of the 50th year, the year of the Jubilee, Mosaic Law prescribed the cancelation of debts among Jewish people every seven years. The reasons are many, and all valid, see, e.g. Gorga (2016). The most important one can be found in the very nature of money[1]: money has real value only at the moment of the exchange; money in my pocket is just paper. If money is concentrated in a few hands, the circulation of money is reduced. When the circulation stops, namely when there is a financial crisis, the value of money is reduced to extremely low levels. Chaos ensues.

Is it not much more rational to face these issues in a timely fashion in order to avoid certain disaster?

Thus the Concordian proposal. It calls for the systematic reduction of zeros in seven years: Start with a 30% reduction in the first year and reduce all debt by 10% per year every year for seven years. The proposal goes on to suggest that wealthy people will remain wealthy, as at the beginning of the escalating creation of zeros in their accounts—because wealth is a relative thing. If you and the Joneses have one million dollars each, you are equally rich. Your neighbor's estate grows to 10 million dollars; they are ten times as rich as you are. Yet, once you have increased your wealth to 10 million dollars, you are **again** just as rich as your neighbor.

This proposal recommends further to be alert and find ways to isolate the smart ones, who might not join you at the outset.

A much longer discussion can be had on the analysis of the economic worthiness of the content of financial estates. For instance, if billions of dollars are evaluated, the difference will be found mainly to reside in financial accounts with more zeros. There was no addition of one chair or one table or one service in the real economy. There was only an addition of zeros in financial accounts wherever they were held. In a regimen of low interest rates as at present, there is no economic value to those zeros. Even with high interest rates, once the reduction of zeros is systematic, the relative value of any two accounts remains the same.

---

[1] This, of course, is a much disputed subject. There are two fundamental theories, the commodity theory and the credit theory; neither is acceptable. Nor has a satisfactory combination of the two been found yet.

7.2.1.3 The Seven-Year Solution

Ancient Israel created the institution of the Mosaic Seven-Year Jubilee. At the coming of the seventh year, all debt among the Israelites, but not debt involving foreigners, was extinguished. The slate was clean, and business relationships came alive again. It might be wise to use the same structure today, at least until better structures are designed and proven effective. There is nothing to prevent a study of eventual effects that might suggest an improved structure.

Without rhyme or reason, many Kings and Emperors worth their boots issued a debt jubilee upon accession to the throne.

7.2.1.4 A Bit on the Mechanics

It is assumed that there are many ways to reduce the debt, and if more ideas are proposed and implemented, that would be splendid. I will concentrate on two possibilities, one at the international level, and the other at the national level.

Technically, this work proposes for the International Monetary Fund (IMF), or a new institution created specifically for this purpose, to create an international facility to account for the Systematic Reduction of Debt (SRD) between nations. [Lately, as we shall see later on I have concentrated on the Bancor to perform this function.]

Local Central Banks are invited to replicate this facility within national borders to take care of the systematic reduction of debt within each nation. Whenever the Central Bank might refuse to perform such function, a new institution—or institutions—could be created specifically for this purpose.

7.2.1.5 A Bit on Cultural Conditions

Just as it is important to distinguish consumer credit (read, consumerism) from capital credit, so it is important to realize that to ask for a loan is to make a commitment to repay it; to default is to renege on that commitment.

The converse is less commonly brought forward: To make a loan, to obtain as much return as possible while knowing that the debtor will eventually default because he or she cannot possibly meet that commitment, is fraudulent. To enter into a creditor/debtor relationship is a two-way responsibility.

7.2.2 *Who Are the Potential Supporters of This Proposal?*

Many people and many institutions come to mind. Potential supporters are expected to come from Jewish organizations, whether they are public or private, secular or religious. Pride of place is not a silly or boastful position to occupy. The expression "Why didn't I think of it" is a glorious recognition of the exceptionality and necessity of any breakthrough like the design of the Jubilee Solution that offers much to be celebrated. To fully understand the reasons for the development of this idea by the ancient Israelites, rather than Egyptians, Greeks, or Romans, requires an in-depth knowledge of the religious, social, political, and especially international constraints/opportunities of ancient Israel. In addition to the idea of one God, the **owner** of all common wealth such as land **and money,** ancient Israelites were the first to come up with the idea of the Jubilee Solution. To this institution, in no small part is due, no doubt, the survival of the Jewish people as a nation, an outward manifestation of a coherent set of shared values, no matter how distant in time or place people happen to be.

The Jewish community may be expected to support this proposal to reduce national and international debt in a systematic, rational way. Yet, Christians of all denominations should not fall that far behind. They are also expected to endorse this proposal for many reasons. Is it not enough for them to do so as reverence for the first public act of Jesus, the expulsion of the money changers from the Temple? His Parable of the Talents, in which hoarding is punished in no uncertain terms; his request of alms for the poor as gifts to himself are a few more of Jesus' injunctions. Then, even though the unremitting struggle against the ravages of usury was eventually given up as recently as 1971 in the United States, this Christian tradition is something to be proud of; it is something that a spark of spirit will revivify in enlightening splendor.

Muslims, of course, are the only religious people who keep the faith against usury alive and well. It is to be noted that they keep such faith, no matter the practical difficulties and the demeaning snickers from those who know-not. It is equally to be noted that their faith is being rewarded in their creativity in financial affairs. Professor Muhammad Yunus, the creator of modern microfinancing and eventually a Nobel Peace laureate, is by faith a Muslim. Those analysts who are fond to point out the minimalist aspects of microfinancing, whether they are Christian or not, ought to remember Jesus singling out the poor woman who gave only two cents to the temple/community—yet those two cents were all she possessed. The few pennies involved in microfinancing often keep a family alive, productive, and living a dignified life. Is there any need to contrast the results of billions of dollars spent on corrupting people and creating too often unnecessary and inefficient public structures?

7.2.3 Some Further Recommendations

There is much that needs to be investigated. There is much to refine before these proposals can be implemented. Ideas that fail practical tests are not worth implementing. They sap the energies of people. So, onward with stern criticism; onward with practical or theoretical suggestions to make these germinal ideas come alive and bear fruits in the world for many years to come. But enough of analysis/paralysis. Onward with implementation.

7.3 What Can the Central Bank Do

7.3.1 Operation "Mend the Fed"

How can the Fed be transformed into an institution that serves all the people well?

The Federal Reserve System (the Fed) has pursued roughly the same type of policy for over a century now. To expect different results from the same actions, as Einstein might have warned, is insanity. We have to turn the Fed, our Central Bank, from serving the few, rather badly, to serving everyone well. If we do this, as Bryan (1896) pointed out long ago, "all other necessary reforms will be possible, but until this is done there is no other reform that can be accomplished." The Fed is the pivot.

Professor Galbraith (2001) was absolutely right, "The process by which banks create money is so simple that the mind is repelled." They create money on the basis of our credit; the Federal Reserve System creates money on the basis of our national credit. The Value of the national currency is created by the blood, sweat, and tears of all the people of a nation. Therefore, that value should be returned to all the people of a nation. See Gorga (2016).

The Federal Reserve System in the United States, and any Central Bank in the world, creates money, not out of thin air as it is commonly believed, but on the basis of our national credit—the credit, the creditworthiness of the people.

To repeat, the value of the money created by Central Banks is given by the blood, sweat, and tears of the people of the nation. Therefore, that money, by right, belongs—not to bankers, not to financial speculators—but to the people, as it is recognized by the United States Constitution. Democratic sovereign people of a nation have the right of access to national credit, not as a grant, but as a loan. National credit is a pool of common wealth; it is our common wealth. The integrity of the pool must be re-established by returning to it the money we have borrowed.

After doing its good work, by repaying the loan we **destroy** the money that was first created. This is an important distinguishing feature that separates this proposal from other similar-looking "money creating" proposals like those of Milton Freedman, Ben Bernanke, or Adair Turner.

The ordered destruction of the money created as loans is one fundamental reason why the call to exercise our right of access to national credit will not create inflation. Another reason flows from the conditions of the loan, conditions that form the suggested new regulatory procedures of the Fed.

By its own will, the Fed can issue the following:

1. Loans only for the creation of real wealth such as tables and chairs and foodstuff;
2. Loans to benefit all people of a nation. Hence, loans, vetted by committees of local bankers, can be issued through local banks to individual entrepreneurs, co-operatives, corporations with Employee Stock Ownership Plans (ESOPs) in their constitution, and public institutions with taxing power, so that they can repay the loan;
3. Loans at cost.

7.3 What Can the Central Bank Do

To repeat, loans must benefit all the people of a nation. Hence, loans, vetted by committees of local bankers, can be issued through local banks to individual entrepreneurs, co-operatives, corporations with Employee Stock Ownership Plans (ESOPs) in their constitution, and public institutions with taxing power, so that they can repay the loan.

Just as banks use our credit to give us a loan, so the Fed can use our national credit to issue loans that will be repaid by us, thus making good on our credit/credibility.

Unlike other money creating programs, this proposal is distinguished also by the fact that the initiative for the creation of new money in the form of loans resides, not with the Fed or the Central Bank or the Treasury Department, but with the people. Thus, it is very unlikely that the process of money creation under the proposed regimen will be influenced by political factors and favoritism and corruption in high places.

The last but not least distinguishing feature is the call for the creation of new money, not on the basis of arbitrary hunches and figures, but in response to real needs, real needs that are expressed as real resources that need to be energized by the pointed infusion of money into the economy. A chain reaction of positive events is thus expected to be set in motion: innovation and entrepreneurship will be unleashed; human beings will reach their full potential in freedom and dignity; needs will be satisfied; a fair distribution of income and wealth will ensue; calls for redistribution of wealth will cease; infrastructure will be improved; politicians will no longer be subjected to inherently **conflicting** demands; citizens will act as sovereigns. Money will get out of politics, because people will get into politics—and rich economics programs.

The monetary system will be placed on a most stable and just basis: Federal Reserve loans will be issued through local banks, the banks that nearly never failed during recent financial crises. And the world can let the too-big-to-fail operations fail, if they fail, without tearing the national monetary system apart. The taxpayer will no longer be pressed to bear the cost of market failures: no need for bail-outs; no need for bail-ins.

Let the Market rule, as it is supposed to do in theory. Let the Government rule over a legal framework designed to foster an economic system that serves all men and women of a nation **well**, rather than—unwittingly, indeed contrary to all best intentions of all members of a sane society—**enslaving them**.

This proposal results from much **history** and much respect for the very dictates of the United States Constitution, Article 1, Section 8.

7.3.2 A Bit on the Rationale of This Proposal

The monetary system is broken—the world over.
  It is not working for the poor.
  It has led to the collapse of the middle class.
  It is not working well for the rich, except in an illusory and transitory way.

We have to turn the Fed from serving the few, rather badly, to serving everyone well.

If the proposed Three Rules are employed, let Wall Street tremble and financial behemoths collapse, Main Street will continue to prosper.

In theory and practice, we are so far away from the American conception of money, that it is worth spending a few more moments on its rationale.

It has been assumed that the function of the Fed is to curb the "animal sprits" of mankind. See Gorga (2015).

Curb the "animal spirits" of mankind? Spirits that in the short term lead to inflation or deflation and fabulous financial crises in the long run? Is that what we expect of the Fed? Is that the ultimate aim of economic theory? Is that the task of a "civilized" society? If that is what we want, we fail. And we fail miserably, because we want to change human nature. This is an impossible task; it is not a task for humans.

No sooner was my piece calling for a restructure of Fed's procedures published a while ago that this realization appeared to me limpidly and forcefully. After many years of working, primarily in economics and only a faint acquaintance with psychology, I abruptly realized that society is imposing an impossible task upon the Fed, the task of curbing the "animal spirits" of mankind. The existence of this Darwinian conception, of course, has been fully discredited in most disciplines, but it still seems to reign supreme in economics.

As usual in cases like this, as soon as I searched, I found solid evidence to support the validity of not giving such a task to the Fed. A brand new report published by the Royal Society for the Encouragement of Arts, Manufactures, and Commerce (2015), titled Wired for Imprudence, explores six "behavioral hurdles" that make it hard for us to manage money well. The report emphasizes that "Cognitive overload, empathy gaps, optimism and overconfidence, instant gratification, harmful habits, and the influence of social norms can all be problematic for financial capability."

Into this socio-psychological din do we want to throw the Fed? Is that what we really want? If the Fed wages this fight, the Fed is doomed to fail—again and again. There is another way. Concordian economics research suggests that the Fed will have a much better chance of success if it administers national credit on behalf of the nation as a whole. The essence of these recommendations is contained in many publications now. They call for the issuance of loans, not grants; loans at cost; loans for the creation of real wealth; and loans for the benefit of all members of society.

You will find in these recommendations a procedure that would allow the Fed—not to work alone against, as Keynes branded them, the "animal spirits" of people. But to work together with its natural allies. Natural allies are individual entrepreneurs, co-operatives, corporations with Employee Stock Ownership Plans (ESOPs) in their constitution, government entities with taxing power, and especially local banks. These entities are all interested, as the Fed constitutionally is, in the stability of the monetary system: steady credit at steady cost. There are many consilient reasons on which to base these recommendations.

The Reason of Customary Praxis

The Fed already works with these entities, but on a last resort basis. It should be the first resort.

7.3 What Can the Central Bank Do

The Reason of Order

The rule today seems to be "first come, first served." This is a rule that engendering fears of scarcity, naturally leads to disorder. The proposed procedures are rules of order.

The Common Wealth Reason

National credit is our common wealth.

The Historical Reason

Hear Ye, Hear Ye

The Massachusetts Bay Colony was the first public organization to issue paper money in the Western world in 1690. In China, paper money was made by the Tang Dynasty in 740 B.C.

Benjamin Franklin explained the rationale for the issuance of paper money in 1729.

As Zarlenga (2002) especially emphasizes, the American Revolution was waged to assert this right of the Colonies.

Continentals were issued by the American Revolutionary Government and counterfeited by the British Army.

Lincoln and Kennedy are two American Presidents who made use of this right.

The Populist Movement worked strenuously for a reform of our monetary system.

"Depression Money" was formed as local currencies that kept many communities afloat during the Great Depression.

All this history points to the surging of an innate right to national credit in the spirit of every true American.

The Legal Reason

The proposed recommendations spring directly from the intent of the framers of legislation that established the Fed in 1913. In Paragraph 2, Section 13 of the Federal Reserve Act you find the straightforward injunction that the Fed has to satisfy the financial needs of the nation by "discounting" eligible industrial, commercial, and agricultural paper. There is no eligibility for faltering financial paper there.

How, when, and why the Fed lost its way is a rather well-known story that cannot be recounted here. Here it is only important to realize that, in implementing the proposed recommendations, the Fed would respect fully the legislative intent of the United States Congress—and might open the road to monetary reform in many other countries of the world as well.

The Constitutional Reason

That legislative intent, in turn, is in full agreement with the Constitutional mandate of Article 1, Section 8, which maintains that, in the United States, the power "To coin Money, regulate the Value thereof, and of foreign Coin" belongs to the people, not the bankers.

The Reason of Unity

If its natural allies are steadily provided with credit, the job of the Fed is done—and done well. A huge sigh of relief will be heard on Main Street. Our communities will be united.

The Political Reason

Our country, and most of the world, is ideologically split as never before. At bottom, the reason is money. It seems that people on the left of the political spectrum want to take money from some people and give it to others. They make an appeal to compassion. The right answers with undeniable issues of justice and efficiency. Neither position is amenable to compromise. And yet, full agreement can be developed on the monetary ground. Concordian economics advocates that new money, money created by the Fed be allocated—not as a grant—but as a loan to all qualified "natural allies." National credit is like a lake; it needs to be replenished. Once the issues are thoroughly examined, both the right and the left will agree that this is the right and just way to proceed. Most factions will disappear.

The Neutral Reason

Money should be created and allocated by the Fed without political interference; this is well-agreed upon in our society. And it is confirmed in Concordian economics. In the proposed restructure of the procedures of the Fed, the call for a loan is initiated at the local level; it is vetted as any other loan by a committee of bankers well-experienced in dealing with fiduciary issues of money. Neither the Fed nor any other government agency has any right to deny or approve the loan. There is no possibility of "political" influence on the issuance of such loans.

The Economic Freedom Reason

Political democracy is empty without economic democracy. That is why the political class is in such low repute today. If new money created by the Fed is indeed allocated on the basis of economic meritocracy, a huge step will be taken toward establishing economic democracy in this country, and eventually in the world. Democracy means freedom—freedom for all, not only for the few who know how to play the political game. Make no mistake, no monopolies, and no outrageous aggregations of wealth in a few hands would be possible within the sphere of true economic democracy. The ownership of any "natural" monopoly, for instance, will be fully shared among all the participants to their mutual economic success.

The Political Freedom Reason

Do we want political freedom for all? Let us start with the assertion of the right to a fair allocation of the new money created by the Fed. And when that is done, let us have a **thorough review** of the need for governmental regulations of economic affairs. That is the road we have to travel to regain the political freedom we have lost in this country.

7.3 What Can the Central Bank Do

The Sovereignty Reason

Who issues the money is the sovereign.

The Justice Reason

The reason for the existence of so many important and concordant foundations of the proposed recommendations is that their ultimate source is justice. The value of money is created by all the people in a nation—yes, all the people, consumers included. Hence, it is right and just to allocate the new money on the basis of rights rather than privilege. Rights unite; privileges divide.

The Virtue Reason

Only virtuous people can create and keep their money in a virtuous way. In time, the Fed will accommodate the virtues of the right as well as the left of the political spectrum, and thus ease the dangerous political impasse that has lately enveloped our country—and, indeed, the world.

The Practical Reason

Einstein might have pointed out that it is insanity to pursue the same course of action, again and again—and expect a different result. Whether knowingly or even fully unknowingly, the Fed has tried to curb the "animal spirits" of mankind for over a century now. We have had one worse financial crash after another. Is not time now to change approach?

The Concordian Reason

The chief expected benefit of the proposed recommendations is that the next financial crisis would not threaten the stability of the monetary system, a scary event indeed in a monetary economy. At the same time, the Fed would allow the forces of the market to play themselves out, and thus the Fed would work in accordance with the best available economic theory. No need to curb animal spirits any longer. "Animal spirits" should be left free to roam the country and the world. No one should interfere with the use of PRIVATE money. No one can.

Thus, we would move along the road to the creation of a Concordian world in which we do not vainly attempt to curb the animal spirits of mankind. Our purpose is much more modest and achievable: Free capital from the capitalist who is wicked; the wicked are the creators of poverty.

In fact, these recommendations are rooted in Concordian economics, the result of 50 years of research and publication—27 of them assisted by Professor Franco Modigliani, the eminent Nobel laureate in economics at MIT, and for 23 years assisted by Professor M. L. Burstein, one of the sharpest minds in economics. Quite a few papers have been published in economics journals and some in peer-reviewed journal; many papers have been published on economics websites, one of them is in the Top 100 Website for Enlightened Economists. I have also published eight books, one translated into eight foreign languages. I have received a Council of Europe scholarship for my dissertation on "The Political Thought of Louis D. Brandeis." I also received a Fulbright Scholarship.

Needless to say, these recommendations will not be implemented without much discussion and vetting. Your assistance, O Reader, is essential. Many indications also suggest that time is of the essence. Please, do coalesce around a new website created just for Concordian economists:

And Another Thought

Jesus threw the money changers out of the Temple; and they came back; and they came back. They will stay there until, not Jesus, not any external force, but We the People will throw them out. But how? By exercising our rights, our political and economic rights. Let us exercise our right to national credit; let us take money out of politics through **people entering the political process in force**—people, as Dr. Peter Bearse (1976), (1982), (1986), (1987), (1999), (2019) recommends.

Afraid of the wrath of old economists and bankers, perhaps, because these recommendations are not coming from their ranks? Be more afraid of the wrecking they are inflicting upon the economic system. Economists know economic theories; they know nothing of the economic process. They believe the economic process is mainly made of money; they do not recognize that even in the sale of a car there are three elements: the car, the money, and the deed of ownership. Bankers, on the other hand, know how banks operate; but they know not the interactive cultural system in which banks operate.

Do not wait for the approval of old economists and bankers. We might wait in vain and until it is too late.

Old economists and bankers are not openly against a Concordian world either. They cannot be. They would not be able to defend their positions. In fact, quite a few economists and bankers who have entered the Concordian world are all for it.

7.3.3 *Some Expected Effects of Both Operations*

William Jennings Bryan's words are as true today as they were when first uttered more than one hundred years ago: "When we have restored the money of the Constitution, all other necessary reforms will be possible, but until this is done there is no other reform that can be accomplished" (Cross of Gold Speech, 1896). Our two operations, Defuse the Bomb and Mend the Fed, are designed to do just that. They are designed to restore the money to the Constitution, meaning that they are designed to reconnect with the best in the American-Judeo-Christian tradition, and they are designed to transform the present monetary system in such a way as to assure us all a future that is stable, lasting, and just.

The mechanics are as simple as they can possibly be. They are simple, but not simplistic at all. A few of the expected results are given below. In the process we will be untying as many knots in our reasoning as possible.

7.3 What Can the Central Bank Do 141

A much longer list, affecting many more aspects of our social, political, and cultural life, could easily be provided. With the first operation, the Federal Reserve System (the Fed), the organization that performs the task of a Central Bank in the United States—with the help of many organizations—is expected to help gently deflate the financial bubble from inside rather than letting it explode to enormous damage to the real economy; with the second operation the Fed is expected to create money by issuing loans in accordance with these procedural specifications: a. Loans only to create real wealth; b. Loans to benefit all members of society; c. Loans at cost.

Implementing the recommendations of these two operations will cause a deep cultural change: From the worship of power and money, we shall pass to the practice of love and justice. Deep cultural changes are organic; they gradually affect each and every nook and cranny in society; therefore, they are impossible to predict with any precision. But these are some of the most likely effects to occur. We shall focus on financial affairs.

On the Meaning of Money

Of course, we cannot even talk of justice in financial affairs unless we truly understand what money is. Technically, money is not wealth; it is a representation of wealth. But this technical definition barely scratches the surface of what money is for us.

Money is so powerful that, to create a new and better world, some want to do away with it altogether. They confuse the thing itself with some of the nefarious uses that are made of it, chief among them is the use of money to control people. This use is not inherent to money but a consequence of the scarcity of money, namely, inherent to the conditions under which money is created and distributed; and these are the conditions that we aim to change with the proposed changes in the procedures of the Fed.

Money, as my barber next door knew well, is the best labor-saving device. If you have money, you can pay people to do work for you—and people will find you even if you live in the North Pole. That is indeed important: Money is a store of value. It is this word "value" that gives us an opening into the true meaning and use of money.

Remember when we bought "pet rocks?" Some of us did. And what did we exchange in the purchase of pet rocks? As Rudolph Steiner (1922) pointed out, in any exchange we exchange values. We gave our money in exchange for what? Rocks? No, we gave money away, because we loved pet rocks.

Money then is a representation of what we love—and not only that. Money is at the same time its converse. Money is a protection against what we fear most.

And what is that? We each have our personal fears, and money unifies us in that as well. Money allows us to purchase economic security. *Its loss is what we fear most.*

> This is just like untying knots in our reasoning, isn't it?

And here the issue gets tricky and technical. As individual persons, we can never purchase economic security. Economic security comes as a result of what we do for our community—and what our community does for us.

Money then is the most syncretic expression of our most varied relationships with other people.

Individually, we cannot either acquire or give economic security—to ourselves or to others. It is only an organized community that can give economic security to individual persons.

On to money in politics, then.

Expected Effects on Politics

Today, money controls politics. No, that is a wrong impression: Money attempts to control politics.

And we attempt to take money out of politics. That is an impossible dream. Money will get out of politics only when people get into politics.

Hence, a citizenry always gets the government it deserves. If we think we deserve better than the government we have today, we have to get involved in politics. From passive voters, we need to become active Sovereigns.

To get involved in politics is the same as learning how to live in concord. This is our most difficult task. But if we do not get this goal into our range of expectations, we will never achieve it. Today, this seems to be an impossible task. Too many communities are broken; too many are in a state of war. And money, of course, is the source of much political grief. Love of money is the source of all evil. But there is another way to approach the issues.

Money is a common good. Once we truly understand it, money offers us our best last hope to live in harmonious relationship with each other.

The day in which the Fed transforms the privilege of access to national credit reserved for the few to a right available to all citizens, that day many consequences will follow one from each other.

Many Effects.

First of all, that day we will give wings to our entrepreneurship and innovation.

Entrepreneurship and Innovation

Let us free the twin angels of entrepreneurship and innovation and, in a very short time, they will create an amount of new real wealth that will dwarf all the wealth created in the past.

Ecologists, fear not! No waste will more than compensate for increased activity.

On the Prevention of Accumulation of Wealth into a Few Hands

If new money created by the Fed will be spent only for the creation of new real wealth, many of the existing conditions that favor the Pac-Man Economy will be altered. The Pac-Man economy is that social organization in which money is used to purchase existing corporations, mostly to the detriment of present workers and future owners. If public money created by the Fed will not be permitted to be used for this purpose, much stability will automatically be added to the economy. The right to the protection of one's wealth will be enhanced. And liberty will be preserved because such operations can still be carried out with private money, but at greater interest costs.

No More Waste of Technological Innovations

To make our lives easier we produce technological innovations. But of what use are they, if their ownership gets concentrated into the hands of existing owners of capital? The majority of us will have to work at two hard-to-get jobs, just to keep pace with the increasing cost of living. The solution to the problem of concentration of wealth into a few hands does not lie in overturning, violently or otherwise, the legal system of the country, but in using the existing laws to benefit the largest number of people possible.

How? It is at this juncture that the future work of unions comes into play: By gradually and legally transforming workers into owners (nay, capitalists), the stage will be set for a broader distribution of the benefits of innovation among as large a number of people as possible. Indeed, when more people, through a fair distribution of equity, will obtain more income, there will be less need for more jobs. With a less frantic need to create jobs under pressure from nearly all sectors of society, less destruction of scarce resources can be expected—and, indeed, even less damage to the environment.

Also, if the frenzy of the Pac-Man economy is somewhat restrained due to the prohibition to use public money for the purchase of existing physical (and financial) assets, we are going to live a much quieter life.

Fair Distribution of Wealth

And the forthcoming wealth will be fairly distributed if we tie fresh loans to ESOPs and co-operatives. From a fair distribution of wealth and income, another benefit of inestimable value will ensue: We will need less consumer credit.

Less Consumer Credit

If we earn a living out of our capital and our work, there will be less need for consumer credit.

No more work to earn money to repay debts but work to create the amount of wealth necessary for healthy and "rich" living; no more ecological waste; no more exploitation of human resources. As Emerson realized, from consumers we need to become producers.

The current insatiable need for consumer credit can be abated with the widespread use of Consumer Stock Ownership Plans (CSOPs).

Consumer Stock Ownership Plans (CSOPs)

Consumer Stock Ownership Plans (CSOPs) will be the cherry on top of our future social organization. What is never realized in a modern economy is that the poor are an essential component of the economic process. The rich get richer with the increase of production and consumption of the Gross National Product. The rich do not have the numbers to consume the Gross National Product; it is the poor who by their numbers perform this essential function. Should the poor not be compensated for performing this essential function for the rich? Certainly, they should. But how? Certainly not with another demeaning hand-out program. Consumer Stock Ownership Plans are perhaps the best possible tools to be used in the near future. The Harvard University Cooperative Store has done this for years. With the development of computers today, it will be an easy task to administer such plans. Can you imagine the world in which Burger King, Stop and Shop, and Microsoft at the end of the year distribute a fair portion of their profits among the consumers who have been keeping them alive all year long?

All the way through, what is the best function that unions can perform in the future?

The Work of Unions in the Future

What benefit does the worker receive, if the day after the minimum wage is raised by law or by union power, the market raises the price of goods and services? While people on fixed income suffer immeasurably, room is made only for lower-priced regions and countries to enter the market. Unions, to be effective in the future, will have to learn how to tie their dues, no longer to higher wages, but to a fair distribution of the profits—a distribution of equity, a distribution of shares of ownership stock.

And Inflation?

And Inflation? Will not there be inflation with the creation of new money by the Fed? No. There will not be any inflation with ESOPs and co-operatives in action. Wages are distributed ahead of market decisions; profits are distributed after the market has decided in favor of the product or service being provided.

Besides, under this proposal new money will be created only in correspondence with the creation of new real wealth. The balance between the two will be dynamic and continuous; hence, no inflation will be possible.

Finally, there are substantial differences between the present proposal and similar-looking ones such as the "printing money" of Milton Friedman, Ben Bernanke, Adair Turner, and the adherents of Modern Monetary Theory. These are all varieties of arbitrary grants issued by the monetary authority. The present proposal is based on citizens' rights, loans are initiated by citizens, and citizens assume the responsibility to repay the loans. To say the least, this proposal does not carry with it any danger of inflation, because as soon as the loan is repaid, the new money is destroyed. It has been absorbed into the economy.

More Technicalities

Continentals and Greenbacks created in the past as cash were effectively grants that the US Government awarded to itself; interest currently paid on bank reserves are effectively grants awarded to private interests.

Buying and selling bonds from and to the US Treasury and the public, the Fed creates—or destroys—money as debt. Cash on Federal Reserve books is accounted for as debt (borrowed from US Treasury).

Our proposal calls for the creation of money as an asset: The proposal is for the Fed to create a new facility, if need be, a facility preferably to be named National

7.3 What Can the Central Bank Do

Credit Notes (NCNs)—lately, I have suggested that these notes ought to be called Bancors; carrying these notes as assets on its books; these notes are to be exchanged at par with existing Federal Reserve notes, in the form of cash (or digits); and creating **new** notes exclusively as loans to create real wealth, as loans to benefit all inhabitants of the land, and loans issued at cost.

So far, we have concentrated our attention on private personal wealth. By allowing access to national credit to public institutions with taxing power, we will also positively affect our public communal wealth.

Public Money for Public Works

Of what benefit is personal wealth amidst public squalor? Of what benefit is private wealth amidst a crumbling infrastructure of roads, bridges, and schools? Certainly, the door to national credit ought to be open to satisfy these needs as well: **Public money for public works.** Public money for public works should be a refrain to cascade harmoniously from the lips of economists, financiers, bankers, politicians, and administrators of the public treasure.

There is much talk about the need to create State Banks. This is not a place for a critical analysis of that proposal. Here we shall simply confine our attention to the analysis of this proposition: We can **fund** State Banks precisely as we will fund any other project with the approval of the Federal Reserve System.

A specific proposal to fund local public works with public money, on which Stuart Weeks and I have been working for more than thirty years, has been classified as The Concord Resolution, Gorga (2018).

And We Will Add Fiscal Stability to Cities, Towns, States, and the Nation as a Whole

With public money for public works, we will be able to repair our crumbling infrastructure here in the United States of America, still one of the richest countries in the world. We will be able to do this because loans out of our national credit will be issued at cost. Let the private sector get rich in due course, out of executing these public works in the most efficient possible way. Not only will we be able to refurbish our public infrastructure; not only will we be able to create all the jobs that we need, and we want; we will also add fiscal stability to cities, towns, states, and the nation as a whole.

Let the message be lost, opening the channels of national credit to satisfy personal and public needs is the way to gain a stable monetary system; more than that, that is the way to gain monetary stability for the nation as a whole. The difference is sectoral stability vs. overall stability. Systems cannot be cured part by part; their immune **system rejects temporary and partial remedies.** Systems have to be cured systematically as a whole complex entity.

The Deeper Meaning of the Two Operations

The implementation of the proposed operations to straighten out our monetary system has a deeper intent than just fixing our financial "mess." They go to the core of values of inestimable worth.

Personal Dignity

What do we gain through the implementation of a rational plan of systematic reduction of debt coupled with the gradual transformation of privileges into rights? Apart from all economic and financial benefits, we gain a whole set of values of inestimable worth.

Rather than using power to crush human beings under a mountain of debt, we use rational solutions that turn to mutual benefit. When we transform the privilege of access to national credit reserved to the few under the current prevailing monetary system into a right belonging to each and every one of us, we foster the personal dignity of each and every human being.

Personal Economic Security

And personal dignity will be built on economic security for everyone: the poor, the middle classes, and the rich. Even the rich will live in a regimen of steady security, rather than under the threat of the pitchforks. No more threats of redistribution of wealth. No more fear of the Tax Man. Thus, there will be certainty of protection of personal wealth for everyone. No more fear of losing one's wealth overnight; no more fear of a financial collapse that will unravel all commercial relationships at once.

Economic Freedom for Individual Human Beings

Economic security built on the basis of the dignity of each and every human being automatically leads to economic freedom for all.

Justice in the Economic System

In turn, economic freedom for all will ensure that the social and economic system works with a maximum of social and economic justice for all. We have largely been reduced to a catatonic state in which we do not any longer know what is just; and most certainly, we are intimidated from asking that political and economic justice be done to us and to every human being.

Morality to Economics

Thus, shall we restore morality to economics: not by preaching; not by practicing methods of moral extortion; but by allowing people to exercise their God-given rights—their "natural" rights.

Economic Freedom to the Nation

Once we restore morality to economics, we will have automatically assured economic freedom to the nation as a whole. And the chain does not stop there.

Freedom in the Political System

With justice in our social organization, we shall also have freedom in our political system. Money will get out of politics because engaged and knowledgeable people will enter the system in droves. Most of all, we shall abstain from asking our representatives and politicians to play Robin Hood, to steal from the rich to give to the poor. While preserving the right of the rich access to national credit, we will most assuredly allow the poor and the middle classes to exercise this right as well.

Fear of Scarcity is the Mother of All Evil

Fear of scarcity is the mother of all evil. When the Fed creates money, not in relation to gold, not in relation to the hunger of voracious national and international bankers but in relation to the real needs of the country, scarcity will be replaced with sufficiency. And all the potential beneficial uses of money will be unleashed within the nation.

Love and Justice

We do much disservice to ourselves when we forget two essential things: 1. Love is a virtue, a characteristic of our human make-up—just as Justice is a virtue. 2. One cannot be implemented without the other.

Hence, we are going to betray them both when we keep them separated from each other. Indeed, the work has to be extended in the other direction; We must not separate them from all basic virtues such as prudence, justice, temperance, courage, wisdom, science, understanding, hope, faith, and love. Indeed, the practice of all the virtues has to be integrated into one solid unit, for the virtues to become powerful tools of action and thought.

This Is the Minimum: It Takes Love to Give—And to Receive—Economic Justice.

7.4 From Money Controlling People to People Controlling Money

7.4.1 Oh, the Rich

Why did we ever think that the (few) rich know how to administer money?

The Federal Reserve System (the Fed) has pursued roughly the same type of policy for over a century now. To expect different results from the same actions, as Einstein might have warned, is insanity. We have to turn the Fed, our Central Bank, from serving the few, rather badly, to serving everyone well. If we do this, as Bryan (1896) pointed out long ago, "all other necessary reforms will be possible, but until this is done there is no other reform that can be accomplished." The Fed is the pivot.

How can the Fed be transformed into an institution that serves all the people well?

As seen in many communications to EconIntersect, Mother Pelican, and a few more venues on the Internet, this goal can be reached by establishing the following three simple procedures for the creation and distribution of new money issued by the Central Bank: 1. Money has to be issued only for the creation of real wealth, not for the purchase of financial assets; 2. Money has to be issued to people who offer an assurance of repayment of the loan, namely individual entrepreneurs, co-operatives, corporations using an Employee Stock Ownership Plan (ESOP), and public entities with taxing power; and 3. Money has to be issued as a loan at cost, not at arbitrary interest rates.

It is all that simple, but not simplistic at all. Once these three procedures are in place, a shift will be operated in the monetary system of any nation of the world that adopts them: from *money controlling people*, we shall pass to a monetary system in which **people control money.**

What does this mean? Specifically, recognizing that the main prerogative of the Sovereign is to issue money and that in a democracy the citizen is the Sovereign, we shall pass.

> From privileges that divide to rights that unite.
>> From begging for fairness to exercising rights, the right of access to national credit.
>
>> From passive voters to active Sovereigns.
>
>> From automatons, pulling down an electoral lever every so often, to becoming personally and socially integrated citizens.
>
>> From sporadic interest in public affairs to continuous control.
>
>> From electing Representatives "to rob Peter to pay Paul" to instructing them to let us exercise our constitutional rights.
>
>> From vain vengeful attempts at retributive justice to economic justice for all.
>
>> From vain programs of redistribution of wealth to fair distribution of wealth.
>
>> Without taking any right away from anybody,
>
>> but letting everybody meet their own specific economic responsibilities.
>
>> To repeat: Not one cent of wealth that belongs to others needs to be redistributed.
>
>> Nay: A program of amnesty for past wrongdoings needs to be instituted.
>
>> But: A program of severe justice needs to be instituted.
>
>> Deceit and lies will be of great concern to people practicing justice.
>
>> From creating money out of thin air to explicitly using national credit.
>
>> No need to worry about lack of money for capital expenditure any longer.
>
>> You can protect your personal, private money only by investing it in your community, hence, the wisdom of Local Interdependence Funds (LIFs)
>
>> and Mutual Assurance Funds (MAFs).
>
>> From bankers' valuation to value of blood sweat and tears of the people.
>
>> From "End the Fed" to "Mend the Fed."
>
>> From a Fed governed by no rules to a Fed governed by firm rules.
>
>> From credit to financiers to credit to the people.
>
>> From consumer credit to capital credit.
>
>> From money that enslaves to money that liberates people.
>
>> From a Fed directed by vague goals to a Fed directed by one clear goal:
>
>> monetary stability.
>
>> From inflation and deflation to monetary stability.
>
>> From scarcity for the many and abundance for the few to sufficiency for everyone.
>
>> From the whim of bankers to the will of the people.
>
>> From benefiting the few to benefiting everyone.

7.4 From Money Controlling People to People Controlling Money

From financial assets to real assets.
From consumers to producers.
From workers to owners.
From creation of money as debt to creation of money as an asset.
From acceptance of market failures to refusal of taxpayers' burden.
From obfuscation to information and accountability.
From private money for public projects to *public* money for *public* projects.
From misguided "favors" from world-wide financiers
to providing credit.
to national agricultural, industrial, and commercial interests.
From financiers' wealth to common wealth.
From control by politicians and bureaucrats to people's control.
From centralization of power in Washington and New York to decentralization.
From working with financiers to working with business and enterprising people.
From berating "animal spirits" to appreciating
the business and enterprising spirit of mankind.
From vain attempts to shackle private money to liberating private money.
From money as a tool to control people to money as a tool to *build community*.
From mainstream economics to Concordian economics.
From a methodology (the use of supply and demand) in search of a subject
to study of the economic process.
From economic independence to economic interdependence.
From a world of competition to a world of economic interdependence.
From morality and justice as an afterthought to the integration of ethics in economics.
From morality and justice as disposable "values"
to morality and justice as our guide stars.
From an economy composed of money
to an economy composed of things, money, and rights.
From misunderstanding (or not-understanding) to understanding money.
From money as a "veil" covering real wealth to money representing real wealth.
Away from, often, money representing only zeros.
From economic justice to political freedom.
From a pittance of wealth created in the past
to sufficiency of wealth we are going to create in the future,
while fully respecting ecological and esthetic good sense.

7.4.2 Time Is Running Short

As against such a bright long-range future, we have a short-range future that is fraught with horrible possibilities. Let us remain positive. Let us remain focused.

Some plaintive questions:

Can we ever rebuild our infrastructure without Mending the Fed?

Can we ever restore our educational system to its former glory without Mending the Fed?

Can we peacefully enlarge the ownership base of our economy without Mending the Fed?

How are we going to accomplish all this?

The Fed has the legal and administrative power to adopt the three procedures pointed out above. I have entered into conversation with the Fed. Here is where we stand so far: After putting together in one document a group of articles published in Mother Pelican, I sent it to the Fed and the Fed has shown some interest in these proposals.

Clearly, these proposals will not be implemented without much vetting through a national discussion. So, please analyze these two petitions:

A patriotic petition to restructure the Fed.

The Jubilee Solution: A systematic reduction of zeros.

Discuss them. Circulate them.

When implemented, we will finally have rules to which Central Banks will be moored, as Peter Conti-Brown in *The Power and Independence of the Federal Reserve* (2017) implicitly recommends; we will finally obtain *The End of Alchemy* (2016) through which Central Banks create money today, as Lord Mervyn King is explicitly recommending; and money created in accordance with the above proposals will finally be one of the major generators of *Good Profit* (2015), as Charles G. Koch is proving it can be generated even under prevailing unfavorable business conditions. Out of the good profits from innovation and entrepreneurship we will be paying for the "entitlements" which we feel entitled to receive. No more vain calls for and dangerous expectations to receive the wealth of others. Of course, charity will cover the remaining cases of people who cannot or do not want to participate in the economic process. Peace and prosperity shall return to our land.

O Men of little faith. Why should you assume that the Fed will not implement these proposals? Why should you assume that the Fed, and all other Central Banks of the world, will not have a profound interest in serving the public good—when they know how to serve it?

If the Fed should refuse to do so, the Congress has the constitutional power and the duty to instruct the Fed to adopt those rules. And if the Congress should refuse? Well, the traditional recourse is a well-established one: We shall throw the "rascals" out and elect true representatives of the will and the interest of all We the People.

Underneath it all, what becomes painfully evident? An age-old truth becomes manifest: We have met the enemy and it is us. We the People have to agree as to what is that we want. Today we all have our favorite solutions to our problems.

We must stop fighting each other and agree on what comes first. We must do it. We will do it, because God—Nature?—has so created us that we accept a good thing when we see it.

References

Bryan, W. J. (1896). Cross of gold speech. History.Com. Available At https://www.History.Com/Topics/Us-Government-And-Politics/William-Jennings-Bryan. Accessed 20 October 2023.

Conti-Brown, P. (2016). *The power and independence of the federal reserve.* Princeton University Press.

Galbraith, J. K. (2001). *Money: whence it came, where it went.* Houghton Mifflin Harcourt.

Gorga, C. (2015, September). The world of economics since 2008. *Mother Pelican A Journal of Solidarity and Sustainability, 11*(9). Available at http://www.pelicanweb.org/solisustv11n09page4.html. Accessed on 18 October 2023.

Gorga, C. (2016, January). Toward a systematic reduction of debt. *Mother Pelican A Journal of Solidarity and Sustainability, 12*(1). Available at http://www.pelicanweb.org/solisustv12n01page4.html. Accessed 18 October 2023.

Gorga, C. (2018). The concord resolution as key to enter the realm of Concordian monetary policy. Available at http://www.pelicanweb.org/solisustv14n12page21.html. Accessed 4 December 2023.

King, L. M. (2016). *The end of alchemy: money, banking, and the future of the global economy.* Norton.

Koch, C. G. (2015). Good profit: how creating value for others built one of the world's most successful companies. Penguin Random House.

Krugman, P. (2014). What have we learned since 2008? New York Times, February 14. Available at https://archive.nytimes.com/krugman.blogs.nytimes.com/2016/02/14/what-have-we-learned-since-2008/

Piketty, T. (2017). Capital in the twenty-first century. Translated by Arthur Goldhammer. Belknap Press.

Piketty, T. (2014). www.lazy.com/watch?v=j62dLzzAzww

Pilkington, P. (2014, November 9). Authoritative arguments in economics. *Econintersect Blog.*

Zarlenga, S. A. (2002). *The lost science of money: The mythology of money, The Story of Power.* American Monetary Institute. www.monetary.org.

Chapter 8
Project Financial Independence

Abstract Financial Independence for anyone can only be built on the Financial Interdependence of everyone. Let us neglect long-term plans for the system as a whole for a while. Let us concentrate our attention on the most practical thing of all on earth: Cash, Money in our very own pockets. (Even though economists study ONLY the theory of money, they seem to disdain money. On the other hand, many people try to obtain the effects of financial independence through a *philosophical* understanding of Positive Money; their position will eventually be much strengthened through advocacy of a transformation in the operations of those institutions that create and distribute money). If we do that, we reach some fundamental understanding of some egregious problems that beset our contemporary life: Why is there such a thing as the bane of consumerism? (We shall leave the bane of hedonism well enough alone in this book.) Why is there such a thing as political oscillations between the extreme right and the extreme left? Why are communities disaggregating under our very eyes? No, the forces that catapult such issues forward are not psychological or political forces. They are economic forces.

8.1 Introduction

Crisis, what crisis? Well, name almost any issue today, and you are faced with a crisis. Soldo (2023) has well epitomized the current crisis with this expression uttered by many people in many parts of the world: "I do not recognize my own country anymore."

Are we going to transform *any* crisis from a crisis into an opportunity? The opportunity, now and always and everywhere, is to realize a dream that has been with us since the dawn of organized society: the dream to create financial independence for all of us and for our children—without requesting the contribution of even one cent from the affluent; see, Gorga (2021a, 2021b). This is a potential that we can realize on the strength of the new economic paradigm, Concordian economics. Concordian economics is not so pure a science as to disdain the sound of a jingle in our pockets.

Indeed, let us follow its spur and be so gross and crass as to fill your pockets and mine—and our bank accounts—with the weight of Cash, namely Money.

This goal can be reached because Concordian economics, unlike modern economics, is all poised to deliver on such a promise. Concordian economics fills the black box that exists at the core of modern economic theory, a discipline so inveigled in the crater of its own crisis to be able to seriously face any outside issue. Indeed, this discipline has been in a state of crisis ever since the publication of Adam Smith's *The Wealth of Nations (1776)*. As Pilkington (2014) sharply points out, "Mainstream economics moves forward not through logical development and integration, but through forgetting."

Modern economists believe that they stride safely through the economics minefield because they proceed in their work with the help of the "scientific" tools of supply and demand—all with the assistance of mathematical logic.[1] Yet, what is not generally realized is that these are tools of economic analysis; they do not form a theory of economics. That is the reason why economists cannot decide whether the BIG DATA they are analyzing trends toward growth, decline, or stability; see, Volume 1, Chap. 2 of this set on Concordian economics.

Indeed, modern economics, for all its obsession with money, does not even have a definition of money; and cash is nowhere to be seen in high theory. Concordian economics instead offers an integration of theory, policy, and practice and in all three of its central manifestations, we see a predilection to recognize our needs to fill our pockets with cash.

Concordian economic theory is all enclosed in the following diagram.

This Figure encapsulates three processes: the process of creation of real wealth, the process of distribution of ownership rights as soon as real or monetary wealth is created, and the process of consumption, namely the expenditure of financial assets to acquire real wealth. Even in the purchase of a chocolate bar, we find these three elements of the economic process: the exchange of monetary wealth for the purchase of real wealth—as well as the automatic distribution of ownership rights brought forward by the sales slip. Without the sales slip one exits the store at one's own risk and peril.

The theory of distribution of ownership rights over wealth as it is created is concerned with nothing but the fair and square distribution of money in our pockets. Why? Because if money is not in our pockets, we cannot even buy a chocolate bar. And if we cannot buy a chocolate bar, as Fig. 8.1 makes abundantly evident, the economic process is dead in its trucks. No economic process, no economic theory. Is this conclusion to be emphasized at all?

Concordian economic policy is all enclosed in this diagram:

---

[1] Oh Reader, do you remember that math cannot solve problems of economics? Math is paralyzed, unable to decide when faced with two diametrically opposed models, the Original Keynes' Model and the Revised Keynes' Model. Logic helps, And Logic reveals that the Original Keynes' Model does not respect any one of the fundamental principles of Logic.

8.1 Introduction

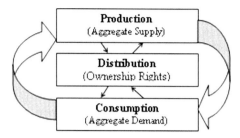

Fig. 8.1 The economic process

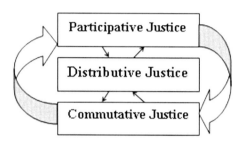

Fig. 8.2 Concordian economic policy

Figure 8.2 below derives from Fig. 8.1: Participative Justice expresses the right to participate in the process of creation of wealth; that is the source, that is the spigot that opens up and directs the flow of money in our pockets; Distributive Justice expresses the right to a fair distribution of the wealth thus created; Commutative Justice expresses the right to obtain an equivalent portion of what one gives. In Concordian economics, it is *impossible* to separate theory from policy just as it is impossible to separate a person from her shadow.

Concordian economic practice is all enclosed in this list of economic rights and responsibilities that one needs to exercise if one wants to practice economic justice. Money and chocolate bars do not grow on trees. They are the result of the blood sweat and tears that flow down our brawn during our daily labors. These labors do not occur in a scatter shot format. They are the result of highly coordinated events: First, one designs the chocolate bar, then one goes collecting the cocoa beans, and so on and so forth. What is hidden in plain view is the function of money throughout the entire economic process. If financial plans are not wisely laid out, if they are not flawlessly executed, the chocolate bar does not reach my breakfast table. Is a chocolate bar essential to life? By itself, certainly not. But do subtract products one by one from our table, and rather than life we observe famine and death.

A tablet: four economic rights and responsibilities

1. The right of access to land and natural resources	1. Pay taxes on land and natural resources that are under our control
2. The right of access to financial resources imbued in national credit	2. Repay loans obtained through access to national credit

(continued)

(continued)

3. The right of access to the fruits of one's labor	3. Perform tasks required in the process of wealth creation
4. The right of access to the fruits of one's property	4. Respect the property of others

These are economic rights and responsibilities that arise from the needs of the four (modern) factors of production. One cannot even bake bread without the exercise of these four economic rights and responsibilities.

8.2 How to Obtain Financial Independence?

In a more extended presentation than is allowed here, it is possible to analyze the process through which, in a well-ordered society, the exercise of all four economic rights and responsibilities leads to economic independence for all of us and for our children. Here we shall concentrate on monetary policy. Cutting to the chase, among the many recommendations of Concordian economics, we shall concentrate on three as most urgent.

Invest Your Money Locally

Defuse The Bomb

Mend The Fed

Clicking on each heading, one will find three Internet petitions that I am highlighting, hoping that better times and perhaps better writers than I am will eventually bring them to the right level of consciousness in the soul of the Reader.

Dear Reader: Study them. Discuss them. Sign them. Circulate them.

The rationale for the *first petition is this*: If you invest your money locally, if you move at least 10% of your financial wealth from Wall Street to Main Street, your money will grow at a slower pace, but it will grow steadily and securely. Once financial independence is achieved, then we can wisely test our fortunes on Wall Street again.

A financial instrument has been designed in cooperation with all local banks to agglomerate all such deposits to form the Local Interdependence Fund, so that the fund becomes a powerful tool of community development. Funds remain in each one of the banks in which you conduct operations today, so the wealth of the Fund will be automatically spread around. Local funds should invest only locally, so to increase the chances of success. Each fund should invest only in enterprises that create real wealth of tables and chairs and foodstuff. Each fund should make loans (not necessarily at cost but certainly) at reasonable rates of interest.

The first time this type of fund was recommended to my local community was just before the dot.com debacle; the second time, just before the Great Recession of

8.2 How to Obtain Financial Independence?

2008. How much richer would my community be today, if the idea had been carried into implementation then?

Any time along the arc of the business cycle is a good time to invest locally. There are actually three types of interdependence funds, Gorga (2023), plus one: Golden Saturday Funds, Gorga (2021a, 2021b). Perhaps, this is not the place to elaborate on the small variations among these funds. Each community should have them. The more, the better. The sooner, the better.

The rationale for the *second petition* has already been discussed a number of times throughout this two-book set. Some essential characteristics are worth repeating. New subtleties, I call them wrinkles, are worth emphasizing. The basic rationale for the second petition is represented by an attempt to adapt to a modern secular society and the economic wisdom of the Mosaic Laws of the Debt Jubilee. If the Debt Jubilee is proclaimed about all debts—not just student debts—and implemented systematically over a seven-year cycle, the periodic collapse of Wall Street values will be avoided—at an inestimable advantage for everyone. Rather than letting the financial bubble *explode on its own terms*, let us gradually deflate the bubble from the inside so to reduce the damage of an eventual explosion to minimal terms.

Two economic realities stand behind the validity of this recommendation: First, much of the growth in the financial economy is not related to real economic growth. Thus, a debt jubilee does not affect real wealth at all. A debt jubilee, under these conditions, amounts to a mere reduction of zeros. The second consideration is possibly more important. Since wealth is a social construct, a *systematic* reduction of zeros leaves all economic operators in the same relative position as they were at the beginning of the jubilee. People are just as rich in relation to each other as they were before the proclamation of the debt jubilee.

Needless to say, one of the immediate benefits of a debt jubilee is to leave financial resources in the hands of debtors, people who are more liable to spend their money than to hoard it. The need for the circulation of money during these days of extreme financial needs for so many people is widely acknowledged and very hard to satisfy.

The rationale for the *third petition* can be found in this key proclamation: Do not destroy the Fed; Mend the Fed. It is indeed possible and necessary to Mend the Fed by changing the rules it uses to create and distribute money. Specifically, it is recommended that the Fed create money by making loans:

1. Only to create a real wealth of tables, chairs, and foodstuff;
2. To entrepreneurs and corporations with ESOPs and to public agencies with taxing powers; and
3. At cost of administration—not at interest. (The Fed is a public—quasi-public?—agency; it should not be allowed to make a profit).

Mirabile dictu, in 2015 I presented the last two proposals to the Fed, and the Fed graciously responded: "Given your proposal (for creating a new monetary system), I suggest that you contact your state and federal representatives."

The Fed has traditionally fought "political interference" into its operations with the classic tooth and nail approach.

Alone, I have been able to do extraordinarily little to pursue this recommendation. I have not had either time or energy or money to contact my state and federal representatives systematically. Now, dear Readers, *all together*, or nearly all together, we might be offered an opportune time to concentrate our attention on this task.

When these Three Rules are implemented, we will finally have practices to which Central Banks will be moored. Conti-Brown (2016), King (2016), and Koch (2015), to mention only a few prominent advocates for an improved Fed, have been calling for similar conditions. Profits from innovation and entrepreneurship will take care of the needs of all participants in the economic process. And a little bit will be left over to cover the cases of people who cannot or do not want to participate in the economic process. No more vain calls for and dangerous expectations to receive the wealth of others. Peace and prosperity shall return to our land.

These considerations are not at all silent rejections of such avuncular recommendations as "a penny saved is a penny earned" or "penny wise and pound foolish" or "waste not, want not." There are age-old truths in them that are part and parcel of the (necessary) virtuous society. What cannot be found in the "old" wisdom is the recommendation to grow any such novelties, for instance, as cash-back programs. All these approaches converge toward one goal: financial independence.

8.3 A Bit of Politics

There are two distinct political advantages to the implementation of a program of action of this sort. Once it is fully explained to the constituency, it ought to garner solid, beyond partisan political support. More important than this initial advantage are the long-term benefits. Since it does not favor any one segment of the population to the detriment—perceived or actual detriment—of another, this program of action will not give immediate rise to any faction sworn to the eventual demolition of the program, and perhaps even society as a whole.

The seeds of our current, dangerous political dysfunction were sown into the very constitution of the programs pursued during the last two or three hundred years. If workers were favored, "capitalists" were ready to rise in opposition; if one class was favored, all other classes were ready to rise in opposition; if one "race' was favored, all other races were ready to rise in opposition. It might have taken a long time, but the party that was disadvantaged would certainly rise in opposition. And so, the pendulum swung: from extreme left to extreme right—and vice versa.

This cycle of dysfunction, even the cycle of love/hate can be broken only if a program is pursued that aims to create economic justice for all; only if we appropriately change our institutions; only if the common good is the guiding star of political action.

An indirect benefit of financial independence will be this. Do you think that those who sell arms to a civilian population or poach wild beasts are happy people? Well, with financial independence, they can stop being unhappy.

Not to put too fine a point on it, should I recite the litany of nefarious actions that engulf our lives today—only to put a jingle in our pocket?

I will not, but I cannot refrain from adding: Do you think that there is any other way to reach an "integral ecology"?

8.4 Time is Running Out

Nerves are frayed. And cases of explosion of inner rage are all around us—both at the national and the international level. The sooner we set things aright, the better it is.

As against a bright long-range future, we have a short-range future that is fraught with horrible possibilities. Let us remain positive. Let us remain focused.

Other plaintive questions:

Can we ever become financially independent if we overburden ourselves with loans, consumer loans more than capital loans, that bear a compound interest charge?

Can we ever hope to become financially independent when we subconsciously opt for a serial collapse of our financial structure?

Can we ever hope to become financially independent when we refuse to consider the rational alternative of a debt jubilee every seven years?

Can we ever hope to become financially independent when we refuse to consider the rational alternative of–at least–an abrupt total transformation of loans burdened with compound interest to loans that carry simple interest?

Can we ever hope to become financially independent when we refuse to consider the rational alternative of a massive adoption of substantial cash-back programs in our retail commerce?

Can we ever build personal financial independence without Mending the Fed?

Can we ever rebuild our infrastructure without Mending the Fed?

Can we ever restore our educational system to its former glory without Mending the Fed?

Can we peacefully enlarge the ownership base of our economy without Mending the Fed?

How are we going to accomplish all this?

The Fed has the legal and administrative power to adopt the Three Rules pointed out above. I have entered into a conversation with the Fed. Here is where we stand so far: After putting together in one document a group of articles published in Mother Pelican, I sent it to the Fed and the Fed has shown some interest in these proposals.

Clearly, these proposals will not be implemented without much vetting through a national discussion. So, let us repeat them; please analyze these two petitions; nay, let us add the third familiar petition:

>Invest your money locally.
>The Jubilee solution: a systematic reduction of zeros.
>A patriotic petition to restructure the fed.

Study them. Discuss them. Sign them. Circulate them.

O Men of little faith. Why should you assume that we will not implement these proposals; why should you believe that the Fed will not implement these proposals? Why should you assume that the Fed, and all other Central Banks of the world, will not have a profound interest in serving the public good—when they know how to serve it?

To repeat, if the Fed should refuse to do so, the Congress has the constitutional power and the duty to instruct the Fed to adopt those rules. And if the Congress should refuse? Well, the traditional recourse is a well-established one: We shall throw the "rascals" out and elect true representatives of the will and the interest of all We the People.

Underneath it all, what becomes painfully evident? An age-old truth becomes manifest: We have met the enemy and it is us. We the People have to agree as to what is that we want. Today we all have our favorite solutions to our problems.

We must stop fighting each other and agree on what comes first. We must do it. We will do it, because God—Nature?—has so created us that we accept a good thing when we see it.

8.5 Three Fundamental Reasons for the Urgency of Financial Independence

There is a hidden rationale to the first petition. The most important reason for the first petition has remained hidden to me up to this writing. There is a fundamental reason why we have no longer respect for or understanding of our fellow next door. The reason is this: We invest in far away lands. For all that we know, the fellow next door might be working against our interests. All this insecurity, all this suspicion vanishes if we invest in the same community, if we invest for our common good.

If our communities are disaggregating under very eyes it is largely because we do not invest our intellectual and financial resources any longer in our local community.

Hence the overarching need for Local Interdependence Funds.

Equally hidden to me so far has been a fundamental reason for financial independence. This reason is counterintuitive, that is why, perhaps, it has taken so long to come to the fore. With widespread financial independence, we will defeat the destructive forces of consumerism. Borrowing for consumer expenditures is directly correlated with lack of financial independence. To fill the hole in our psyche created by lack of financial independence, we buy and buy more and more consumer goods even when we do not need them. Consumerism has been identified as one of the banes of contemporary existence. But what are the tools to fight against the baneful effects of consumerism, except empty rhetoric? To wage an effective battle against the many nefarious effects of consumerism, we need a change in our institutions. We need to build solid financial independence for the whole nation.

Here is another major reason for financial independence. The MAGA phenomenon in the United States is a phenomenon that has secular roots in most *countries of the world. During the last several centuries we have seen violent oscillations from the* political left to the political right and vice versa. What was the cause of such gyrations? Political passion? Or the promise from the powers in charge at the moment to put more jingles in our pockets?

Financial independence is that important.

Financial independence will reduce the swings from extreme left to extreme right of the political system—and vice versa. Financial independence will reduce the internal urges to buy and buy more and more consumer goods. Financial independence, derived from local investments, will be a major aggregative force that will annul the powerful disaggregative forces that overcome communities today.

8.6 One More Effect

Anya Leonard (2023), the Founder and Director of Classical Wisdom, has recently asked a poignant question: "Can We Be Humane In the Face of Horror? What is needed to stop violent cycles?" At the cost of being tagged again as an incorrigible optimist or perhaps sounding a one-note cymbal, I must suggest that an answer to Anya's deep question is the same that I have given in relation to many other issues: If we want to cut a chain of hatred and violence, we need to change our institutions. More specifically yet, we must obtain financial independence for an entire nation.

8.7 Conclusion

Our current series of crises offers us the opportunity to explore new ways of organizing our communities. Is this the time to aim for the creation of financial independence for everyone—without requesting even one penny from the affluent? Is not personal financial independence a goal we have been aspiring to achieve ever since the dawn of civilization? If we do make good use of the current crises, each crisis becomes a blessing rather than a curse. Financial Independence also yields financial security.

References

Bhutta, N., Goldin, J., & Homonoff, T. (2016). Consumer borrowing after payday loan bans. *Journal of Law and Economics, 59*, 225–259.

Brady, M. E. (2013). John Maynard Keynes's upper and lower valued probabilities: A study of how statisticians, philosophers, logicians, historians, and economists failed to comprehend Keynes's breakthrough application of G. Boole's interval approach to probability in the 20th century. *International Journal of Applied Economics and Econometrics, 21*, 254–272.

Coase, R. H. (1937). The nature of the firm. *Economica, 4*, 386–405.

Coase, R. H. (1960). The problem of social cost. *Journal of Law and Economics, 3*, 1–44.

Conti-Brown, P. (2016). *The power and independence of the Federal Reserve.* Princeton University Press.

Durr, J. (2016). Personal communication, September 14. In *Public affairs office, board of governors of the federal reserve system.* Available at file:///C:/Users/cgorg/OneDrive/Attachments/ECONOMICS/Documents/2nd%20Jean%20Durr,%20FRS.pdf

Ferrini, V. (2002). Gorga worthy of note. *Gloucester Daily Times*, December 11, p. A6.

Gladwell, M. (2002). *The tipping point.* Back Bay Books.

Gewirth, A. (1985). Economic justice: Concepts and criteria. In K. Kipnis & D. T. Meyers (Eds.), *Economic justice: Private rights and public responsibilities.* Rowman & Littlefield.

Gorga, C. (1994). Four economic rights: Social renewal through economic justice for all. *Social Justice Rev., 85*(1–2), 3–6.

Gorga, C. (1999). Toward the definition of economic rights. *Journal of Markets & Morality, 2*, 88–101.

Gorga, C. (2002, 2009). *The economic process: An instantaneous Non-Newtonian picture.* University Press of America. Third edition by The Somist Institute (2016b).

Gorga, C. (2010). Roots of property law: From the moral contract, and the doctrine of economic justice, to the social contract. Is the legal contract next? World Institute for Research and Publication (WIRP), June 4. Available at SSRN: https://doi.org/10.2139/ssrn.1600595

Gorga, C. (2011). Some shortcomings of the social contract. Available at SSRN: https://doi.org/10.2139/ssrn.3143002

Gorga, C. (2015). Two proposals in the form of two petitions designed to stabilize the monetary system. The Somist Institute, December 3. Available at two proposals.pdf.

Gorga, C. (2016a). Wake up America. Wake up from your 250-year-old slumber. *Mother Pelican, A Journal of Solidarity and Sustainability, 12*(6).

Gorga, C. (2016b). Two proposals to stabilize the monetary system. *Econintersect,* August 21.

Gorga, C. (2017a). A cascade of errors (1517–2017). *OpEd News,* October 31.

Gorga, C. Concordian economics: An overall view. *Econintersect,* January 2.

Gorga, C. (2017c). Money, banking, and the economic process. *Econintersect,* July 12.

Gorga, C. (2018). *The redemption of the bully: Through love toward the beloved community.* Scholars' Press.

Gorga, C. (2019). The free rider problem. *Mother Pelican, A Journal of Solidarity and Sustainability, 15*(2).

Gorga, C. (2021a). Toward economic, ecological, and human interdependence. *Mother Pelican, A Journal of Solidarity and Sustainability, 17*(6).

Gorga, C. (2021). Project financial independence. *Talkmarkets*, February 18. Available at https://talkmarkets.com/content/project-financial-independence?post=298689. Accessed on October 21, 2023.

Heller, M., & Salzman, J. (2021). *Mine! how the hidden rules of ownership control our lives.* Doubleday.

King, L. M. K. (2016). *The end of Alchemy: Money, banking, and the future of the global economy.* Norton.

Koch, C. G. (2015). *Good profit: How creating value for others built one of the world's most successful companies.* Penguin Random House.

Leonard, A. (2023). Can we be humane in the face of horror? What is needed to stop violent cycles? Classical Wisdom. Available at https://classicalwisdom.substack.com/can-we-be-humane-in-the-face-of-horror?utm_source=substack&utm_medium=email. Accessed on October 23, 2023.

Locke, J. (1689 [1965]). In P. Laslett (Ed.), *Two treatises of government.* Awnsham and John Churchill, A Mentor Book, Bk. II, Ch. V, paras 25–27.

References

Neill, R. (2011). *Slavery in the writings of Thomas Aquinas.* Yumpu.com. Available at: https://www.yumpu.com/en/document/read/12426173/slavery-in-the-writings-of-thomas-aquinas

Nozick, R. (1974). *Anarchy, state, and Utopia.* Basic Books.

Pazzanese, C. (2021). Amartya Sen's nine-decade journey from colonial India to Nobel Prize and beyond. *The Harvard Gazette*, June 3.

Piketty, T. (2014). *Capital in the twenty-first century.* Harvard University Press.

Pilkington, P. (2014). Authoritative Arguments in Economics. *Econintersect Blog, 9* November.

Rawls, J. (1971). *A theory of justice* (pp. 12, 72, 136, 538). Harvard University Press.

Ryan, J. A. (1906). *A living wage: Its ethical and economic aspects.* Macmillan.

Ryan, J. A. (1916). *Distributive justice: The right and wrong of our present distribution of wealth.* Macmillan.

Sen, A. K. (1998). The possibility of social choice. In T. Persson (Ed.), *From Nobel Lectures, Economics 1996–2000.* World Scientific Publishing Co.

Soldo, N. (2023). "Niccolo's L'Avventura." Niccolo Soldo from Fisted by Foucault, October 23. Available at https://mail.google.com/mail/u/0/#inbox/FMfcgzGwHLmHjbdXgRQjLdXVFcTQBxWM. Accessed 24 October 2023.

Tierney, B. (1959). *Medieval poor law: A sketch of canonical theory and its application in England.* University of California Press.

Wood, D. (2002). *Medieval economic thought.* Cambridge University Press.

Part III
Physical Interdependence

Chapter 9
Toward Economic, Ecological, and Human Interdependence

Abstract Deep problems of ecological insanity are menacing our very existence. To ignore them is more than shortsighted, it is suicidal, hence this chapter. In it we shall emphasize some positive effects that Concordian economics—with economic justice at its core—can have on our ecology. Properly applied, economic justice reveals hidden ecological treasures. Let us give a quick look at them. In Sect. 9.1 we will observe some of the positive ecological effects that will automatically flow from the eventual implementation of Concordian economic policies. In Sect. 9.2 we will reverse our perspective. We will start from some issues that exist in the real world of land, air, and water, and we will see how the resolution of those issues can have a positive outcome if the world calls upon the help that only Concordian economics can offer.

9.1 Some Ecological Effects of Concordian Economics

9.1.1 Introduction

A lovely expression has been around for quite a few years: Econ-Ecol. When I heard it, I became full of hope that such a marriage was indeed going to be consecrated any time soon. In 2008, I even published in a peer-reviewed journal, a journal for and by physicists, a paper titled "Economics for Physicists and Ecologists." I reprinted the paper in Mother Pelican in 2018. The initial enthusiastic reaction from one economist made me think that we would soon get there. Instead, I had to assume that, since this economist did not find in the paper a continuation of the linear math practiced by modern economists, he lost interest. And other economists, evidently, never have even looked into this paper. The geometry of Concordian economics is mostly fractal and the math is the math of non-linear, chaos theory.

I might be wrong, of course, but until the seed planted in that paper comes to full bloom the Econ-Ecol marriage has to be still in waiting. What I can do, and I have been doing in the meantime, is to give some specifics about the points at which there is a clear intersection between Economics and Ecology; see, e.g., Gorga (2021a). Some of these intersection points follow.

There is a deep reason why these intersections have to be brought to life now more urgently than ever. The necessary current Coronavirus relief program of over $1.0 trillion does nothing to resolve long-term problems of inequality, poverty, economic growth, and ecological despoliation.

It is only Concordian economics that will eventually take care of these pesky long-term problems. Besides, should we not worry that the replenishment of the current rescue program will not have smooth sailing in the Congress of the United States next time around? Where America leads, most of the world follows.

As there are four (modern) factors of production, so in Concordian economics there are four rights of access to the factors of production and four corresponding responsibilities, whose exercise actually gives birth to the rights. Passing from the abstract realm of jurisprudence to that of political science and politics, through an extension of Concordian economics one passes on to building four economic policies out of these four economic rights and responsibilities. Ecological implications of Concordian economics are better observed in the context of these four economic policies: Concordian monetary policy, fiscal policy, labor policy, and industrial policy.

9.1.2 On Ecological Effects of Concordian Monetary Policy

Create money only to create real wealth while enlarging the ownership base of the nation and reducing the costs of capital formation.

The primary goal of Concordian monetary policy is the achievement of financial independence for each and every human being. There are many reasons for the call to the achievement of this goal. Not the least are the reasons for the creation of a sane ecology.

Let us start with the financial causes of ecological degradation. There are many; in my humble opinion, the fundamental one is our level of indebtedness, as a consequence of which we create jobs, not to satisfy any real need, but because we need to repay our debts.

To alter this condition, we need to reform the monetary system. There are many things that are wrong with our monetary system. Rather than engaging in the exercise of listing any of them, I prefer to outline the solution to the key wrongs—while emphasizing ecological benefits in the process.

For a large number of reasons, the key solution involves fundamental changes in the operations of the Federal Reserve System (the Fed), our Central Bank. These changes start with the creation of money as an asset to the nation, not itself a debt by borrowing from existing wealth owners. Then, by creating money to create real wealth, while the creation of *financial* wealth through public money is starved. Enlarging the ownership base of our wealth through an equitable distribution of income we might foster a reduction of indebtedness. Finally, to keep the list short, by creating money at cost, the piling of interest and compound interest at that is prevented.

Reduce indebtedness, and you reduce the churning of waters to repay debts.

To repeat, three policy recommendations offer a synthetic presentation of Concordian monetary policy, a policy of creation and distribution of money by and for *We the People* rather than *They the Bankers*:

> INVEST YOUR MONEY LOCALLY.
> DEFUSE THE TIME BOMB.
> MEND THE FEDERAL RESERVE.

The content of these petitions is rather simple: A: Invest at least 10% of your money on Main Street rather than Wall Street. B: Make full use of the economic wisdom of the Mosaic Laws of the Jubilee, namely apply as soon as possible a systematic Debt Jubilee on a seven-year cycle. C: *Mend the Fed*, do not *Destroy the Fed*.

Implicit in this outline is the fundamental distinction between capital credit and consumer credit. Capital credit frees us; consumer credit enslaves us. With capital credit, we repay the loan through the productivity of the loan. With consumer credit, we pledge to the lender the fruit of our own future productivity, an activity that is not assured at all. What happens if we remain unemployed for a long time?

9.1.2.1 Two Key Ecological Consequences

To enjoy financial independence means not to be in debt to anybody. Two extraordinary ecological consequences will result from a regimen of widespread financial independence. First, do we ever stop to consider how many trees are felled, not to create tables and chairs, but to generate income to repay debt? Second, in the process of generation of monetary income, there is a subtle form of waste that cannot be overemphasized. These consequences occur under our very eyes, but we hardly ever take them into account. Under the pressures of a consumerist society, how many items we buy that we do not use and that go to waste? In the meantime, trees are felled.

9.1.3 On Ecological Effects of Fiscal Policy: Present and Future

If We the People are offended by the obscene display of power in too many Tax Plans that transfer wealth from 99% to 1%, there is no reason to despair. We need to change the Tax Code. But before engaging in such a venture, it behooves us to know the characteristics of the current Code as well as what we want in the Tax Code of the future—no matter how distant that future might be.

9.1.3.1 Some Characteristics of the Current Code

Fiscal policy is mostly involved in a dangerous zero-sum game of Robbing Peter to Pay Paul (RPPP).

Will Rogers identified one characteristic of the current fiscal policy, the fiscal policy under which we in the United States have been living and suffering for more than a century. Will Rogers said: "*The income tax has made liars out of more Americans than golf*."

He was right; nearly all of us try to hide as much wealth as we safely can from the Tax Man. And this is not the worst characteristic of the system. The worst is the economic consequence of this action. Once we hide some wealth from the Tax Man, we are induced to hide it from other people as well. Technically speaking, we are induced to hoard our wealth. Some of the consequences of hoarding are self-evident. If we hoard our wealth, we cannot invest it. Thus, no new wealth is created; no new jobs are created. We are somehow even doomed not to enjoy that wealth; and not to give it to others who might sorely need it.

Quite apart from these consequences, what legal right does the Tax Man have to our wealth? None. Except the power that the Tax Man arrogates to himself through the exercise of sheer political power[1]; no right except a kind of gentlemen's agreement that I have to compensate my government for the benefits I am receiving through its many services—many of which I might violently disagree with, such as adding fluoride to my municipal drinking water, for instance? The conversation might become too granular to be useful. Better to remain on the broad general issue.

What moral power does the Tax Man have to the wealth that I have produced? None. Thus, We the People tolerate an immoral economic system. Any wonder some rich people retaliate and try to hide as much of "their" wealth as possible? No wonder the social, economic, and political world today is tossed into such upheavals that no one is certain of anything any longer.

We must change The System. But how?

The question to investigate is, "How does wealth inequality arise?" The Tax Code tends to make a bad situation worse; through the exercise of political power, it increases the inequality. But it does not create inequality.

Inequality is created elsewhere. Inequality is created within the economic system. Inequality is created by the lack of recognized and enforced economic rights and responsibilities that prevail in the economic system.

9.1.3.2 Four Horses of Inequality

When people do not pay the full share of the taxes they owe, especially taxes on land and natural resources, they steal from fellow citizens who are burdened with the

---

[1] When we come to analyze corporate taxes, we realize that the Tax Man exercises the power to tax that wealth twice: First, when it is within the ledgers of the corporation, and then when it reaches the hands of the stockholder.

total share of the costs of running a country. When the central bank sells a pool of common wealth—i.e., national credit—to preferred customers, the central bank sells for a mess of pottage a national treasure that belongs to the entire population. Private appropriation of common goods—such as land and money—without compensation is expropriation and plunder. When stockholders cash in the value of their stocks and bonds, they rob the workers who have originally contributed to the creation of that value, namely its capital appreciation—and are excluded from that bounty by the faulty legal institute of the "wage contract." When one purchases a whole corporation, and uses other people's money to concentrate the wealth of the nation into fewer and fewer hands, one robs at least the workers, if not also the previous as well as future potential stockholders, of the ensuing capital appreciation of the corporation. Robbing people of their wealth makes them destitute and renders many actually homeless. How much ecological degradation occurs in our cities because of forced homelessness?

Speaking of the ecological disaster represented by the downtown of so many cities and towns, how to recount the full story? A couple of points will be singled out here. Cars are certainly like so many projectiles aimed at the physical structure of the downtown. But then there has been the misbegotten accounting carried out by enthusiastic accountants and economists that, by accusing the mom and pop merchant of overcharging, have instigated the abandonment of downtown locations in favor of far away places where parking and misuse of the land by parking is abundant. By destroying the independence of mom and pop merchants, many locations were deprived of the income that went to far away stockholders. Inequality grew.

Indeed, when inequality reaches a certain intolerable level, many people, many groups of people rise in insurrection and even open warfare. Do we ever calculate the ecological cost of insurrections and wars?

Set these four economic mechanisms of wealth accumulation aright, and inequality is cut at its root. You Give to Caesar What Is Caesar's. Do not steal is a commandment. You do justice and receive justice. With a just distribution of wealth, there is no need for its redistribution. Moreover, the purpose of reducing inequality is not to achieve equality. Equality is a faulty, impossible, and unnecessary ideal. Control these four horses of inequality and you automatically make room for the development of a just and free economy, Ultimately, you build a healthy and vibrant ecological society.

9.1.3.3 The Healthy Fiscal Policy of the Future

The fiscal policy of the future will not have double taxation of corporate wealth; the fiscal policy of the future will not have income taxes. In a modern application of Henry George's prescription (and Ricardo's, Stuart Mill's, and 8 Nobel Laureates in economics), taxes on values of land and natural resources will suffice to keep the structure of the state in good health. The proviso is that the functions of the state will shrink to those that truly belong to the state; namely, safety, national security, and promulgation and administration of justice.

There is one positive aspect of the welfare state that ought to be noticed and, *mutatis mutandis*, might need to be kept alive. This is the field of social insurance. It might make sense to have one public or private national insurance corporation dealing with the health care system; one insurance corporation for social security; and one corporation for old age pensions. But there is no need for these corporations to be organized and administered by the stare, a detailed supervision of economic justice might suffice to preserve the integrity of the private system.

9.1.3.4 The Transition

It is hard to foresee the future, and whatever plans for the future are to be made should be flexible. It is possible to imagine that the transition will be very gradual and self-organized. As one enters fully the free economy, one has all the incentives to voluntarily leave the welfare state. As one increases, the other decreases.

Who will not prefer to live in the dignity of self-sufficiency?

Surely it will be possible to find double-dippers. But they will not last long–and for sure they will not have large effects. They might even be expunged from the system.

The current fiscal system is at a breaking point. It remains alive for two reasons. One is inertia; the other is lack of alternatives. As soon as the alternative becomes available, the welfare state will dissolve. These are some of the results of Concordian fiscal policies.

9.1.3.5 Additional Ecological Results of Georgist/Concordian Fiscal Policy

Pay Taxes on Land Values.

The long-term roots of Concordian fiscal policy can be found in the persistent thought of Henry George and the brigade of faithful Georgists. Henry George was neither the first nor the last to extol the merits of land tax value as the basis of a national fiscal policy. Eight Nobel laureates in economics eventually joined the choir, but there is no visible stirring in creating a national movement to implement such basic policy as a tax on land values. Indeed, **eventually**, a tax on such values *only*: thus, no income taxes; no corporate taxes, or at least a corresponding reduction in income taxes and corporate taxes. Clearly, this policy will have to be coordinated with all other economic policies; basically, the welfare state, the overwhelming bureaucratic state will have to shrink considerably, organically and internally—an outcome that can only be the result of a capillary application of economic justice.

Perhaps, the coming of the implementation of a Georgist/Concordian fiscal policy can be shortened by a day or two if we link this form of taxation to an older national policy: our understanding of the tragedy of the commons. Ecologists are supposed to care for the land. Deep ecology will never come to light if ecologists do not go to the bottom of this cultural tragedy. *There never was a tragedy of the commons; there has only been a steady tragedy of the enclosures.* The commons have been in existence

9.1 Some Ecological Effects of Concordian Economics

for millions of years; they have always been a safety valve for the poor, people who need so little as to take only what they need out of the land—or the oceans.

Once kings started selling ownership rights to the commons, rights that they did not have, rich land owners literally *enclosed* the land; then, to recoup their purchasing costs, they overexploited the land and the enclosures collapsed. By the same token, large estates could not be tended by the few landowners and their fertility was wasted.

Is this not an incidental way to touch upon the problem/opportunity of the commons? Land and money are commons. Do not privatize them; as Elinor Ostrom taught us, let the appropriate community develop rules and regulations to control access to the commons.

Henry George was right. Too many things hang on land value taxation. We set the issue aside at our great risk and peril; risk and peril of not understanding the issues; risk and peril of perpetuating the damage that a poor treatment of land value taxation automatically carries with it.

One way to reestablish the holy alliance between people and the land is to tax land values, so large homesteads—large tracts of land hoarded—can no longer be afforded. The organic breakup of the large estates will again allow the poor, the majority of the population to care for as much of the land as they can afford to till.

Large tracts of land owned by the few exist not only in the downtowns of many cities, but especially in that band of the land encircling the cities. These are lands that strangle the cities from within and without. Much poverty arises from the fiscal stranglehold on those lands. An inordinate amount of waste is taking place on those lands. Will ecologists ever become alerted to these close relationships between economics and ecology?

Just one observation: Is not poor land tax value the fundamental cause why we witness long commuting lines between work and lodging? Is the "commuting" not an inordinate waste of carbon fuels? Is not the injection of such fuels into the atmosphere a primary cause of the climate crisis? So ecologists tell us.

When will city planning, brilliant city planning, and humane city planning be carried out in full accordance with the dictates of economics and ecology?

Conversely, does anyone have serious proposals on how to avert the disastrous consequences of climate change; on how to reduce emissions of carbon dioxide and other greenhouse gases? Have environmentalists ever seriously tied their expectations to create well-planned urbanism?

9.1.4 *On Ecological Effects of Kelsonian/Concordian Labor Policy*

Rather than higher wages, aim for equity distribution of ownership rights over wealth created by workers.

The roots of Concordian labor policy can be found in the genial thought of Luis O. Kelso. To really understand Kelso's thought, one has to consider all the implications of his long-term pivotal essay titled Karl Marx: The Almost Capitalist. In it, Kelso points out that much of the malady of today's world could have been avoided, and can still be avoided, if our aim is not to pit one social class against the other, but if we foster policies that legally, gradually, orderly transform workers into owners of whatever they produce. A large group of consequences will ensue: **inequality will be abated; poverty will be curtailed; financial resources will not be wasted** in pursuit of ever larger financial gains. Corporations will then rather pay undisturbed attention to what they are doing.

If people were spending their own money, rather than a capitalist's money, would not financial resources be used sparingly? Would not natural resources be used to take care of real needs?

From the ecology point of view, one of the major expected benefits of transforming workers into owners of their corporations is this: Only insiders know the deep effects of corporate operations. Would widespread ownership and control of our large corporations by "We the People" prevent the performance of operations that pollute our atmosphere, our rivers, our aquifers, and our oceans? And the list of positive effects and reduction of negative effects—to say nothing of curbing corruption of our political system—can be much extended. Ecologists do consider this a revolutionary possibility.

9.1.5 On Ecological Effects of Concordian Industrial Policy

Internal growth of the corporations: unlimited; external growth by purchase: prohibited.

The long-term roots of Concordian industrial policy can be found in the progressive thought of Luis D. Brandeis. Brandeis was one of the leaders of the Progressive Movement. His major concern was the behavior of exploitation of the large corporations to the detriment of everything in sight: land, people, cities, and cultures. During the last four to five hundred years, the literati have been involved in dreaming of windmills; engineers have devoted their lives to constructing the windmills; and the oligopolists have been single-handedly devoted to taking control of the windmills. Most economists, often dumbfounded, have left events go by.

Brandeis and the Progressives devoted much of their attention to anti-trust policies, policies to interrupt this deep cultural blindness. Rules and regulations they devised were trying to keep the irrepressible power of industrialism under control; the attention of leaders of the Progressive Movement was mostly concentrated on how to keep the industrial trusts under control and, when their power became overwhelming, how to break them up.

Concordian economics has focused its attention on the future rather than the present or the past. Hence, the Brandeis Rule: Let corporations grow internally as large as the market allows them to grow; but, definitely prevent the growth of these corporations through outside purchase. Let us start with the largest 100 corporations and prohibit them in no uncertain terms from purchasing or being purchased by other entities for a year or two; analyze the results; and gradually extend this policy to cover the next and the next 100 largest corporations. Would not our great captains of industry give an eye tooth if they could concentrate their attention only on the internal affairs of the corporation rather than keeping one eye to see what happens over their shoulders and another eye on what happens sideways?

How much waste of natural resources takes place in the doing and undoing of the trusts? Will ecologists ever care?

These are not simply technical issues; they are deep cultural issues. One small piece of evidence can be quickly adduced here. The trusts grew at roughly the same time as our modern megalopolises grew; they both grew by the same method, not by internal growth but by external aggrandizement.

9.1.5.1 Some Fruitful Considerations

I tend to be rather against expressions like "climate justice" and "ecological justice." Our atmosphere, our mountains, our plains, our cities, our aquifers, our rivers, and our oceans do not need justice. Their "feelings," their "rights" are stronger than that. They require systemic, sane, and sound utilization. Sanity, not justice, is the touchstone. Ecological insanity comes back to bite us. Exploitative extraction of our natural resources and pollution of our environment are wounds that engulf us.

The apex of malfeasance is the presence of the tax depletion allowance.

It is an integration of sane and sound economic policies with sane and sound ecological practices that will give us peace of mind and perhaps even survival.

By casting away the economics of avarice, envy, and grumbling, if we consistently apply just economic policies faithfully for at least ten years in a row we will discover that *abject poverty disappears from the face of the earth and the rich grow steadily richer, all the while the despoliation of the land is abated.* The reason for this prediction is clear. Economic freedom follows economic justice. With economic freedom at large in the land, people will start producing all the wealth that they need. (Indeed, they will start creating only the children they can possibly love.) And since they will directly bear the costs associated with such production, they will produce just what they need and not one tiny bit more. The avoidance of inefficiency and waste will be the lodestar to guide production as well as consumption of wealth. Mother Earth with her flowers and trees and beasts will be rediscovered as the great giver of life and will again be considered as sacred—sacred, just as men and women are sacred; just as the whole universe is sacred.

It is only if we consider land as sacred that we are going to have deep respect for the land, and we are going to exercise deeply sane and sound ecological practices toward our Mother Earth. That the land is sacred there can be no doubt. The deep studies of Connie Baxter Marlow and Andrew Cameron Bailey as few others reveal that all indigenous people, the four continents over, have a deep sense of the sacredness of the land. A sense of sacredness that allows the Arapaho to state "Take only what you need and leave the land as you found it." American Indians practice a religion I like to call Americanism.

Ancient cultures had this innate natural religious relationship with Nature. There are modern interpretations of Quantum Physics, as again emphasized in the Marlow/Bailey studies, that lead to the same conclusions, the Oneness of Nature; the Oneness with Nature.

That Mother Nature is sacred can also be derived from an extension of the equivalence of matter to energy to include spirit as the third indispensable element of the equivalence. This extension is a logical necessity.

Yes, this is a new paradigm advocated by many sources; this is the love paradigm.

9.2 A Reverse Perspective

9.2.1 Some Tasks Ahead of Us in Community Development

The basic equivalence of Concordian economics, Production ≡ Distribution ≡ Consumption, does not represent a set of formal relations, which as Benedetto Croce said of morality, are to be worshipped from far away and can be impunely neglected from close-by. No, that equivalence opens up an entirely new intellectual world for… for whom? Indeed for Intellectuals. As I have pointed out on a number of occasions, during the last four to five hundred years, intellectuals have dreamed of windmills, engineers have built windmills, and oligopolists have acquired control of the windmills.

Intellectuals can go on dreaming forever. They are free to do that. But Concordian economics offers them—above all—the opportunity to be again masters of the public life, true philosopher-kings perhaps. Physicists are now intellectually equipped to deal openly with money in their daily operations; Economists are now intellectually equipped to deal openly with the physical reality in their daily operations. "Production," to emphasize it in no uncertain terms, deals with real wealth, wealth that exists in the real world of ecology and physics. The changes brought to economic theory by Concordian economics, in other words, make economics again intelligible to intellectuals of any discipline. Intellectuals, therefore, are presented with the golden opportunity not to be cowed any longer by the misleading mathematics of modern economics. Blinder (1999) confirms: "…too much of what young scholars write these days is 'theoretical drivel, mathematically elegant but not about anything real.'" Intellectuals can regain control of the full spectrum of public decisions concerning our life, liberty, and property. Just as intellectuals used to do before Adam Smith.

A tall order, perhaps; but an indispensable one. The ship of state is running through very perilous waters. Only sane and sound economic **and** ecological policies will right its course. All hands aboard!

I am not talking from nowhere. I have personally experienced the magic of interdependence. The ability of the equivalence of Production to Distribution to Consumption to unite the world of Physical Relations with the World of Money is not an interesting intellectual abstraction for me; it concerns real life. I have personally

9.2 A Reverse Perspective

experienced the power of this understanding. Working in close relation with food scientists at the Gloucester Laboratory of the National Marine Fisheries in the 1980s, we were able to introduce fresh fish in the national supermarket chains. Quite apart from the billions of dollars involved in these transactions, one of the reasons I give myself a pat on the back is that, by making fresh fish available in supermarkets in Des Moines, Iowa, we were able to improve the health status of the American population. A wealth of studies continues to discover health benefits do be derived from eating seafood.

Intellectuals, do not be overly concerned. I did not abandon the world of the intellect altogether. With many seafood scientists there, I wrote a bunch of papers and with Louis J. Ronsivalli (1988), the director of the laboratory, I wrote a book titled *Quality Assurance of Seafood*. Every once in a while I am informed that this body of work is still quoted in various parts of the world.

And my involvement with fisheries development did not start nor end there. It started on a much broader plane. It was community-wide. Once intellectuals again assume responsibility for the content of our public discourse, they can eventually participate fully in the performance of some of the most important tasks that are ahead of us here in Gloucester, and most other communities of the world. I have put these tasks in the form of an Internet petition: SAVE THE FISHERIES.

The intent of this petition is addressed in a variety of my writings and more intensively in my book titled To My Polis—with Love (2008). "Save the Fisheries" petition calls for full respect on the part of the National Marine Fisheries Service (NMFS) of the laws of biology—rather than evanescent statistical laws that the Magnuson-Stevens Act (MSA) has imposed upon our fishermen. These administrative regulations have been a disaster—a disaster for the physical operation of too many fishing communities; a disaster for the destruction of jobs; a disaster for the distribution of income; a disaster for the cohesion of the fishing community. Unnecessary dislocations in the family fishing fleet have occurred, as a consequence of which we import—at great burden on our international balance of payments—about 90% of the seafood consumption in the United States. More on these issues can be found in *To My Polis*.[2] Nor have I been bashful. Before and after the publication of *To My Polis*, I have expressed my concerns in a barrage of My View columns published in our local paper, the Gloucester Daily Times.

Biological laws on land as well as at sea tell us that nature keeps a balance in its affairs by allowing predators to do their job until they become so overpowering that their stocks collapse and, in turn, become the prey of the moment. It has to be highly recommended that the U.S. Congress amend MSA to annul its destructive regulations and require the satisfaction of only two mandates: First, NMFS has to do the utmost to prevent overfishing by large corporations, national as well as international corporations; second, NMFS has to allow fishermen to guard against overfishing by the natural predators of the moment and thus work in unison with—not against—the laws of nature.

A cod lays a million eggs at a time.

---

[2] See pp. 27–29, 51–53, 60–65, 137–142, 171–190, 275–309, 319–360.

NMFS has to tell fishermen what are the species of fish that are in abundant supply at the moment. They are the predators. To restrict our observation to only the most important sequence, at times herring and mackerel (the pelagics) that live in the middle of the water column are the natural predators of bottom fish like precious cod; at other times the bottom fish are the predators of the pelagics. When the larvae of bottom fish rise to the surface of the water column in search of food, the plankton, and light, they become a feast for the pelagics. Ditto for the codlings that need to go back down to the bottom of the ocean to live with their friends and relatives.

I was blown away when a Park Ranger in the Far West explained that the same relationships exist on land between trees and the bush underneath them. Ditto, when I learned that lemmings do not kill themselves by jumping off cliffs to make us laugh. They are chased by their predators. Ditto for the relationship between sheep and coyotes.

The forceful insertion of ecologists, and fisheries economists, into this discourse is a strange one. Only one question is allowed here. Do extreme ecologists ever consider that fish die by natural death—and that it is quite appropriate for fishermen to catch them before they die? Do tree-huggers prefer to see trees destroyed by fire, rather than being systematically harvested by lumberjacks? This, of course, is not the place to go into the relationships between family farms and corporate agricultural operations. Nor into the need to create surimi plants to create a market for pelagics, when pelagics are the abundant predators.

For millions of years, human beings used to adapt to these natural ebbs and flows. That was a case of full interdependence between human and natural events. During the last forty years, due to a coincidence of events, fishermen have not been allowed to respect the laws of nature. The consequences have been a disaster for the fishermen and for the Gloucester community, as well as other fishing communities. When will biologists follow the dictates of the laws of nature? And ecologists follow the wisdom of biologists? And when will bureaucrats use **their** best judgment?

9.2.1.1 Need for Surimi Plants

Truth to tell, NMFS is not quite free to adopt this policy. There is a reality to face: There is no great market for the pelagics in the United States. These are mostly black fish such as herring and mackerel; who would ever eat dark fish?

To every problem, there is a solution. The solution is to process dark fish in a surimi plant. There are three basic products that come out of these plants: 1. Skins and bones to be used as fertilizers; 2. Ecosapentaenoic oil, omega-three oils, which is never enough to satisfy a growing market; and, 3. Surimi, a *white* fish paste that can take the shape and flavor of a favorite fish: shrimp, crab, lobster tails. Surimi plants are multipling.

9.2.1.2 Need for Appropriate Boat Design

To add insult to injury, for its own good reasons NMFS has prohibited the construction of appropriately designed boats. The need is for sleek, long fishing boats that would respond to demands of energy efficiency. NMFS permits only the construction of short, squat boats. See, Altenburger (2022).

9.2.2 Coronavirus and Economic Interdependence

It has been said that Coronavirus is changing our understanding of the world. Let us see how much is this true. Let us see what changes might occur if we think in terms of Interdependence rather than Independence.

These thoughts were formulated and published before the specific vaccine against Coronavirus was discovered; see, Gorga (2021b). They can still be of help today. Certainly, this thought process will be most helpful in the future.

There are innumerable posibilities in thinking along the lines of economic interdependence and working within the intellectual framework of economic interdependence, rather than that of individualism or even that of competition.

The Coronavirus pandemic offers us an opportunity to truly practice interdependence and explore how far this vessel takes us.

Clearly, the entire world (the entire world of science at least) is involved in the search for a vaccine. That is the only solution that will alleviate our pains. Should not the scientific world coordinate its efforts by letting each scientist, and each scientific organization, collaborate with each and every laboratory in the world, and see who is the first to get us all through the goal post?

Clearly, property rights interests militate against truly open and complete collaboration. A patent is going to be assigned to the entity whose vaccine is certified first. Because of the prevalent support for the "winner-take-all" mentality, the organization that under current legal practices is going to create the vaccine first is going to "make a killing."

Is not this the fundamental reason why the process of bringing a vaccine to market generally is so dreadfully slow? Recognizing that this legal/political/ideological approach is actually, definitely, leaving behind many human beings dead in the process, should we not experiment with a new legal/political/ideological intellectual approach?

The potential solution is this: Rather than granting an exclusive patent to the organization that reaches a viable solution first, why not share the financial benefits of the patent among *all* organizations that have participated in the process of creating the vaccine?

From day one, each and every organization would publish on a website each and every detail of the experiment it is working on. This information alone would eliminate the waste involved in duplication of efforts. Many organizations would immediately start working on a different approach—or an approach that might have statistically fewer chances of success, but in the end might prove more successful than a "safer" approach.

Results of each experiment would be published as soon as obtained.

As we know, there is no failure in science. Negative results are not necessarily failures. They prove that a specific experiment does not yield positive results. Each and every organization in the world that is made aware of this result will avoid spending time and energy on it—unless, of course, residual doubts of its potential value still persist.

Immediate knowledge of successes and failures would again permit each and every organization to discard Tier One hypotheses and without waiting for internal confirmation would pass on to Tier Two—and then to Tier Three and Four and Five—hypotheses.

Can we imagine how much faster would we reach the goal of a successful vaccine? Can we imagine how much mental energy would be spared, energy that instead of working on hypotheses (doomed) to fail would be working on more advanced and perhaps even more adventurous experiments?

It all depends on the socially conceived and socially permitted reward system. In the "winner-take-all approach" one is motivated to reach the goal *first* and *alone*. In the world of interdependence, the *common* goal remains to reach the goal the **fastest** possible way. The sharing of the knowledge of individual "failures" would result in the fastest way to reach the goal together.

The key to enter the world of interdependence lies in the distribution of profits from the patent. If, instead of the "winner-take-all approach" we were to institute this, the "all winners approach," we could **distribute profits on the basis of the expenses** incurred in the process of discovery of the vaccine. These expenses can be easily accounted for and verified.

Not the least benefit of this application of the principles of interdependence to Big Pharma is an expected considerable reduction in costs, for the simple reason that this approach invites a reduction of needless duplication and thus a reduction of waste. The reduction of costs turns especially to the benefit of consumers on fixed income. (**Note:** It is not Big Pharma that is "the problem"; it is "the system" within which Big Pharma operates that needs to be cured.)

Can we imagine how much shorter will the road from here to the discovery of a vaccine be? Can we imagine how much will the tempi of final success be accelerated? Can we imagine how many fathers and mothers will be spared the loss of a child, and how many children will be spared the loss of a parent?

Needless to say, this level of exchange of information would do much to favor transparency—and even honesty?—in a field as literally vital as pharmaceuticals.

Two more benefits of interdependence, once seriously experienced, are effects near and dear to the heart of any Concordian economics' proposal: an increase in transparency and an effective reduction of inequality.

The increase in transparency, through an increase in mutual trust and respect, turns to the benefit of the entire community; in equal measure, the reduction of inequality turns to the benefit of everyone—rich and poor alike. Economic inequality is the long-term, hidden cause of steady economic instability and even cyclical financial crashes.

Another Benefit: The degree of interdependence and transparency suggested here would make it nearly impossible for any "industrial complex" such as Big Pharma to control any public agency such as the Food and Drug Administration (FDA).

9.2.2.1 IMPLIED: A Deep Cultural Shift to Meet the Coronavirus Challenge

A crisis is an opportunity. The Coronavirus pandemic offers us an opportunity to start almost from scratch. Let us see the cultural implications of meeting this challenge.

Some Historical Origins of Current Economic Crisis.

Undoubtedly, the current crisis is a crisis of *both* Capitalism and Socialism. Neither form of organization of society has been capable of solving our major social, economic, and political problems. The most acute problem is the persistence of poverty amidst plenty—a problem made more acute by the Coronavirus pandemic.

Our current crisis is nothing new. We have been living with it for the last four to five hundred years. It actually started with John Locke's decision to abandon the Aristotelian/Aquinian project of economic justice in favor of a policy that exalts the *justice of property rights*.

Not for naught, John Locke is recognized as the intellectual father of Individualism and Capitalism.

Did John Locke ever suspect the potential retort: Do you want to talk of the justice of property rights? Let me tell you of the *injustice of property rights*. That is what the Socialists and Karl Marx did.

Karl Marx and the Socialists, of course, are widely recognized as intellectual fathers and mothers of Collectivism and Socialism/Communism.

This is where the political and economic discourse still stands today.

9.2.2.2 The Modern Curse of Property Rights

Being related to existing property, property limited in amount at any given time, property rights have become a curse. Everyone wants them; indeed, everyone wants *more* of them. It is this inevitable social dynamic that leads to an avalanche of profound, but largely disguised errors. Essentially, it leads to the combined abyss of scarcity and poverty.

To escape poverty, our social, economic, and political imagination has given rise to the phenomenon of the Masters of Mankind. It was no other than Adam Smith who tagged them in this fashion: "All for ourselves, and nothing for other people, seems, in every age of the world, to have been the vile maxim of the masters of mankind."

Concordian economics recognizes the sacredness of private property rights and suggests different solutions to the tween problems of scarcity and poverty.

9.2.2.3 A Long Story Cut Short

An interesting dynamics has dominated the world during the last four to five centuries. The literati, unable to free themselves of the deep cultural genius of Cervantes, have written about the windmills; the engineers have focused on creating the windmills; and the oligopolists, the Masters of Mankind, have concentrated their attention on owning and controlling the windmills.

9.2.2.4 A Centuries-Old Cry of MAGA People

The consequences of the actions of the Masters of Mankind have been felt most by those who today are identified as MAGA People.

There is much more than words that our political leadership owes our country men and women—and children. There is a whole array of injustices that have to be set aright. Set these injustices right and you unify the country. We must realize that, while *MAGA People are at the forefront* of the affront of injustices, no sector of the population escapes scot-free.

As pointed out on other occasions, the affections that hold MAGA People together are the resentments and the afflictions that society inflicts upon them. Their lives are being eviscerated by the latifundia; yes, who knows about the latifundia any longer? Ever since Constantine converted to Christianity, latifundia have disappeared from polite political imagination; but vast tracts of land—whether in the wilderness, in dilapidated downtowns, or in the undeveloped band of land that strangles the cities— are still controlled by few people and rich corporations. As a consequence, MAGA People tend to be corralled into crowded lots.

MAGA People's lives are being eviscerated when money is lent to people with money **on easy terms** and the People without money are left to pay outrageous interest.

MAGA People's lives are being eviscerated whenever two mega corporations are glued together; then the few gain more power and the people within and without both corporations suffer many afflictions.

MAGA People's lives are being eviscerated by robots that take their jobs, their livelihood, away.

No, economic oppression is not due to the ill will of anyone. It is systemic; it springs from the system, a system that we have built helter-skelter, adding a patch here, and a patch there. No one has designed it. There has never been any real understanding of *the economic process* as a whole—only understanding of parts of the elephant. In its development, we have overlooked many essential elements. It is now time to try to put it all together.

We have built a system that ultimately affects negatively everyone. Do we ever consider the condition of the billionaire who goes to bed tonight with the fear that he or she will wake up to the news that, due to the collapse of the Stock Market somewhere in the world, this poor soul has lost a good chunk of the wealth so painfully accumulated over the years?

Have we considered the psychological reflection on the affluent when society opts for a "preferential treatment for the poor"? If we are going to love the poor so much, to the extent of giving them a preferential treatment, don't we implicitly say that we hate the rich—or at least we have less love for the rich?

Have we seriously considered that we have built *a society of beggars*? While the poor beg for food and shelter, the middle classes beg for a job. And the affluent are constantly begging for a subsidy and/or a tax reduction.

Yes, these horrible conditions that weigh so heavily on the life of nearly everyone today can and must be changed.

9.2.2.5 From Property Rights to Economic Rights

To set things right, we need a major **cultural** revolution. We need to shift our attention from property rights to economic rights. We need to shift our attention from the *finite* amount of property rights to the *infinite* amount of economic rights.

At a fundamental level, all these negative conditions spring from our uncontrollable pursuit of "happiness"; they spring from a world engulfed in rights without responsibilities. There is no short cut. Only the full assumption of responsibilities will set the world aright. Much discernment does indeed suggest that only the performance of four economic rights and responsibilities will gradually set our mutual social, economic, and political relationships aright. We must switch our attention from many expressions of wishful thinking to the reality of what can and must be done. This is the only way for the moral leadership of our country to gain the allegiance of MAGA People, the people who have forever switched their allegiance from the hard right to the hard left, or vice versa—and consistently been deceived.

9.2.2.6 TO REPEAT, Four Economic Rights and Responsibilities

First, **Money**. Money is not created out of thin air. Money is created out of our national credit, our creditworthiness. Since we individually create the value of our national credit, we are individually fully entitled to access it as we need it, on the basis of loans, loans to create real wealth; loans obtained at cost. Our responsibility is to repay the loans.

LAND. We are not angels. We need access to land and natural resources to be productive—indeed, to be anywhere or do anything. We have the responsibility to pay taxes on the land and natural resources on which we have exclusive control. Latifundia exist because some people pay no land taxes; let everyone pay the appropriate amount of land taxes and latifundia will be dissolved; land and natural resources will gradually become available to all who need them—at fair market price.

LABOR. We must acquire ownership of all the wealth we create; if we work for corporations, we must have a fair share of the value of capital appreciation that we create. Employee Stock Ownership Plans (ESOPs) are ideal legal instruments to achieve this goal. Needless to say, we have the responsibility to earn our compensation.

CAPITAL. Corporations should be free to grow as large as they internally and organically can. They should be prohibited from acquiring other corporations through mergers and acquisitions. This form of growth is tantamount to industrial murder.

To learn about the subtleties of these four economic rights and responsibilities, forget Keynes, forget Hayek. Do study four giant American thinkers: Benjamin Franklin, Henry George, Louis O. Kelso, and Louis D. Brandeis.

9.2.3 A Deep Cultural Shift

Moderna did not hear me, but my work is far from obsolete. New pandemics are scheduled to arrive. In the waiting, I have thought to *generalize* **the proposed application** of Concordian economics to one and all developments of medicines. And I like to interpret the term in its most extensive meaning: undoubtedly all DNA studies and applications fall under this rubric. Come to think of it, should not all foods fall under the same category?

Come to think of it, should not items that give us clothing and shelter fall under the same category? Indeed, I should find it hard to exclude even the production of frivolities.

And what about the looming specter, the bright promise of AI?

To apply this "application" of Concordian economics to as large a panoply of economic affairs as possible is never too late; let us start as soon as possible.

* * *

It is undoubtedly hard to experiment with the full application of Interdependence because it runs against such traditional "values" as vainglory, pride, and self-reliance. Time will tell whether we will ever become capable of overcoming the limitations we impose on ourselves through the negative powers of these traditional values. They incorporate the *Spirit of the Age*.

Macroscopically, the Spirit of the Age is manifesting itself through this operation: We are killing people who work, by overwork; and the people who do *not* work, by starvation and homelessness.

The Spirit of the Age is manifest in this expression: *Let us make the money*. Notice the subtle connotation of "making the money"—not through the product we produce, but directly: How are we supposed to make the money, the money that is already in circulation? Is this not a dream? Is this not an impossibility?

9.2 A Reverse Perspective

The consequences of these Ill Winds are all there to be seen. We might be able to deny the macroscopic reality. Harder it is to deny this reality if we look at it under the microscope.

Aware or unawares, art dealers in New York killed Basquiat. The market was "hot." The dealers were paying high prices to buy more and more "things" that came out of Basquiat's art. The young Basquiat found no better way to enjoy the fruit of his success than using drugs. He died of an overdose.

Not so in the past, not so in Borneo. Rarely in the distant past was the artist even signing his or her artwork. A few years ago, while in Borneo, we learned that the artist was still taking seven years—seven years–to recover his spirit from the production of an art object. The artist was hard at work making art, not making money. It did take seven years to recover his or her powers.

The ranks of highly technical psychologists and sociologists are invited to fill in the gaps—or correct the misunderstandings—I, untrained in these waters, untrained in these very complex issues, am daring to leave behind.

* * *

Well, if this desired degree of industrial interdependence might appear too pollyannish, the concerted, persistent application of Concordian rights and responsibilities **right now** should quite simply be a question of "law." And why not a question of morality as well? Let the Spirit of the Age purge itself at its own pace. There is plenty that can be done, plenty that ought to be done, plenty that must be done right now.

9.2.4 A Few Issues About Fluoridation

Issues of public health ought to be of deep concern to everyone. There are a few fundamental issues about the use of fluoride in our public waters we all should take a position on. Until these issues are addressed, not one additional ounce of fluoride ought to be added to our public water supply.

9.2.4.1 The Issue of Science

There are two kinds of fluoride, the natural one and the industrial one. Every municipal Department of Public Works uses the industrial one. The industry is honest. It clearly labels the sacks of fluoride it sells to the public as POISON.

The discussion ought to end right there. Who in the world would ever think of poisoning our public water supply?

But, no. The discussion goes on. Proponents of fluoridation seem to be confused by THEIR science. They conflate the two types of fluoride into One: They have the audacity to maintain that **all fluoride is fluoride.**

This is a veiled attack against Mother Nature that I must unmask: They are basically stating that Mother Nature is Poisonous. One must defend Mother Nature.

Of course, Mother Nature can be "naturally" poisonous. But she is discreet; she doesn't tell anyone. And she leaves it to chance. Besides, natural poison might be there to toughen our immune system. And another difference. Mother Nature offers her "poison" free of charge!

9.2.4.2 The Issue of Smallness

Proponents of fluoridation try to convince themselves and others that permitted ppm (parts per million) of fluoride are SO small that we need to drink a great amount of water before we go beyond the official guidelines of safety. True, BUT.

They do not acknowledge that many of us DO, INDEED, DRINK THAT UNSAFE amount of water OVER TIME. The "small" doses of fluoride are not expelled; rather, they ACCUMULATE in our bodies and cause incalculable damage, especially to all our soft organs.

In tune with ancient wisdom, those who do systems analysis know very well that it is the last straw that breaks the camel's back. Chaos theory recognizes that the swing of a butterfly's wing in Brazil can cause a tornado in Texas. It is the last "small" dose ingested that, added to all other "small" parts, can cause incalculable damage to our health.

9.2.4.3 Oh, The Fish

Once the issue of fluoride in our public water supply is analyzed in its entirety, another issue comes to the fore. Fervent believers in the value of fluoridation say that the largest amounts of fluoride "pass though" our bodies.

Well, where does this fluoride end up? In the oceans, of course.

Oh, the fishes, the poor fishes. If only they could talk.

Will fervent believers in fluoridation change their attitudes when the next whale, dolphin, or seal that crashes on our shores reveals "small" parts of fluoride in their bodies?

9.2.4.4 Ah! The Do-Gooders

Who are the people who support fluoridation? Apart from those who are heavily influenced by a misguided cynicism, you know "We all have to die once; the guy with the most toys wins." Apart from these people, there are the gullible.

Who are the gullible? The do-gooders, of course.

Strangely enough, some of the most vociferous supporters of fluoridation are people who sport the moniker DDS on their lapels. They are Doctors in Dental Surgery—as if dental surgery had anything to do with toxicology.

It is FOR OUR GOOD, of course, that these people want to add fluoride to our public water supply.

9.2.4.5 A Fast Cost/Benefit Analysis

The "good" they offer is a potential reduction of cavities by 25%. This is the best that flawed studies of the 1950s could come up with. (Later studies have emphasized that benefits from fluoride derive from topical applications to the teeth; not the scatter shot of spreading fluoride in the public water supply).

Whatever the estimated benefit, notice the implicit acknowledgment. The use of fluoride is 75% INEFFECTIVE.

Now this outcome might even be tolerable, if the cost/benefit analysis of fluoride were not so unbalanced. Measured against such a miniscule POTENTIAL BENEFIT, this is the risk: "This review identified a number of potentials and **established** (emphasis added) adverse effects including cognitive impairment, hypothyroidism, dental and skeletal fluorosis, enzyme and electrolyte derangement, and cancer."

The source of this study is: National Research Council (NRC), *Fluoride in Drinking Water: A Scientific Review of EPA's Standards,* National Academies Press, Washington, DC, USA, 2006.

9.2.4.6 Authorities Are Running Away from Support

One more thing, at least, our Good Doctors have to explain in order to convince us of the validity of their position: Why is the trend AWAY from fluoridation? Dear Doctors, please, tell us why so many authorities and so many cities and towns, all over the world, are running away from the old flush of fascination with fluoride.

9.2.4.7 Author's Note on Personal Cost

Ever since I discovered the dangers of fluoride, I have been drinking only "Spring Water," at a cost of about $5.00 per week. I am the only one in my family who drinks fresh water. Now multiply this cost by the 52 weeks of the year, and then by the thousands of people in my community who drink "Spring Water." To this cost, you have to add the yearly cost of purchasing fluoride added to our water supply, and the municipal cost of administering such a program, an expensive program since my Municipal Authorities have, by law, to take many samples of water many times a year, keep a record of such numbers, and provide the workers with much expensive (I am sure) protective gear. Do these workers garner the highest wages possible? I hope so. What is the incidence of these costs on my property tax bill?

And how did I discover that I was personally affected by the fluoride added to my municipal water supply? I discovered it seven years ago when I chewed on a piece of lettuce and I cracked a molar. Is not this a personal experience of dental fluorosis? That is not the end of my story. You still have to add the cost of taking care of that cracked molar. Now, to give you an idea of the natural strength of my teeth, I have to report that a much earlier dentist had to ask for help from her husband to extract one of my molars.

Now, dear Reader. you may ask, "What Is the Function of Concordian Economics in Relation to Fluoride?"

Many functions. Let me count the ways. The era should be over when the literati, many economists no doubt included, refuse to touch matters of science. The era should be over when the literati, many economists no doubt included, refuse to touch matters of deep interest and concern to their communities. The era should be over when the literati, many economists no doubt included, refuse to open their eyes to many frankly fraudulent operations—way beyond fluoridation[3]—going on in our communities.

The era should be over when many specialists, Doctors of Dentistry in our case, accept bribes—as it is claimed in the case of fluoridation of our municipal waters—in order to support decisions that turn to the detriment of the community.

The era should be over when industrial corporations make a buck selling poison to gullible municipal officers.

That is not the last pedestal from which Concordian economics blares out its merits. The purpose of Concordian economics is to create financially independent people. Financially independent people are less likely to fall prey to despicable actions. Financially independent people are less likely to work for corporations that produce poisonous products. Financially independent people are less likely to work for corporations that sell poisonous products. Financially independent people are less likely to work for—public or private corporations—that use poisonous products.

9.3 Appendix

The following diagram is from Lafayette's Fluoride Frenzy (David MacNeal, *YellowScene Magazine*, June 18, 2013). MacNeal mentions that many people get "artificial" fluoride exposure not only from treated water but also from other sources such as toothpaste.

---

[3] It seems that water fluoridation is a kid's play in relation to the widespread use and abuse of Per- and Polyfluoroalkyl Substances (PFAS).

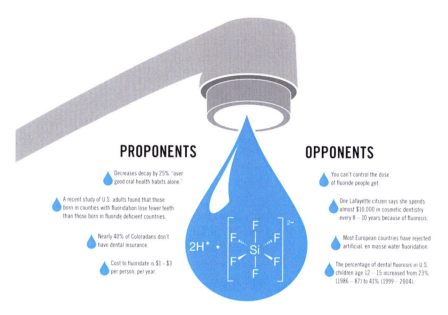

9.3.1 Rebuild the Downtown Through Racial Harmony

I could not let this day dedicated to the remembrance of Martin Luther King. Jr. go by without bringing forward what, Congress willing, the Federal Reserve System (the Fed) will do to rebuild our downtowns through racial harmony.

A few days before Martin Luther King was assassinated, reconnecting no doubt to President Franklin D. Roosevelt's legacy, he issued a call for economic rights.

Access to national credit is one of the pivotal economic rights to be exercised by the people. Through the exercise of this right, citizens ask for the Fed to create money only for the creation of real wealth in the form of loans at the cost to individual entrepreneurs and co-operatives or corporations with ESOPs in their operations.

Let us see what can the Fed do.

Assisted no doubt by the host of social agencies devoted to the many problems afflicting the downtown of every city, and quite a few towns, today, the Fed will fund the operations of new and old contractors who have solid plans for the renovation of the abundant, but dilapidated, housing stock covering acres and acres of land—and the building of new houses on those many lots filled with weeds and rubbish.

Public institutions with taxing power will, no doubt, also want to obtain loans at cost from the Fed to build or rebuild schools and the much-talked-about, depleted physical infrastructure of our country.

The minds of inhabitants of our cities and towns, young and old, male and female, will be diverted from fear of drugs and destruction of lives toward the reconstruction of their environment.

They who willingly or unwillingly serve as custodians of our physical and cultural inheritance represented by the awesome buildings of the last centuries and the civic\\ institutions of neighborhood associations and town halls will have a chance to prove the validity of the old American way. The way created by Franklin and praised by Tocqueville.

Progress has not been an undivided blessing.

It is high time that we benefit from real progress in medicine and communications, to say the least, without being cowed into the acceptance of the destruction of the dignity of human souls and harmony of our physical environment.

Will young and old, male and female human beings living in our cities and towns respond to the opportunity of becoming building contractors—and all other business operations that accompany the task? The list is considerable: from interior and exterior designers, to suppliers of the many items that go into building a home, and then tools and car repair shops. Not to speak of lawyers, doctors, and accountants. Let us not forget the insurance man—or the firefighter. And why not build movie theaters and museums at the same time? In the rear guard come house painters and artists (does the name Hopper tickle the mind?) and photographers and recorders of history and kibitzing.

If assisted by the schools and by the civic agencies, a few will jump to the opportunity of buying homes and renovating them. Many will gradually follow the few intrepid ones who will see the light offered by this opportunity.

But they must repay the loan. How will contractors—and associates—do that? One way is to provide rental space to friends and relatives. The other one, perhaps more satisfactory and comprehensive, is this. Assisted by the social agencies, even before asking for a loan, contractors ought to secure a buyer for the new or refurbished house.

Who are these buyers?

Well, they are readily available. In addition to those who "save" their pennies and wisely invest them, buyers are the ones tired of living in the social isolation of the suburbs. They are the ones who preach social integration: Now they have the opportunity to practice what they preach.

A further opportunity—provided by the implicit overcoming of racial barriers of the past through zoning ordinances and building codes—is that of creating racially integrated neighborhoods.

More.

Buyers are those who are utterly concerned about the damage caused by global warming. By avoiding long commuting lines, they will save energy: Most jobs are still in the center of cities and towns.

These good souls will no longer be part of a vociferous, scared multitude. They will be part of the solution.

They can look forward to another unexpected set of benefits. They might be able to go home to share lunch with their loved ones. They might have more time to read, watch any performance they like, or relax. Above all their nerves will no longer be frayed by driving in noisy, smelly, dangerous traffic.

These are some of the benefits we shall reap if we adopt the suggestions offered by Concordian economics.

9.3.2 Why Wall Street Ought to Favor a Gradual Decline in the Cost of Land

When a friend expressed concern for the high price of land, this is what I told him.

Working together, here is how we will gradually reduce the cost of land to manageable proportions: As Henry George, many classical economists recommended, and, *mirabile dictu*, not one but eight Nobel laureates in economics all agreed, the price of land will gradually decrease if taxes are imposed on the value of land. The reason is simple and is ingrained in the mechanics of the market. When taxes are imposed on land, many landowners will prefer to sell their land; latifundia will gradually disappear; hence, with an increase in the market supply of land, its price can be expected to decrease. No state intervention is necessary: Those who want to preserve the environment as it is, they simply need to pay their fair share of taxes on the land.

Hidden in this proposition is the expectation that land value taxation will not just be "another" tax. It will gradually replace congeries of taxes, from income taxes to corporate taxes.

With the reduction of corporate taxes, corporate Wall Street will benefit as all other industrial and commercial corporations will benefit.

Hidden even deeper in this chain of discoveries is the expectation that the cost of Government will have accordingly to decrease. And it will decrease, not by denying access to all sorts of currently available social services, from Welfare to Medicare, but by finding new/old methods of payment for them.

To discover new methods of payment for social services, there is no other way than to restructure the private economy by making it more productive through an equitable distribution of income and wealth—equitable, not equal. This appears to be such an impossible dream because we have not really given much serious thought to it.

We have been inveigled in the ideology of equality. To insist on it, we need equity, not equality. This means that all participants in the economic process will receive what is due them, neither more nor less. As is widely demonstrated, by this simple equity "trick" people become more productive.

In so doing, the rules for the distribution of income and wealth will no longer be dictated by an abstract efficiency of the market, but by a set of concrete rules established by the private market itself ahead of engaging in the process of creation of wealth.

In the fishing industry, for example, ancient established rules still determine the percentage of the value of the catch going to the owner of the vessel, the percentage going to the captain, and the percentage going to the crew. Everyone knows the rules in advance; an agreement is reached not only because the justice of the rules has been determined by deep cultural and moral decisions, by themselves well tested by trials and errors over the centuries; but also because these are abstract and inflexible rules. They govern the industry as a whole and forever. People who do not like them are free to apply their abilities elsewhere.

This, then, is work to be done in each industry; the sooner it is done, the happier will everyone be.

In addition to eliminating rules and regulations that have hamstrung the economy, a comparable fundamental restructure will have to be undertaken within the fiscal policies of the government. Why not start with an agreement on the gradual elimination of all subsidies to private industry? A subsidized market is not a free market; it is a slave market.

And if the community should develop a hankering for a new industry, just like the green industry, for example, the government should own the enterprise—and sell it at an auction as soon as the idea becomes financially feasible. Full speed ahead. Damn the torpedoes. Let foreign competition wallow in the shallow waters of possible temporary comparative advantage through existing low wages.

With a gradual comprehensive restructuring of our public and private economy, "We the People" of the United States will become increasingly rich. And therefore, we will be able to afford to pay for current entitlements; and, by paying for them with our own cash, we will acquire access to those services at reduced cost, since much paperwork will be eliminated. We will then acquire access to those services as God-given rights. No questions asked. No begging for assistance.

But gradually increasing taxes on land and reducing all other taxes is not the only way to reduce the price of land—and to benefit financial as well as all other individual and corporate activities.

The price of land will gradually decline when the Federal Reserve System (the Fed) stops allowing the use of public money for the purchase of financial assets and restricts the issuance of loans to the creation of real wealth. The creation of real wealth necessarily calls for the use of land and natural resources.

True, an increased demand for land and natural resources will gradually increase their price; but this increase will be restrained if entrepreneurs purchase land outright, rather than purchasing land through mortgages, which implies borrowing money at relatively high interest rates in private financial markets.

Ditto for the purchase of land and natural resources through accumulated labor earnings. With the widespread use of ESOPs and CSOPs, future potential entrepreneurs will have a better chance to receive higher compensation for their present labors, hence they will have a better chance to accumulate savings with which to pay for land and natural resources.

Then there is a fourth way in which the price of land and natural resources will gradually decline, or at least increase less rapidly than it is currently increasing. If the Fed rejects the use of public money for mergers and acquisitions, frenzied accumulations of wealth will decrease, hence the price of land and natural resources will gradually decrease.

As it can be seen, these four avenues for the gradual decline of the price of land and natural resources correspond to the exercise of the four economic rights and responsibilities addressed in a variety of publications on Concordian economics to meet the requirements of our four modern factors of production: land, labor, financial capital, and physical capital. The exercise of these four rights and responsibilities will grant us gradual sane and sound fiscal, monetary, labor, and industrial policies.

In addition, Concordian economics is advancing another major measure to stabilize the monetary system. This is the application of the ancient practice of the Jubilee to reduce all unpayable debts systematically over a seven-year cycle. This operation will have the effect of reducing all prices gradually and systematically so that relative positions will be preserved, and people will be as rich at the end of the cycle as they were before the recommendations of Concordian economics were implemented.

The question arises. Why should Wall Street foster the adoption of the recommendations of Concordian economics? There are many reasons:

Wall Streeters will regain the "approbation" of mankind, for doing the "right" thing rather than the selfish thing;

Wall Streeters' life will be incredibly less stressful, which does not mean at all that all risks and all large profits will disappear from sight;

Wall Streeters will regain the respect of the young generations;

Wall Streeters can look forward to spending an old life amidst financial and spiritual comfort.

These are the soft reasons. The hard reason is that Wall Streeters alone today have the political power to enforce these rules. *Amazingly, Wall Street is the only institution whose members are still united in the pursuit of their common good.* They only have to expand their vision to include the common good of the community at large.

This political action will not occur in a vacuum. Much good will can be expected from the center of the political spectrum. More concretely still, as a letter from the Fed indicates, Wall Street will be met with open arms by the Fed.

Taking care of the common good of the community at large is a temporary political action that Wall Streeters will have to perform. It is once in a lifetime action. Once the right policies are set in motion, they can be expected to soon go back to their usual activities. Then, they will discover that an unexpected benefit is yielded by the pursuit of the common good.

Eliminating absurd practices followed during recent years, absurd practices arising mostly from the falling apart of society, Wall Street will voluntarily restrict its activities to perform many complex functions, which it is organically called to perform. Wall Street will "magically" transform small, useless savings into richly performing assets; Wall Street will produce a reliable current valuation of assets; Wall Street will make "the market" perform efficiently.

Go Wall Street, go. You have nothing to lose, but the pall of many misguided ideas. They are ideas that did not arise from within your ranks, anyway. These were ideas generated by too large a number of defunct, and some still alive economists.

9.3.3 Why Countries Shouldn't Sell Their Natural Resources to Foreigners

On December 11, 2016, I posted on *EconIntersect* an essay that focused its attention on Cuba. It was titled "Own Cuba – Don't Sell Her." It is now time to enlarge our focus onto Africa, namely on each and every nation of Africa, and the rest of the world for that matter.

Here is what I said then:

With the passing of Fidel Castro, will Cuba finally be truly free?

On Feb 10, 2016, Luis Gutierrez wrote to gaiapc@yahoogroups.ca:

> I am not a fan of the Castro regime. Not that what we had before was much better, but the cure has been even worse than the disease. Pity, because the Cuban revolution could have been a good turning point but was betrayed and corrupted by absolute power. Communism is extreme capitalism turned upside down and inside out; even more materialistic than capitalism, and with human rights either ignored or manipulated at will by the state. Not recommendable, but let's see what they can do now that they no longer blame the embargo for the Cuban disaster.

What they will most likely do is what Russia and China have done after the collapse of Communism. They have sold juicy morsels of the people's labors to a few exploiters and created billionaires. Back to the worst forms of capitalism, in other words. Not even Adam Smith was favorable to this type of capitalism. In fact, tucked very tightly within the folds of the Wealth of Nations, there is this strong maxim that ought to keep Neoliberals on their toes:

> All for ourselves and nothing for other people, seems, in every age of the world, to have been the vile maxim of the masters of mankind.

9.3.3.1 A True Alternative, a Revolution from the Center

The pendulum swings wildly back and forth, a revolution from the left predictably spurs a revolution from the right. How can one evaluate this long historical tradition? Even without adding the effects of the next expected collapse of the world financial system, it can objectively be said that the social, economic, and political condition of We the People of the World is getting progressively worse. One cannot expect anything much better from a continuation of ongoing economic policies.

We the People have not yet really experienced a revolution from the center. This is a real alternative, I believe, to the structural weaknesses of both Individualism/Capitalism and Collectivism/Communism.

Socialism (and, strangely enough perhaps, the ideology of social justice) has, of course, been the traditional preferred alternative. But Socialism tends to carry with it the structural weaknesses of both Capitalism and Communism. In the course of fifty years of ongoing research and publication, the real alternative that I have discovered and strongly recommend to Cuba and all other nations of the world is this: If the intention is to build a world of solidarity and sustainability, Concordian economics

9.3 Appendix

is the economic framework one may want to embrace. Concordian economics leads to a revolution from the center,

9.3.3.2 Concordian Economics

Concordian economics is a candidate to replace mainstream economics. Concordian economics offers an integration of economic theory, policy, and practice.

Here are two diagrams that present theory and policy back to back (Figs. 9.1 and 9.2).

Concordian economic theory presents the integration of **Production** of real goods and services; **Consumption** or expenditure of financial assets to acquire real goods and services; and the **Distribution** of the value of ownership rights over goods as well as money. One cycle of the process is completed when goods pass from producers to consumers and money from consumers to producers; for the exchange to occur—in a civilized way—both producers and consumers must have ownership of what they exchange.

Even in the purchase of a car, there is an exchange of three items: (1) the car; (2) the money; and (3) the deed of ownership.

Since in any transaction, there are three entities, real wealth, people, and money, a full economic analysis has to take care of all three bottom lines: planet, people, and profits. A brief explanation for this broad coverage is that Production, Distribution,

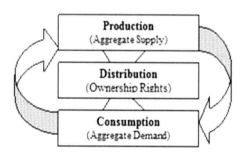

Fig. 9.1 Concordian Theory

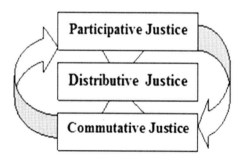

Fig. 9.2 Concordian Policy

and Consumption are synthetic terms; but they are universal. Therefore, they encompass all real wealth, all financial instruments, and all ownership rights—whether they are produced by or belong to private individuals, to governments, or are held in common as in "commons."

Concordian economic policy presents an integration of the three essential planks of economic justice: the right to participate in the economic process (**participative justice**); (in order to obtain) the right to a fair share of what one produces (**distributive justice**); and the right to receive an equivalent value of what one gives (**commutative justice**).

And here is how theory and policy are translated into action. Concordian economic practice presents an integrated set of rights and responsibilities in relation to the four essential factors of modern production: the right of access to land and natural resources and the **responsibility** to pay taxes on that portion of land and natural resources that fall under our exclusive control; the right of access to national credit and the **responsibility** to repay loans acquired through national credit; the right to the fruits of one's labor and the **responsibility** to contribute to the process of creation of wealth; the right to the enjoyment of one's wealth and the **responsibility** to respect the wealth of others. The exercise of these economic rights presupposes, not the absence, but the full bloom of such political rights as freedom of speech and the responsibility to exercise the voting franchise.

NOTE: While the introduction of economic justice at the core of Concordian economics is an automatic operation, we must be aware of its historical importance. With economic justice, we return to the intellectual world that prevailed from Aristotle to Adam Smith—with adjustments, of course. The core of the "old" world was encapsulated in John Locke's formula: we all have the right to "*life, liberty, and property.*" To return to that world, in other words, is to undo what Jefferson somewhat mischievously did. We all know that Jefferson erased the word property from the draft of the Declaration of Independence and substituted it with the expression "*the pursuit of happiness.*" By crossing out the word "*property,*" Jefferson broke with Tradition and thrust us toward the la land of "*happiness.*" This is a land of entitlements. This is a land of "*rights*" and no responsibilities. Jefferson had to do that, because otherwise, he would have not saved the union. Property then covered the horrible practice of ownership of human beings, and the South was not ready to free the slaves. But thanks to Abraham Lincoln, slavery does no longer plagues us. We can safely go back to the ancient formula of "*life, liberty, and property.*"

9.3.3.3 The Crucial Importance of Ownership

The best way of summarizing the core of the new/old train of thought represented by Concordian economics is to touch upon the crucial importance of ownership. The Framers of the US Constitution did know in their bones the relationships among personal freedom, political liberty, and culture. They knew that these relationships were all rooted in the ownership of property; they knew this reality to such an extent that they denied the voting franchise to the propertyless. This solution was obviously wrong and became unsustainable.

The right solution, as George Mason recommended, is to extend the "*means of acquiring and possessing property*" to everyone. A copy of the Virginia Declaration of Rights, which embodies this high principle, faces me every time I go upstairs in my house, a colonial house. George Mason's goal is finally within reach.

The way to reach this goal is to expand upon a recommendation I advanced in a series of essays collected in To My Polis, With Love in the early part of this century (2008). Then I pleaded: "*Do not sell Gloucester—Own It.*"

Today I will enlarge the field of observation and heartily make the same recommendation to Cubans: "*Do not sell Cuba - Own her.*"

And now, April 21, 2017, I would like to enlarge the scope of this Chapter by focusing on Africa as a whole, namely on each and every nation in Africa—and the rest of the world, for that matter. This is my recommendation: "*Do not sell African natural resources to foreigners—Own them and develop them yourselves.*"

Technical experts from all over the world will be at your feet, if you pay them well.

Here are a few specifics to make this recommendation a reality.

9.3.3.4 Where Are the Financial Resources?

Where are the financial resources to reach this goal? As I pointed out then and have continued to explore in the pages of Mother Pelican and EconIntersect (here and here), there are two major sources of financial funds that are readily available for the asking: One is a local interdependence fund; the other is the Central Bank. All that is required is a bit of knowledge and much political will.

The interdependence fund that I recommend—there is a great variety of them—asks the community to cash in at least ten percent of its wealth, and put it into a fund, administered by its owners/depositors, to be devoted exclusively to local economic development projects. The essential rules for a safe and sound administration of the funds are these: 1. Issue loans only for the creation of real wealth; 2. Issue loans at cost, not at variable interest rates; 3. Issue loans to benefit all members of the community, which implies that loans ought to be issued only to individual entrepreneurs, co-operatives, corporations with Employee Stock Ownership Plans (ESOPs), and public agencies with taxing powers, so the loans can be repaid. In a society thus gradually made securely and justly rich, love/charity will easily take care, with great dignity, of the few who for any reason do not want to or cannot participate in the economic process. In a healthy society, those who do not want or cannot participate in the economic process are naturally few. What is generally not recognized is that most people love to work; indeed, need to work to earn self-respect—from themselves and from others. The essential proviso is that they should be free to and have the opportunity to do what they love. In due time an appropriate amount of resources ought to be devoted to cultural projects as well.

The Central Bank of Cuba—or any African nation—can apply these same rules when creating new money. Thus, local entrepreneurs, co-operatives, local corporations with ESOPs, and local agencies with taxing power will have access to national credit. Rather than selling their assets to local and especially to foreign interests, owners of existing assets will have the financial resources to hold on to their possessions and make them prosper.

Cuba will finally be Cuba Libre, indeed.

Of course, this is precisely what I am recommending to the American political structure as well. I hope that in this period of exciting ferment, the American public as well as the Cuban—and African—public will listen. Amazingly, given all due differences, Cuba, the US, and the rest of the world are in the same intellectual boat at the moment. The scale is enormously different, of course; yet, the human perils and opportunities are largely the same.

9.3.3.5 One Immense Difference

The immense difference between USA and the rest of the world is that the US Dollar is the preferred means of exchange in international commerce. This is a reality that might or might not change in the future. For the time being, how best to operate within this reality? There are two solutions: One is to teach the people of the world to buy local; two, is to raise tariffs on import of foreign goods. The ultimate solution on which we all have to work in order to have a peaceful world is gradually to reach an equivalence of value in the exchange of foreign currencies. Later we shall give a look at the possibility of creating the Bancor International Order (BIO).

9.3.3.6 A Word on Implementation

Considering that each one of the rights and responsibilities (Rs&Rs) recommended above (with the exception of the Brandeis Rule) have been exercised on a piecemeal basis with great success for a long time all over the world gives much hope for the future. These Rs&Rs stem from an integrated application of the thought of Henry George (land), Benjamin Franklin (financial capital), Louis O. Kelso (labor), and Louis D. Brandeis (physical capital). Thus, this is an All-American policy. And it will have to become an All-World policy. Forget Keynes; forget Hayek.

One would think that just by mentioning them, most Cuban, American, and African people would want to see these economic rights and responsibilities implemented; but that is not going to be the case. What is required is that ten percent of the population rally around them; that ten percent will convince the other ninety percent of their necessity. What it takes is political action.

Since money is the most common need and the most likely tool of future community building, we need–at first–to concentrate our attention on the implementation of the second set of Rs&Rs. We need to exercise our right of access to national credit, because access to financial capital—as distinguished from access to consumer loans

9.3 Appendix

that enslave us—will free us all: Cubans, Americans, Africans, and eventually all other people of the world.

If loans to fix our public works infrastructure are financed this way, their repayment could be achieved through a tax on land and natural resources, thus we would automatically be implementing the other fundamental set of Rs&Rs as well, namely the exercise of our right of access to land and natural resources: These taxes, by reducing hoarding and accumulation of land in a few hands, increase the supply of land on the market and thus reduce their price for all people.

If access to national credit were to favor the creation of ESOPs, we would be automatically implementing the third set of Rs&Rs concerning labor.

For the fourth set of Rs&Rs concerning physical capital, we need to be fairly bold and innovative. Apart from a stringent application of anti-trust regulations, some ideas concerning the Brandeis Rule are introduced in other Chapters. In the course of implementing these Rs&Rs, we would be automatically implementing the highest values of democracy as well.

It was a poet, Walt Whitman, who ultimately understood the deepest demands and promises of democracy. He said: "Did you, too, O friend, suppose democracy was only for elections, for politics, and for a party name? I say democracy is only of use there that it may pass on and come to its flower and fruits in manners, in the highest forms of interaction between men, and their beliefs—in religion, literature, colleges, and schools—democracy in all public and private life."

We have challenging work to do.

9.3.3.7 A Momentous Recent Development

A momentous development occurred since the publication of this essay. After examining a set of integrated policy recommendations, the Federal Reserve System seems to be ready to implement them—if proposed by the Congress. See, Fed response in Chap. 2.

9.3.3.8 The Most Exciting Part of the Work Ahead

The most exciting part of the work ahead in Cuba, the United States, and the African nations is that in the course of application of Concordian economics, we will automatically discover that economic justice is a new/old field of action and thought that offers progressively larger solutions to our current many-sided social, economic, political, and cultural ills.

These solutions are simple, but far from simplistic constructions of the mind. They are forms of humanism in full bloom. Why is economic justice, a construction that is integrally imbued in Concordian economics, so important? Because justice is a virtue, and any virtue can be fully exercised only if it is aided by all other virtues. Hence, to give and receive economic justice we need love. And love is, not a fickle sentiment, but the highest of all human virtues. Indeed, it is a theological virtue. "*The*

Other" to embrace in our love is not only our neighbor, and ultimately our enemy, but Mother Earth as well. If we are not that inclusive, we are going to commit ecological suicide.

9.3.4 Conclusion

Cuba, the United States, all African nations, and gradually all nations of the world have a once in a lifetime opportunity to choose among fundamentally different paths of cultural and economic development. The proposed Concordian economic path is a new path. Much is there to be said to differentiate the paths thoroughly. This presentation, supplemented perhaps by readings of other writings by this writer as well as the works of Benjamin Franklin, Henry George, Louis D., Brandeis, and Louis O. Kelso, might suffice.

We only need to stress what Dr. Gutierrez pointed out in the paragraph quoted at the beginning of this exhortation, "Communism is extreme capitalism turned upside down and inside out; even more materialistic than capitalism, and with human rights either ignored or manipulated at will by the state."

Both systems, Capitalism and Communism, are based on privileges for the few without any responsibility. Concordian economics, instead, is based on rights for all validated by correspondent responsibilities.

Go Cuba, go. Go America, go. Go Africa, go.

Be free and thus help us all to be free.

Viva Cuba Libre. Viva America free. Viva Africa free.

9.3.5 Functional Integration of Management Tasks

If we do not sell them for a cheap immediate gain, our natural resources are here. The financial resources are also there, if we properly draw on our *national* credit. Are these personal convictions perchance putting us in danger of going overboard and letting us fall into a presumed Age of Plenty? Between the scourge of scarcity and the corruption of abundance, enough is a feast. This issue deserves a moment of our attention. It is the ambitious subtext of this book to convert the Reader to a mentality in which, in Stuart Weeks's felicitous phrase, "Enough is a Feast." Between abundance and scarcity there is the golden mean of sufficiency; see, Gorga and Weeks (1997).

We fully realize that this vision is so different from our usual horizons as to require a sea change in us and in our environment. It takes a real effort of the imagination. After all, are we not supposed, obsessively, always to want more? This is the conclusion effectively reached by Paul Margulies, founder of Anthroposophy Working, while observing the dynamics of Rocco's desires. Rocco is the gangster in the movie "Key Largo" who, in response to Bogart's challenge, "I know what you want. You want more," blurts out: "Yeah, that's it, I want more."

In the scramble to divide either the fruits of scarcity or those of abundance, some acquire more than they need and others do not have enough. Enough. Is not that what we are really after? Enough is a feast. Do we not hope to have always enough of whatever we want, whatever we need? When there is enough, wants and needs become one. Of course, we are and we must remain the ones to define how much is enough for us; yet, this is not absurd Individualism. By ourselves, we will never be able to achieve much. We need to join forces with others. We even need to institutionalize our beliefs. We need to create appropriate institutions to help us practice all our virtues. We need to create institutions that become intermediaries between us and the state: Institutions that enter into combat with our own worst individual instincts as well as the worst instincts of society as a whole.

Instead, are not too many existing institutions helping the modern world to go fast forward into social disorganization? The peculiar forms of this disintegration might be totally different from one country to another, but the general trend is evident. In the North as well as in the South, in the East as well as in the West, we bemoan some aspects of contemporary life. The very roots of each one of our ancient civilizations are being threatened by forces that no longer operate from the outside in. They operate from inside our very soul.

How to stem this tide? We submit that the key tool is Organization. The Way to get there is to work together with others.

We need to create new institutions in conformity with a new principle, a principle that we like to call Functional Integration. This is a form of organization that attempts to obtain the complementary benefits of vertical and horizontal integration as well as those of total independence. The Functional Integration (FI) Model attempts to gather activities together that are already related in accordance with their function. This is a new form of organization that is designed to lead to social harmony and civic responsibility. After all, do we not all share a common goal? The Common Good. Simply put, is not this goal the achievement of a civilized society?

Figure 9.3 suggests the forms this type of integration might assume within the seafood industry. Let us conceive of all participants in the seafood industry as owning in common all the hardware: From fishing boats to seafood processing plants; from institutes for the industry to educate the consumer, and be educated by the consumer, to laboratories for the research and development of all possible means of utilization of renewable marine resources; from trucks to stores. The hardware would be under the stewardship of a group of people organized into a SuperESOP, whose Board of Directors is elected by all the owners. The owners exercise all the rights and enjoy all the privileges of owners, as the stockholders of democratic organizations do and ought to do. The SuperESOP would attend to the financing and maintenance requirements of the hardware, and independent teams of entrepreneurs would be making that hardware operational, by leasing it—from whom? from themselves. If each team organizes itself with the assistance of individual ESOPs, so much the better. The essential point is that the independence of each team is fully preserved

Fig. 9.3 Functional integration within the seafood industry

by concentrating the *operation of functions*, rather than concentrating control over people (Fig. 9.3).

The nearest equivalent to this type of social integration is a shopping mall that would be owned by all owners and employees of stores operating within the mall. This is in contrast to the conventional structure in which the malls are owned and operated by independent concerns, in which instance stores simply rent space within the mall, pay rent, and are provided with all the services that are needed in common. In this case, quite rightly, all capital gains (or losses) that accrue from the operation of the mall belong to the owners of the mall. In the FI Model, capital gains or losses accrue to owners of the hardware; and whatever profits accrue from the rental of the hardware belong only to the teams that rent the hardware. Beyond the legitimate concerns of health, safety, and public welfare, the state, or the public in general, should have no say on any of the operations of the FI Model. In contrast, the State ought to have much to say, and it does have much to say, in any form of pure vertical or horizntal integration. Indeed, for these frm we have recommended te Brandeis Rule: let firm grow **internally** as large as the market allows them to grow, but do prohibit growth by **external** purchase.

This structure might not be born full blown. It might be necessary to assemble it piece by piece. And there might be two or more SuperESOPs for each port. But, clearly, the more trust, the more cohesion, the more benefits. If, through a SuperESOP, the participants in the industry own as much of the hardware as possible, many things can be done more efficiently. At a bare minimum:

I. The SuperESOP can enforce the requirements of quality assurance to the consumer: This assurance can be provided only if the various elements of the industry collaborate with each other. Today this collaboration occurs quite rarely, and when it does it is mostly due to chance: One processor here, two fishermen there;

9.3 Appendix

II. The SuperESOP can enforce efficiency standards for the utilization of each and every piece of hardware undreamed of by individual entrepreneurs. Unnecessary duplication of equipment and even operations would cease. For instance, boats might be treated like airplanes, they would *not* be waiting for the crew to rest before they would be turned around to go fishing again. And the boats might not need to be the same as those of today. They might be smaller, faster, more efficiently operated and equipped;

III. The SuperESOP can reach efficiency standards in purchasing supplies and equipment, borrowing money, and attending to all other financing requirements of a modem business—including purchasing insurance—that individual entrepreneurs cannot obtain;

IV. The SuperESOP can set up maintenance schedules of all machinery and equipment in a way that individual entrepreneurs cannot achieve;

V. The SuperESOP can create and administer a first rate information system regarding marketing and biological data with the aim of rationalizing the capture and raising of each species as well as the timing of landings of fish, thus ensuring that temporary gluts—with their depressing effects on pricing—would no longer occur;

VI. The SuperESOP can nurture first rate research and development laboratories. Special attention could be given especially to development, thus easing the process of technology transfer from the laboratory to the industry;

VII. The SuperESOP can foster specialization of activities that small, independent, individual entrepreneurs cannot achieve. A boat owner, a fish farmer, or a seafood processor today has to be at least an expert in finances, engineering, and real estate. What do these operations have to do with catching fish, raising it, or processing it? With a SuperESOP, the boat owner, fish farmer, and the seafood processor would simply organize a team of people and devote all their time and expertise to catching the fish, raising it, or processing it. And all teams would preserve their independence at the same time. Whatever money the team that leases boats or fish farms or stores makes is its own money, its own reward.

This model of social and economic integration can be applied to any set of industrial or commercial enterprises. To name one specific example, one day it might be possible to organize along these lines commercial establishments on Main Street of any city or town in the United States or any other nation in the world. The first such SuperESOP might even be called "Main Street USA."

So far, we have dealt with largely mundane issues. Can we now elevate the discussion a notch or two? Let us think about the issues in the broadest possible terms for a moment. At the core, the issues dealt with here are not technical issues at all. They are issues of economic justice. And issues of liberty. Issues of liberty and justice for all.

We have been repeating these words for a few centuries now. And some might say that they have led to the excesses of the French Revolution and the Red Revolution. In the United States, those excesses are parodied in the excesses of the "Age of

Entitlements." The way to avoid all such excesses is not to leave the content of the expression "liberty and justice for all" to the imagination, but to define it precisely. The economic content of that expression can be defined by these four rights: 1. The right of access to land and natural resources; 2. The right of access to national credit; 3. The right to own the fruits of one's labor; and, 4. The right to protect the blessings of one 's wealth.

And then these rights have to be anchored to the reality outside us as well as to the reality inside us. As believers, we reserve the right to speak of God, but we fully accept the wish of others who might want to speak of Nature or Chance. For us, the most fundamental proposition to consider is this: To think that God would not provide for all his children is blasphemy. For others who might prefer to speak in secular terms, we would like to submit the following equivalent reasoning: To think that Nature or Chance would not provide for all their children is contrary to the factual propositions that Nature is bountiful and Chance is infinite.

Leaving the reality outside us well alone, we can now attempt to relate our discussion to the reality within us, by asking: In practical terms, what is the sin that all of us commit? We submit that, generally, every day, we sin against all virtues. We sin against the four cardinal virtues, because we lack prudence, justice, temperance, and fortitude. We sin against the three intellectual virtues, because we lack wisdom, science, and understanding. We sin against the three theological virtues, because we lack hope, faith, and, last but most, love.

Yes, if we want the renewal of our fisheries and the renewal of our entire practice of economic growth, we must be quite serious about the practice of our virtues. Our virtues, as St. Thomas Aquinas said, are "the peak of power."

References

Altenburger, S. (2022, December 21). How a federal rule is ruining our fleet and port in one generation. *Gloucester Daily Times*. Available at https://www.gloucestertimes.com/news/fishing_industry_news/commentary-how-a-federal-rule-is-ruining-our-fleet-and-port-in-one-generation/article_603a6436-75b6-11ed-958c-07ba7a5ee136.html. Accessed December 13, 2023.

Blinder, A. (1999, September 18). Quoted in "Students seek some reality amid the math of economics" by Michael M. Weinstein. *The New York Times*, pp. A17, A19.

Conti-Brown, P. (2016). *The power and independence of the Federal Reserve*. Princeton University Press.

Gorga, C. (2005, November 12). Fish and future. Gloucester Daily Times, My View. Reprinted in to My Polis, pp. 27–29. Also available at https://fisherynation.com/fish-future. Accessed December 14, 2023.

Gorga, C. (2008a). Economics for physicists and ecologists. *Transactions on Advanced Research, 4*(1), 6–9.

Gorga, C. (2008). *To my Polis—with love*. The Somist Institute.

Gorga, C. (2018). Economics for physicists and ecologists. *Mother Pelican A Journal of Solidarity and Sustainability, 14*(3). Available at: https://www.pelicanweb.org/solisustv14n03page5.html. Accessed on October 21, 2023.

References

Gorga, C. (2021a, May 11). Toward economic, ecological, and human interdependence. *OpEd News*. Available at Toward Economic, Ecological, and Human Interdependence | OpEd News. Accessed on October 21, 2023.

Gorga, C. (2021b, February 18). Project financial independence. *Talkmarkets*. Available at https://talkmarkets.com/content/project-financial-independence?post=298689. Accessed on October 21, 2023.

Gorga, C. (2021c, September 6). Fiscal policy: Present and future. *Econintersect*. Available at Fiscal policy: Present and future. Accessed December 13, 2023.

Gorga, C., & Ronsivalli, L. J. (1988). *Quality assurance of seafood*. Van Nostrand Reinhold.

Gorga, C., & Weeks, S. B. (1997). Fisheries renewal: A renewal of the soul of business. *Catholic Social Science Review, 2*, 145–161. Available at https://www.pdcnet.org/cssr/content/cssr_1997_0002_0145_0161. Accessed on November 10, 2023

Kelso, L. O. (1957). Karl Marx: The almost capitalist. *American Bar Association Journal, 43*(235–238), 275–279.

King, L. M. K. (2016). *The end of Alchemy: Money, banking, and the future of the global economy*. Norton.

Koch, C. G. (2015). *Good profit: How creating value for others built one of the world's most successful companies*. Penguin Random House.

Leonard, A. (2023). Can we be humane in the face of horror? What is needed to stop violent cycles? *Classical Wisdom*. Available at https://classicalwisdom.substack.com/can-we-be-humane-in-the-face-of-horror?utm_source=substack&utm_medium=email. Accessed on October 23, 2023.

Otto, P., & Struben, J. (2004). Gloucester fisher: Insights from a group modeling intervention. *System Dynamics Review*, 287–312.

Pilkington, P. (2014, November 9). Authoritative arguments in economics. *Econintersect Blog*.

Smith, A. (1776). *The wealth of nations*. Modern (Cannan) Library edition with the fore ward by Max Lerner. New York, N.Y.

Soldo, N. (2023). Niccolo's L'Avventura. Niccolo Soldo from Fisted by Foucault, October 23. Available at https://mail.google.com/mail/u/0/#inbox/FMfcgzGwHLmHjbdXgRQjLdXVFcTQBxWM. Accessed October 24, 2023.

Chapter 10
Two Published and Two Unpublishable (?) Urban Plans

Abstract In this Chapter we are going to give a fast look at four urban plans: The outline of two such plans has already been published; two more plans offer such a futuristic vision for our cities and towns that their details might not be published in the foreseeable future. The Chapter also introduces a daring plan for the use of marine water to save perhaps two-thirds of the precious fresh water supply. This plan was conceived by my nephew Giovanni Papa.

10.1 Introduction

My beloved Professor Vittorio de Caprariis discouraged me from pursuing an Academic career because I "would be 40—and still unsettled."

Here I am at 88 still unsettled.

In any case, my non-academic life showed me a couple of interesting experiences. I started my non-academic career in Urban Planning, where I discovered that urban professionals were highly involved with physical issues but neglected the economic aspects of life.

The reverse did I find in my subsequent War on Poverty: no interest in the physical aspects of a community.

As I said in the Acknowledgments to *My Polis*, "John D. Atwood and L. Denton Crews (my "bosses") must have had faith in me at first sight. They hired me without prior experience. And they allowed me to plunge into the mystic worlds of urban planning and community development. The money they paid was not too much; but the intellectual and moral rewards could have not been higher."

In any case, here are "my" programs in Urban Planning.

10.2 First Published One

In my study of Moses Jubilee, I encountered the lost practice of rotating crops in order to leave one plot of land vacant every seven years; see, Gorga (2009). The practice left the land idle "naturally" to recover her productive capacity. Having lost this practice, what have we replaced it with? We have replaced it with the practice of force-feeding the land with fertilizers and pesticides.

This is a financial boon for Big Corporations, but what is the Land left with? The land is left with the need to dispose of those fertilizers once they have accomplished their desired task.

It is this practice that is gradually polluting our underground aquifers, and rivers. The ocean is left to absorb the risk of total defilement. But for how long?

Should not ecologists hop on solutions to this long-term threat to humanity? Waiting for all proper scientific analyses, the gist of the plan is this; let us go back to the old practice of rotating crop production every seven years, No fertilizers; no pesticides.

This is a plea more than a plan that I have issued in more than one of my writings.

I know that the hardest thing for a rational mind is to admit error. Hence the default preference is to cover up errors through rationalizations. But, here is the disposition of a present case. One can ultimately justify an error committed in the past because of ignorance of its effect. One cannot rationalize an error committed in the present. Such a stance is simply deeply irrational.

We must develop the courage to admit our errors.

10.3 Second Published One

Waging my War on Poverty, I peeked into the physical aspects of my community and, in collaboration with a large number of political, business, and civic leaders, I designed a set of plans to render my city a (more) lovely pedestrian place; see, Gorga (2008). The Reader must know a little bit about my community: Gloucester is the first fishing port in the nation; Gloucester is a community in which the vision of a farsighted Park Commissioner, George Stacy, was realized in 1925, soon after the three hundredth celebration of the birth of Gloucester. Houses were removed from the edge of the outer harbor, whereby a splendid view of the ocean was opened up, and the Stacy Boulevard Esplanade was created. Young people, old people, people with dogs, people without dogs thread it year round. Joe Garland, a prominent Gloucester historian, made me feel right at home by making me notice that Gloucester Harbor is a grand reminder of the Gulf of Naples.

A personal note is perhaps appropriate here. As I wrote in the Introduction "*To My Polis—with Love*" (2008), "I am a pilgrim: I go where my Lord leads me. More modestly, most days, I consider myself an immigrant. That is the reason why I am especially sensitive to place, my geographic place, and my place in society—my polis. Unlike indigenous people (have there ever been such people? Are we not all and always migrants?), I have since childhood been blessed and cursed with the need to move from one society to the next. One day I landed in Gloucester, Massachusetts, USA, and I set roots here." During the last few years, I surprise myself repeating, "I love every inch of Gloucester." Or, even more appropriately. "God, it is good to be here."

The details of the physical designs to render Gloucester a pedestrian city can be gathered from pages 32–80 and 319–360 of *To My Polis—With Love* (2008).

In compensation for the lack of presentation of the necessary details, the Reader will find there—among many other plots and plans—the bare bones of a possible application to the downtown of the new form of business organization, the Functional Integration of Management Tasks (pp. 120–124) that was treated earlier in this book. Rather than vertical and/or horizontal integration of economic activities, the suggestion is to let the various functions determine the modes of aggregation of business activities. A whole range of possibilities open up to view: If at least a portion of the downtown is owned in common, all sorts of expenses that are sheer duplication of efforts could be aggregated under one administration. Merchants would concentrate their energies on merchandizing efforts (pp. 46–50). Would it not be easier for them to find a loan or any variety of insurance coverage? Would they not find it easier to address politicians and bureaucrats?

One possibility for the downtown could then be to develop the second and third story of buildings either as large department stores or as a hotel. Overlooking the harbor how much would tourists be willing to pay to spend a few hours there?

Another grand opportunity might be to cover Main Street with a canvass to protect pedestrians from such inclement weather as winter snow storms and summer downpours.

10.4 A First Unpublishable (?) Plan

The bicentennial of our nation, 1976, came along and found me in private consulting mode. The forthcoming celebration was dominated by the vision of rows and rows of cars entering Gloucester, ambulating throughout all our streets in search of a parking spot, and finding none, cars could be seen turning South by Route 128. My concern for such unfortunate visitors recommended a solution: Let us build a sizeable parking lot at the entrance of the city and move people downtown through shuttle buses. This solution I suggested to a few regional and state authorities. The solution did not develop legs, perhaps because people did not flood Gloucester. Does this solution for outsiders coming in apply to any (many?) community on earth?

10.5 A Second Unpublishable (?) Plan

This proposal is in two parts.

Part One. Let us be concerned, not with the people coming in, but the people residing in our crowded cities. Preface. Urban, sorry "ecological" programming, has been controlled by The Car during the last century; perhaps people will be wise enough *to control* The Car during this still young century. Let us make our cities and towns again (!) pedestrian environments: the solution is to build parking lots at the edge of our cities and towns; let us people use their cars for long-distance travel between cities; let us use "Ubers," taxis, and public transportation for in-town short trips; let merchants deliver goods to clients (via push carts, perhaps?)

Some cities might even dare to restore the ancient glory that existed prior to the wrecking ball of Urban Renewal in the United States.

Are ecologists concerned with the exhaustion of oil and fossil fuels—and obnoxious residuals of their use? To make our cities and towns *pedestrian again* is the "final" solution. I am astonished that we are consuming oil and gas at great sufferance to the environment, even when such products should be wisely preserved to produce medicines for an extended future.

This might be an opportune moment to bring forward another clear set of relationships between ecology and economics. Cars emit gases that upset weather conditions. Upset weather conditions upset crop production. Upset crop production affects the costs of production and prices of consumer products. Prices of consumer products affect consumer habits. This is not a made up chain of events but a summary of the long journey between production of oil in Spain and consumption of pizza in Durham, N.C. See, e.g., Nerkar (2023).

Part Two. Megalopolises such as New York and Mexico City did not grow "naturally" but by annexation of one neighborhood after another. Can we reverse the process? Do we have the courage to reverse our errors?

Let us determine the size of each city by pedestrian standards. Along the separation of one circle from another, let us build parking lots and trees to restore our breathing air and to save fuels.

Let us do it.

Galaxies do it.

Implicit Part Three. The "Corporation," whether a municipal or private financial corporation, is not a "natural" unmanageable monster. As Louis D. Brandeis well taught us, the Corporation is a *creature of the State*. With the application of Concordian economics, we are going to fully control the Corporation—in ten years, or less. And The State as well.

The Corporation will be controlled *from within* through the widespread use of Employee Stock Ownership Plans (ESOPs). People who work for *their* corporations, and with so much financial independence to stand on their two feet, will not tolerate any untoward action by the management. Thus the Corporation will be controlled *from within*. Employees/Owners will be Management.

The Corporation will be controlled *from without* through a fearless application of the Brandeis Rule.

Somists will want to be in charge of their municipal affairs, won't they? Will they not choose to live in a pedestrian city? In the same ten years, we shall curb the insatiable appetite of The State as well. Social justice, with its justification of Entitlements–"rights" without responsibilities–will be abated from without: no new Entitlement Program will be justified. The appetite of The State will be curbed from within as well, because an increasing number of people will not need a hand-out. Economic Justice will be triumphant.

10.6 And then… A Proposal by My Nephew Gianni Papa to Use Marine Water

Hard to believe it but fresh water, the world over, is becoming more precious than gold: This report, issued in April 2014, stated that **already** "Over the past 10 years, the S&P 500 Global Water index has outperformed the bellwether gold and energy indices." And it added, "In fact, water outperformed the stock market in the same period." Scarier still, there is talk of "water wars" as a means to apportion scarce fresh water supplies in many parts of the world. Even in the West of the United States water tables are getting dangerously low.

Only 2.5% of the water available in the world is fresh, and only a portion of that is drinkable.

And yet we misuse a good three quarters of our fresh water supply. In this presentation, I will outline a set of mechanisms conceived by my nephew through which we can save as much precious fresh water as possible. Gianni estimates we can save as much as 2/3 of available drinkable water by 2050.

10.7 The Proposal

The proposal is remarkably simple in its broad outline: Let us use marine water to take care of all those current uses for which fresh water is not essential. Much water is used to flush toilets, this amount is estimated to be nearly a quarter of our total daily water consumption in most parts of the world: This water ought to be nearly all replaced with marine water.

Much water is used to wash floors of factories and homes; it is estimated that this use absorbs up to 15–25 L of water per clean floor: This supply ought to be replaced with marine water.

Because of a great variety of applications, data on water consumption in the food, animal husbandry, and paint industry, water to wash linens and clothes in homes and hospitals, and the like are hard to come by. If necessary, a rough estimate can be obtained through this formula:

$$SUWC = DWC - (TWC + WFWC)$$

where
SUWC is Sundry Uses of Water Consumption
DWC is Drinking Water Consumption
TWC is Toilet Water Consumption
WFWC is Washing Floors Water Consumption.

10.7.1 Component Parts of the Mechanical System

The component parts of the mechanical system are: 1. Hydraulic pumps to siphon marine water from the ocean to storage tanks; 2. Saltwater corrosion-resistant tanks to be located in the highest sections of cities and towns; and 3. Construction of a duplicate local water pipe system to hold and dispense salt water for uses that do not require fresh water.

A water meter can be installed in each household and each establishment to charge for the cost of individual consumption.

Such meters will at the same time perform the task of producing accurate measurements of saltwater consumption.

10.7.2 A Field of Possible Innovations

Do we really know the mechanism used by trees to continuously siphon moisture from the roots to the highest leaf? If we do, can we duplicate the driving force of transpiration?

Would that mechanism offer significant cost savings over traditional mechanical pumping mechanism through which water is transferred from a lower to a higher point?

If we do not know and cannot possibly duplicate the mechanism used by trees, a reverse mechanism might be worth exploring:

Rather than pump the marine water upstream, can water be siphoned upwards through a vacuum apparatus? Learning perhaps from the trees, hydraulic pumps might be used only once: Once the air is taken out of the pipes, marine water will flow to the highest point necessary. And then the pump might be used elsewhere.

10.7.3 Broad Cost Estimates

For obvious reasons, cost estimates will vary from country to country.

Initial cost estimates to develop a prototype system along the lines outlined here are likely to be rather high. They can be easily estimated once the social, economic, and political will to build such a system becomes apparent.

The presentation of such cost estimates has to take two considerations into account: Costs of the proposed system will decrease over time—while the costs of obtaining fresh water supplies are definitely going to increase at the same time.

Engineering estimates have to take this dynamic into full account.

10.7.4 Who Will Be the First to Create Such a System?

Saudi Arabia is likely to be the first developer of such a system.

Saudi Arabia, as is well known, is currently importing fresh water from distant glaciers to its homeland.

Comparative cost estimates are likely to encourage a rather immediate application of this proposal.

10.8 Our Survival

Once this program of action is widely discussed, human ingenuity will intervene to make the program financially feasible.

Once the financial feasibility is demonstrated, the political will to create such a system is going to grow exponentially.

Our survival is likely to depend on it.

References

Gorga, C. (2008). *To my polis—with love*. The Somist Institute.
Gorga, C. (2009). The economics of jubilation—blinking Adam's fallacy away. *Social Science Research Network (SSRN)*, October 15. Available at the economics of jubilation—blinking Adam's fallacy away by carmine Gorga: SSRN.
Gorga, C., & Weeks, S. B. (1997). Fisheries renewal: A renewal of the soul of business. *Catholic Social Science Renewable, 2*(145–161). Available at https://www.pdcnet.org/cssr/content/cssr_1997_0002_0145_0161. Accessed 10 November 2023.
Gorga, C. (2017a, June 6). Why wall street ought to favor a gradual decline in the cost of land. *Talk-Markets*. Available at https://talkmarkets.com/content/real-estate--reits/why-wall-street-ought-to-favor-a-gradual-decline-in-the-cost-of-land?post=137645. Accessed 14 December 2023.

Gorga, C. (2017b, April 21). Why countries shouldn't sell their natural resources to foreigners. *TalkMarkets*. Available at https://talkmarkets.com/content/why-countries-shouldnt-sell-their-natural-resources-to-foreigners?post=132343. Accessed 14 December 2023.

Gorga, C. (2021d, September 6). Rebuild the downtown through racial harmony. *Econintresect*. Available at https://econintersect.com/?s=Rebuild+the+Downtown. Accessed 14 December 2023.

Gorga, C. (2021b, September 6). A deeper cultural shift to meet the coronavirus challenge. *Econintersect*. Available at https://econintersect.com/pages/opinion/opinion.php/post/202012100241. Accessed 14 December 2023.

Gorga, C. (2021a, September 6). Coronavirus and economic interdependence. *EconIntersect*. Available at https://econintersect.com/pages/opinion/opinion.php/post/202004260302. Accessed on 21 October 2023.

Gorga, C. (2021c, September 6). A few issues about fluoridation. *EconIntrsect*. Available at https://econintersect.com/pages/opinion/opinion.php/post/201905310251. Accessed 14 December 2023.

Nerkar, S. (2023). Why olive oil is so expensive right now. *New York Times,* October 22, Section a, page 1. Available at https://www.nytimes.com/2023/10/22/business/olive-oil-price.html. Accessed 23 October 2023.

Part IV
Human Interdependence

Chapter 11
Ethics in Concordian Economics

Abstract Ethics enters the structure of Concordian economics at three crucial stages, not surreptitiously in the background, but explicitly and forcefully. Ethics is a fundamental construct of the theory of distribution of ownership rights and this theory lies at the very core of Concordian economic theory. Next stage: Concordian economic policy is guided by the theory of economic justice. Ethics, finally, enters into Concordian economics in the analysis of daily practices, with emphasis on the play between economic rights and economic responsibilities and focus on the methods of accumulation of capital. Ethics is the conduct that keeps everting in harmonic relationship with everything else.

11.1 Introduction

Ethics does not appear in mainstream economics. A long historcal traditon has led econmists to this pass. Today, eonomists are happy to say that they eschew matters of ethics because they follow the dictates of a "pure" science; because they are not controLlled by "value" judgments. Come to think of it, is modern economics "valueless"?

Ethics does appear explicitly at three crucial stages of the structure of Concordian economics; see, Gorga (2012). Ethics is inherent in the theory of distribution of ownership rights over financial as well as real resources and this theory is no longer an afterthought to be dealt with at some mythical ideal future state of the economic system, but is located as the core of the economic process: Hence, no action is ever recognized in Concordian economics that does not involve the full force of the theory of distribution of *values* of ownership rights. In Concordian economics, ethics also enters the economic discourse at the moment of transition from economic theory to the formulation of economic policy: Economic policy is no longer rooted into the political and ideological whims of the moment; economic policy is guided by the age-old theory of economic justice. Ethics, finally, enters into Concordian economics in the analysis of daily practices of economic agents who are endowed with the armor of economic rights and responsibilities and focuses its attention on the processes of accumulation of capital.

Accordingly, the paper is divided into three parts.

Part I deals with ethics in Concordian economic theory. Part II deals with ethics in Concordian economic policy. And Part III deals with ethics in Concordian economic practices.

11.2 Ethics in Concordian Economic Theory

Concordian economic theory has its roots into the mathematical and logical consequences of inserting an age-old word, Hoarding, into the structure of Keynes' model of the economic system, Keynes (1936: 63). This is the model on which all mainstream, Austrian, and even heterodox theory is built. The initial result of these operations, a result that can be easily duplicated by any willing researcher, is the transformation of the structure of that model, which, in honor of the genius of Keynes, I have named the Revised Keynes Model. A cautionary word: substantively, the two models represent entirely different intellectual worlds.

Hoarding is Saving defined as all non-productive wealth.

Prior to its full presentation in Gorga (2002, 2009a, 2009b), the new model was reported in Gorga (1982). It was republished with some explanatory notes in Gorga (2008a, 2008b), and is reproduced with minor editorial changes and an addendum—on ethics and the theory of distribution of ownership rights—in the following paragraphs, which, it is worth emphasizing, contain statements that are as true today as they were in 1982 or 2008.

The current crisis in economic affairs must be due to many factors. But in a fundamental sense it is due to structural and conceptual weaknesses contained in Keynes' model of the economic system.

The proposition that $S = I$ is **not** an equivalence, as Keynes stated at page 63 and as it must be for it to be formally valid relationship.[1] The terms are neither reflexive nor symmetric nor transitive. Saving has the potential of assuming 100,000 meanings. And, by necessity, so does Investment. Consumption means spending; but in contemporary economics this meaning is arbitrarily cut off at spending on consumer goods.

Keynes' model must be revised.

Manipulating the original model, one obtains:

$$\text{Income} = \text{Saving} + \text{Consumption} \quad (11.1)$$

---

[1] Using the looking glass of $S = I$, unable to distinguish saving from investment, the economics profession has fallen through the rabbit hole of "Adam Smith's Fallacy." This is the assumption that private greed turns out to be public good. This is a world in which—as today's events confirm and Keynes pointed out—"nothing is clear and everything is possible."

11.2 Ethics in Concordian Economic Theory

$$\text{Investment} = \text{Income} - \text{Saving} \quad (11.2)$$

$$\text{Investment} = \text{Consumption}. \quad (11.3)$$

The meaning of terms is different in this model. *Saving* means all nonproductive wealth. This term becomes clearer if it is substituted with the word "Hoarding."[2] *Investment* means all productive wealth. And *Consumption* means any expenditure of money (or other wealth).

Through detailed logico-mathematical reasoning,[3] the relationship between Saving (or better, Hoarding) and Investment is changed from equality to complementarity.

Equation (11.3) becomes a formally valid equivalence by inserting in it the theory of Distribution, and substituting the word Investment with its old meaning of Production. One thus obtains:

$$\text{Production} \leftrightarrow \text{Distribution} \leftrightarrow \text{Consumption}$$

Graphically, this equivalence can be represented as in Fig. 1 Chap. 1.

For the full unfolding of this model into the structure of Concordian economic theory, see *The Economic Process: An Instantaneous Non-Newtonian Picture* (2002, 2009) and "The Economics of Jubilation: Blinking Adam's Fallacy Away" in Tavidze (2010, Chap. 1).

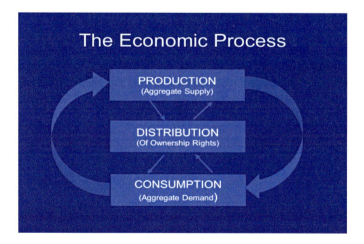

Fig. 11.1 The Economic Process

---

[2] Through the looking glass of Hoarding, the world looks totally different. Strangely, later, to my unending surprise I had to discover that that is the lens constantly used from Moses, through Jesus of the Parable of the Talents, to Locke. Adam Smith offered a discontinuity in this millennial tradition.

[3] *EP*: 3–137.

11.2.1 An Addendum on Ethics and the Theory of Distribution of the Values of Ownership Rights

Perhaps the relationship between ethics and the theory of distribution ought to be made more explicitly clear. Even though ethics enters into economics at each and every moment of its development, the necessary presence of ethics is nowhere as clear as in the distribution of ownership rights. In Part III we shall make this relation emphatically clear; there we shall also introduce the fundamental distinction between ownership of property rights and ownership of economic rights; see, Gorga (1999). For the time being suffice it to say that ethics in economics converges into the application of the theory of distribution of ownership rights and diffuses from there into every corner of daily practices of economics.

When the producer creates real wealth, since the law abhors a vacuum, an ownership right is automatically created; and, since the law is supposed to be rooted in ethics, the values of ownership rights are represented by financial instruments that can be newly created by financiers and are supposed to be created in accordance with the real value of the wealth created. Let us specify: the producer creates a chair worth $200; the value of the corresponding ownership right ought to be worth $200. The financial note to denote ownership of this title ought also to be worth $200. This is the type of values among economic, financial, and legal relationships that the theory of creation of ownership rights obliges us to establish. In simplified fashion, this is how the values of the economic process are created and accounted for at each moment in time. The entrepreneur sets up a joint production with the accountant, the lawyer, and the financier. The financier transforms the static legal note of ownership into a transferable financial instrument.

This is how values of ownership rights are created in theory: how are they distributed? Following customary practical applications of the theory of economic justice, the value of the newly created real wealth and newly created financial instruments is automatically apportioned among the present owners of existing wealth. In Part III we shall enter more deeply into this process by distinguishing property rights from economic rights.

Nor does the story end there. With every market exchange, there is an invisible transfer of ownership rights among buyers and sellers: ownership rights to goods and services are transferred from producers to consumers, and money—or other financial instruments representing ownership of financial wealth—is transferred from consumers to producers.

These legal, financial, and economic relationships are analytically taken into account in the theory of Concordian economics; hence, one can easily observe whether these relationships are carried forward in an ethical or unethical manner. The legal and financial accounting is one thing; the judgment of the ethics of the operations is necessarily another level of abstraction. Yet, the ethical judgment is neither disjointed nor arbitrary: it is synchronous and objective.

11.3 Ethics in Concordian Economic Policy

In Concordian economics each and every policy and each and every activity is advanced and judged in accordance with the dictates of the age-old construction of the theory of economic justice, a theory that today is obscured by the prevalence of the undefined and undefinable doctrine of Social Justice. Interestingly, while nearly everyone talks of Social Justice these days, almost no one talks of economic justice.

Needless to say, this dichotomy is a synthetic manifestation of a major dysfunction in economic policy today—worldwide.

But why is Social Justice undefined and undefinable? Long story. Its fundamental flaw is the disjunction of rights from responsibilities. Each and every program of Social Justice wallows in the la-la land of the pursuit of happiness—happiness bought on the cheap. Social Justice attributes rights to some and responsibilities to others.

It is the "individual" person who has all the rights—and his and her rights are multiplying daily nowadays; the "government" has all the responsibilities.

In a robust program of economic justice, an economic policy program advocated by Concordian economics, rights and responsibilities are located in the same economic entity—constantly.

(A revelation has occurred to me just at this writing: No wonder feeble minds with weak spines, exposed to Concordian economics, fade away like comets; while sturdy minds, once attracted into the orbit of Concordian economics, stay with it forever, forever contributing and forever wanting to know more about it.)

The structure of the theory of economic justice, which, although not practiced, can still be read in the documents of the Catholic Church, was presented in Gorga (2007) and is reproduced in the following paragraphs with two additions: one concerns the enlarging, whenever necessary, the focus of observation from the Church to Concordian economics and to society as a whole; the other concerns making explicit the relationship between Concordian economic theory and Concordian economic policy.

Underlying the millenarian doctrine of economic justice is the Aristotelian/Thomistic division of justice into political and economic justice. The principles of distributive and commutative ("exchange") justice are part of the Church's ancestral patrimony. Since Rerum Novarum (# 34 and 46), the Church has been adding to them the plank of participative justice, offering thus a full-fledged theory of economic justice.

The three planks of the theory of economic justice are related to the tripartite division of classical economics into production, distribution, and consumption. Simply, people who participate in production are empowered to participate in the distribution of wealth; and owners are free to exchange their share for other goods and services, invest it anew in the process of wealth creation, consume it—or give it to charitable purposes.

Anchored in morality, the theory of economic justice establishes the rules, the invisible threads—peculiar to each culture and age—that connect us by mutual rights and responsibilities (RN# 2, 10, 12, 13, 14, 15, 25, 37, 53, 58). These rules transform wealth from a material entity into a force that affects the quality of life of people and society, because property is indissolubly linked to life and liberty.

11.4 The Content of Economic Justice

The Doctors of the Church defined the principles of distributive and commutative justice. They left the plank of participative justice unspoken, for reasons to become apparent forthwith.

Participative Justice. Owning a farm was for ages the main way to participate in economic life; and, since in the Jewish, Greek, Roman, Christian, and Muslim tradition most studies were done by and for landowners, the issue of participative justice did not arise early on. Landowners did not necessarily till the land—just as stockholders do not necessarily sit at the assembly line. Today over the centuries, landowners established relationships with tenants, who did the tilling and received an agreed-upon proportion of the product. The dispossessed had a right of access to the commons, through which they became landowners in fact, if not in title.

With the enclosure of the commons, the economic condition of Europe changed radically. And the need to address issues of participative justice eventually became explicit because, as Pope John Paul II maintained in *Centesimus Annus* (# 33–35), either people and nations participate in the economic process or they are marginalized—are made poor and placed at the margins of society.

One participates in an enterprise through sole proprietorship, partnership, membership in a cooperative, or holding stock in an incorporated business. These are forms of private enterprise traditionally fostered by the Church and acknowledged by society at large.

Workers do not participate in the life of the corporation for which they work because, legally, they are outside contractors: They offer their labor services and receive wages. The traditional support of the Church and society at large for unions is due to the recognition that labor unions tend to equalize the relationship between the individual worker and the powerful combines that have been formed during the last two centuries. But unions do not provide final protection. Hence the challenge to transform human beings into owners, launched by Leo XIII (*Rerum Novarum* # 46), represents the most living and vital portion of the Church—and society at large—moral engagement with the socio-economic structures of contemporary society.

Distributive Justice. Participation in production is not enough. Issues of fairness in the distribution of income and wealth also need to be addressed. Rooted in the Jewish tradition of the jubilee, the doctrine of distributive justice spans the arch from consideration of grace from overpowering financial debt to perennial vigilance against monopolies. The keystone in the construction of distributive justice during the Middle Ages was the status of economic "superfluities" as legally belonging to the poor. The Church collected the surplus and made it available to the poor. No questions asked—urged St. John Chrysostom.

Commutative Justice. The definition of just price as any competitive price, first reached by the Doctors of the Church, forms the foundation of commutative justice. The doctrine covers condemnation of practices that run contrary to doctrine as well as encouragement of practices that foster competition in the market. Usury, defined as the exchange of money loaned for excessive interest payments, an issue very much alive in the Muslim tradition, used to be a primary target of the moral wrath of the Church and society at large.[4] No space was left open to chance—hence the practice of guilds as administrators of fair prices, quantity, and quality was wholeheartedly embraced by the Church and society at large. In commutative justice one finds the moral justification for much contemporary anti-trust legislation.

The attentive reader will have noticed the self-similarity of the structure of the economic process and the structure of economic justice. There is a one-to-one correspondence between participative justice and production; distributive justice and distribution of ownership rights; commutative justice and consumption or expenditure of financial resources. One looks at the world of economics from the point of view economic theory, the other looks at the world of economics from the point of view of economic policy.

This is the structure of economic justice in bare bones: Does an economic activity—or more generally, an economic policy—offer fair participation in production, distribution, and exchange of wealth? Then it is just. Technically, if prices of factors of production are set unfairly high, participation becomes prohibitive; if excessive values are distributed to some, these factors become overpriced and others underpriced; then the basis for objective evaluation of fair prices in the exchange of wealth vanishes. Adumbrated in these positions is the reality that unfair prices do not lead to efficiency.

11.5 Justice and Charity

Through comprehensive application of the theory of economic justice, Concordian economics treats all members of society alike and, by protecting everyone, protects especially the poor who are otherwise abandoned to themselves and absent from the table where vital decisions are taken by the powerful and the efficient. This effect suggests the need for a clear distinction.

The call for justice is not a call for charity. While justice, according to St. Thomas Aquinas, exercises a practical (cardinal) virtue, charity exercises a theological virtue. The need for charity generally signals a failure of justice. More, in *Quadragesimo Anno* (# 4) Pope Pius XI issued a firm injunction against using charity"to veil the violation of justice."

Indeed, the full exercise of economic justice is essential to the success of charity. Only if its need is rather miniscule, the call for economic charity can be fulfilled.

---

[4] President Nixon broke with that tradition in 1971.

We are not saints. Charity, high as it is in the moral sphere, is a last resort in the economic sphere.

11.6 Ethics in Concordian Economic Practices

Each and every action in Concordian economics is judged in accordance with the following mental apparatus, which was presented in Gorga (2009a, 2009b) and is reproduced in the following paragraphs.

11.7 Lack of an Existing Tool Kit

"High" mainstream economic theory is silent on the *practices* (!) of economics. This neglect is not due to chance; rather, it is due to the assumption that, since economic practices are determined by society at large and are supposedly controlled by allied social disciplines, they lie outside the economist's field of expertise. Indeed, having abandoned the field to lawyers, and ethicists, and philosophers, and sociologists, and political scientists, mainstream economists have become passive takers of a proposition that lies at the very core of the issue. This is the proposition that present ownership rights provide practical rules for the distribution of future ownership rights. The proposition has long legs, because it determines the pattern of future distribution of income and wealth. Economists observe every day the manifold negative consequences of this belief, but feel powerless to even address the issues. This is another juncture at which, by taking themselves out of the discussion, economists are threatening to make economics a socially irrelevant discipline.

To regain their power, economists have only to look at it as an economic, rather than a legal, political, or moral issue. If they do that, they discover that their assumptions are faulty. The error is elementary. The reasoning is circular. In order to enter and to break this circular form of argumentation, namely that present property rights determine future property rights, economists need to remember that property rights are pieces of paper: A piece of paper does not—and cannot—create real wealth. It is not even the exercise of property rights that creates real wealth. Property rights are a bundle of rights that link human beings to things. Their current owners may wish as hard as they can, it is not in the nature of property rights to create wealth.

It is not the use of property rights, but the use of property—namely, the use of real goods and services—that creates new wealth. The distinction is fundamental. The discussion is shifted away from the abstract legal field on to a concrete field. The discussion is focused on the observation of the economic reality. The use of real goods and services to create new wealth is infused, not by property rights, but by the exercise of economic power. To an economic power corresponds an economic right. As specified below, temporally, logically, economically, and legally, economic rights precede property rights. Economic rights are the generators, the fathers and the mothers, of property rights. The nature of economic rights becomes clear when the two rights, economic rights and property rights, are observed as separate and distinct entities, and then both rights are placed in contraposition with entitlements. The three terms are often used as synonyms. They are not. As specified in Gorga (1999).

> First, the content of these three entities is different. The object of property rights are *marketable things*, tangible or intangible things such as material goods and services. The object of entitlements are *human needs*, from food to shelter to health. The object of economic rights are *economic needs*. Second, the legal form of these three entities is different. Property rights are *concrete legal* titles over existing wealth; economic rights are *abstract legal* claims over future wealth; and entitlements are *moral* claims on wealth that legally belongs to others. Finally, the quantity that they measure is variable. While both property rights and entitlements relate to existing wealth, and therefore a necessarily finite quantity, economic rights relate to future wealth, an unknown and elastic—if not a potentially infinite—quantity.

Economically, and consequently legally, real wealth is created by the exercise of economic rights—indeed, economic rights and economic responsibilities, as we shall see. Hence economists are fully entitled to extend their competence to the field of economic rights and economic responsibilities. Economists will discover that the field is wholly within their range of expertise and responsibility. At the end of this journey, economists shall be able to offer to lawyers, ethicists, and philosophers, as well as political scientists and politicians, this proposition: Future ownership rights are determined, not by property rights, but by economic rights—indeed, they are determined by economic rights and economic responsibilities. Thus the closed circuit that at present imprisons economic theory, the proposition that property rights beget property rights, is broken. Economists are in charge of economic issues.

11.8 New Tools to Control Economic Practices

The transmission belt that carries principles of economic justice into the complexity of modern economic life, and shapes objective guidelines for the formulation and evaluation of just economic policies is the presence of economic rights and economic responsibilities (ERs&ERs), both lodged in the same person at the same time. These two conditions need to be clarified. Economic rights and responsibilities need to be lodged into the same person, otherwise one does not follow an economic discourse in which everything is strictly related to everything else; rather, one follows escapism: If my father, my uncle, or the state is responsible for my welfare, we are lost, as Keynes used to say, "in a haze where nothing is clear and everything is possible" Keynes (1936: 292). The second condition is equally important. Economic rights are rooted, not in abstract morality, but in our own concrete economic responsibilities; cf., Gorga (1999).

ERs&ERs come forward in response to the well-known requirements of the factors of production identified by Classical economists as land, capital, and labor—with the addition of a modern distinction between financial and physical capital. (This is a Schumpeterian perspective.) Guided by these economic needs, our focus of attention is on the satisfaction of the plank of participative justice; successive iterations that are mostly skipped in this presentation would reveal that the same rights and responsibilities satisfy also the requirements of the planks of distributive justice and commutative justice. A minimal set of economic rights and corresponding responsibilities is as follows:

1. *We all have the right of access to land and natural resources.* This is a natural right. It belongs to us just in virtue of our humanness. Land and natural resources are our original commons. They belong to us all. This is an essential right, because without the possibility of exercising it, we are deprived of the possibility of participating in the economic process. And without this participation, we are marginalized; we are made dependent on the good will of others. The most direct way of securing this right in the complexity of the modern world is neither through squatting nor through expropriation; rather, it is through the exercise of **the responsibility to pay taxes** for the exclusive use of those resources that are under our command—with a corresponding reduction of taxes on buildings and man-made improvements on the land. The exercise of the responsibility to pay taxes on land has a double function: It secures our right to the use of the resources that are under our command and it also makes room for others to access land and natural resources that they need. Land taxation is the economic bridge between hoarding, namely the accumulation of idle land, and the right of access to that land with its natural resources. Paying taxes on the value of land and natural resources gradually encourages dis-hoarding, hence it lowers the price of the land, and correspondingly opens up the resources of that land to all those who need them and can make use of them. Worrisome hoarding is especially that which occurs both downtown and in the belt surrounding major cities and towns. It is to leapfrog over this belt that people go to the suburbs in search for affordable land, thus creating overstretched lines of communication and protection and overlong commuting lines—with consequent waste of fuel that overtaxes nonrenewable resources, the ozone layer, the pocketbook, and the nervous system. Paying taxes on land value is a most fair form of taxation, because it implies returning to the community part of the value that is created, not by the individual owner, but by the community. Land that sits idle does not produce income, true; yet, it produces capital appreciation over time: Rare is the case of capital loss; and even when that occurs, the relative loss tends to be smaller than the loss on other assets. (To see how this pair of ERs&ERs meets also the requirements of distributive and commutative justice, let us simply consider that, if one avoids taxes, the total tax load is not going to be distributed fairly among the population. And if one avoids taxes, one obtains something—i.e., private control over a quantity of resources—for which one does not offer proportionate compensation to the rest of the community.)

2. *We all have the right of access to national credit.* Since national credit is the power of a nation to create money, and since the value of money is given by the

value of wealth left over by past generations and the creativity of every person in a nation, national credit is the last frontier, the last commons. Without access to credit today one is made economically impotent. Worse, since this advantage is granted to the privileged few, it is automatically denied to the majority of the population who are henceforth condemned to pay a higher rate of interest, if they obtain credit at all. (Is this not a root of inequality?) Of course, such a loan should be extended only on the basis of **the responsibility to repay the loan**. And these loans will have a high chance of being repaid because they ought to be issued at cost and issued exclusively to individually owned enterprises, Employee Stock Ownership Plans (ESOPs), and cooperatives, as well as states and municipalities with taxing powers, and issued exclusively for capital formation, namely for the creation of new wealth—not to buy financial paper, consumer goods or goods to be hoarded or to cover administrative expenses of states and municipalities. Capital credit liberates us.

3. *We all have the right to the fruits of our labor.* This right should not be limited to the right to obtain only a wage. It should be extended to cover the other major fruit of economic growth over time: capital appreciation—as well as being subject to capital loss, of course. The only justification for reserving capital appreciation for stockholders, the owners of a corporation, and excluding workers from it, can be found in the fact that loans are given only to owners of past wealth (the Catch-22 of today's economic reasoning: "save and invest and you too can become rich"—as if this proposition were either economically feasible or ecologically sustainable.) But from now on this right can be extended to people who do not have prior wealth through the right of access to national credit—especially by legally transforming workers into owners through individually owned enterprises, Employee Stock Ownership Plans (ESOPs), and cooperatives. Of course, this full right should be extended only in correspondence with **the responsibility to offer services** of value equivalent to projected compensation. And there will be an outpouring of such services because, while in a command and control economy workers are requested to check their brain at the factory gates, in a socially responsible economy—an economy in which rights are exercised on the basis of responsibilities—workers/owners are legally, socially, and psychologically empowered to exercise their brain fully at their work post. Their moral antennas will be up.

4. *We all have the right to protect our wealth.* This right seems to be universally accepted, except in one case that matters most: in the case of the trustification process, the process used especially after the Civil War in the United States to create corporate trusts and repeated in a hundred subtle variations ever since. (People feel free, not only to acquire shares of the stock of one corporation, but free to use that stock to acquire another whole corporation by all forms of trusts, mergers, and acquisition. The very idea of the corporation, forever a public entity, has thus been privatized and monetized.) There are two ways in which corporations grow: One is through internal growth, and this approach ought to be protected in no uncertain terms; the other is through external purchase and, with limits, this manifestation ought to be prohibited in no uncertain terms. This is the

Brandeis Rule. Why? Because this prohibition is the only certain way to protect the wealth of present owners. And if it is assumed that most stockholders of the modern corporation are happy to have their shares bought and sold on the market, it must be granted that growth-by purchase takes wealth away from workers who have contributed to create that value—and many times, in the trustification process, lose their work site as well. All in the name of efficiency—a misnomer that stands for private financial gain generated at the expense of shifting costs onto the shoulders of the community at large. Of course, this right ought to be purchased only at the cost of **the responsibility to respect the wealth of others**. These are two-way streets. We cannot even attempt to restrain the Pac-Man economy, while we use Pac-Man instruments.

These economic rights and responsibilities can be exercised by anyone who does not only want to receive economic justice, but also wants to grant economic justice to others. Indeed, these are the essential conditions for the establishment of economic justice, as well as the establishment of a **free enterprise system**, in the modern world. As a consequence of the dynamics of the implementation of these four marginal changes in our current practices, economic freedom will be expanded to embrace all who want to subject themselves to the rigors of the economic process—and then the few remaining hard cases can be easily taken care of by charity. No. There is no compulsion in any of the above suggestions policies. The landowner can pay more taxes and control more land or can escape the tax levy altogether by reducing land ownership to zero; the applicant for a national loan can escape the constraints suggested for access to national credit by tapping into private capital markets; the worker can escape the responsibilities of ownership by vying for a job rather than an equity position; and the owner of physical capital can escape the constraints implicit in the proposed anti-trust policy by remaining below the trigger of an agreed-upon threshold for growth-by-purchase prohibition. This prohibition should apply to the largest corporations first and be gradually expanded to include eventually all except, let us say, corporations engaged in intrastate or local commerce.

Intellectually, the proposed economic rights and economic responsibilities perform functions outlined in the conception of "general abstract rules" by Hayek (1960: 153), the "original position" by Rawls (1971: 12, 72, 136, 538), the "reverse theory" by Nozick (1974: 238), and the "Principle of Generic Consistency" by Gewirth (1985: 19); practically, they will function as Gladwell's (2000) "tipping points." Economic rights and responsibilities transform the abstract discussion on justice, especially economic justice, into a very concrete set of directives. Ultimately, it was a poet, Vincent Ferrini (2002), who caught the essence of economic rights and economic responsibilities by identifying their ability to provide "the answers to universal poverty and the anxieties of the affluent."

Operating as tipping points in our *modus vivendi*, ERs&ERs will set in motion a process of interdependence that respects the reality of economic affairs, and the reality of human relationships. Recognizing that most people and most businesses always act morally, the increasing number of "bad apples" that at times seem to receive all the attention (and envious support) of a superficial intellectual world will

11.8 New Tools to Control Economic Practices

be recognized as dangerous exceptions, perhaps ostracized, but certainly no longer applauded. Once the tendencies of these people are kept in check, all wealth will be distributed, not equally—that is meaningless utopianism—but fairly. The assurance for this result resides in the transformation of the current social contract into a legal contract: When landowners pay their share of land taxes, they will sell their hoards and access to land and natural resources will automatically be opened up for most people; when people will get access to national credit, many will become independent entrepreneurs; when workers are transformed into owners, they will have the legal tools to demand a fair distribution of income and wealth; when growth-by-purchase will mostly become a forbidden activity, most corporations and most employee/owners will preserve their independence.

These measures, by consistently curbing the excesses of the few for a period of at least ten years, will cumulatively lead to a fair distribution of income and wealth. To reassure ourselves of this outcome, let us comprehensively look at the issues from another point of view. If land owners were to use their possessions of land and natural resources efficiently (with efficiency measured through lower private capitalization and higher effective demand), would there be such wanting in the world? If national credit were made available to all entrepreneurs at cost, would we not translate the immanent reservoir of creative powers into economically profitable ventures? If workers were transformed into worker/owners, would we not increase our extant productive capacity incommensurably? If corporate growth-by-purchase—with accompanying translation of that economic power into corruption of our political system—were curbed, would we not obtain less concentration of economic power into a few hands?

All four ERs&ERs naturally lead to a fairer distribution of income than prevails today. Eventually, with a fair distribution of incom]e and wealth, there will no longer be any need for redistributive programs, which are an expression of double utopianism (first, people as if living in la la land are allowed to accumulate much, no matter how; and then they are expected to peacefully discharge their ill-gotten wealth). Preserving their current wealth, the rich will grow richer at a steady but slower pace; and the poor will no longer be poor, because they will have all they need. Lacking fuel at both ends, violent oscillations in the business cycle will be abated.

We will thus recover the essential truth of economics. This is the truth that there are two conditions of growth: economic freedom and economic justice, as concrete expressions of freedom and morality. Both are essential. The relationship between the two is quite clear: While freedom does not necessarily bring justice with it, justice unavoidably brings freedom. One can abuse freedom by denying freedom to others, one can never abuse justice. Hence, the initial condition of freedom for all is proof positive of the existence of economic justice in the land. This is economics that is socially relevant. And the relevance is not an afterthought. The relevance is implicit. The social import of economic theory is realized when the distribution of ownership rights is seen as an integral part of its constitution; and the social import of economic justice and economic rights and responsibilities is simply stated: We must prevent all foreseeable injustices from occurring. Once an injustice has occurred, there is nothing that can be done to undo the dastard deed. This is the bosom of realism.

11.9 Conclusion

Ethics enters most forcefully the field of Concordian economics at three crucial stages: At the center of Concordian economics, namely at the center of the analysis of the economic process, lies the theory of distribution of value of ownership rights—with ownership rights being composed of both property rights and economic rights. Thus the central problem that bedevils contemporary economics is brought into the field of economic analysis and under control.

The economic process is defined as the integration of the production (of real wealth), distribution (of ownership rights), and consumption (expenditure of financial instruments).

The theory of economic justice controls decisions in the field of Concordian economic policy. And the clear attribution of economic responsibility determines the creation of economic rights in daily Concordian economic practice. Thus rooted, not only present and future, but also past property rights will be able to withstand any ideological ill wind.

The theory of economic justice comprises three planks: participative justice, distributive justice, and commutative justice. The theory of economic justice is the mirror image of the economic process: one cannot be separated from the other, just as it is impossible to separate a person from her shadow.

Rather than trying to summarize what has been said above in the field of Concordian economies practices, allow me to give you in a few sentences the brutal core of this analysis both in a negative and a positive format. This core was offered on December 12, 2011 as a set of comments to Radford (2011). Here it is:

Economics without ethics is an empty mental exercise. The ethics of economics are exceedingly simple. They can be reduced to this one maxim: Do not steal.

If you do not pay taxes on land and natural resources that are under your exclusive command, you steal from members of your community who will have to pay correspondingly higher taxes.

If you enjoy exclusive use of access to national credit, a common good, you steal from others in your community.

If you pay wages, you steal from your workers the fruits of capital appreciation.

If you agglomerate wealth into your hands using unethically acquired financial resources, you steal future capital appreciation from existing owners.

It would not be healthy to leave this text on a negative and perhaps frightening note. Let us therefore observe the same economic reality with an optimistic eye. The basic recommendation of this Chapter is this simple: Foster economic policies that avoid all these four temptations to steal, nay, equalize the initial conditions among all citizens of a nation, and you will automatically put the economic world aright. Once distribution of wealth as it is created occurs fairly, the need for its re-distribution will vanish.

The economic condition of the world has been allowed to deteriorate to such an extent that these words might appear as a practice of magic rather than hard economic analysis. This would be a wrong inference. For detailed analyses of the expected consequences, see especially Rawls and Hayek. Above all, to see how realistic they are. Concordian economic policies and practices have to be put in the context of time. Then it will be realized that the expected result will be obtained not overnight but as a consequence of perhaps ten years of steadfast transformation of Concordian economics into daily reality. As in tipping points theory (and chaos theory), a new world will automatically arise in the very application of these practices.

References

Ferrini, V. (2002). Gorga worthy of note. *Gloucester Daily Times*. December 11, A6.
Gewirth, A. (1985). Economic Justice: Concepts and Criteria. In K. Kipnis, & D. T. Meyers (Eds.) *Economic justice: Private rights and public responsibilities*. Rowman & Allanheld.
Gladwell, M. (2000). *The tipping point: How little things can make a big difference*. Little, Brown & Company.
Gorga, C. (2002, 2009). *The economic process: an instantaneous non-newtonian picture*. University Press of America.
Gorga, C. (2007). Economic justice. In *Catholic social thought, social science, and social policy: An encyclopedia*. Scarecrow Press.
Gorga, C. (2008). *To my polis—with love*. The Somist Institute.
Gorga, C. (2008). *To my polis, with love: may Gloucester show the world the ways of frugality*. The Somist Institute.
Gorga, C. (2009, October 15). The economics of jubilation—blinking Adam's fallacy away. *Social Science Research Network* (*SSRN*). Available at the economics of jubilation—blinking Adam's fallacy away by carmine Gorga: SSRN.
Gorga, C. (2010). *The economic process: an instantaneous non-newtonian picture*. University Press of America. An expanded edition.
Gorga, C. (2012). Ethics in Concordian economics. RIO+20 PORTAL, *BUILDING THE PEOPLES SUMMIT RIO+20,* Documentos, February 19. Available at http://rio20.net/en/documentos/ethics-in-concordian-economics/. Accessed 15 December 2023, Reprinted in *Mother Pelican*, June 2015. Available at http://www.pelicanweb.org/solisustv11n06page4.html. Accessed 15 December 2023,
Gorga, C. (1982). The revised keynes' model (an Abstract). *Atlantic Economic Journal, 10*(3), 52.
Gorga, C. (1999). Toward the definition of economic rights. *Journal of Markets and Morality, 2*(1), 88–101.
Gorga, C. (2009a). Concordian economics: tools to return relevance to economics. *Forum for Social Economics, 38*(1), 53–69.
Hayek, F. A. (1960). *The constitution of liberty*. University of Chicago Press.
Keynes, J. M. (1936). *The general theory of employment, interest, and money*. Harcourt.
Nerkar, S. (2023). Why olive oil is so expensive right now. *New York Times,* October 22, Section a, page 1. Available at https://www.nytimes.com/2023/10/22/business/olive-oil-price.html. Accessed 23 October 2023.
Nozick, R. (1974). *Anarchy, state, and utopia*. Basic Books.
Radford, P. (2011). Ethics in economics—Where is it? *Real-World Economics Review, 58*, 2–8.
Rawls, J. (1971). *A theory of justice*. Harvard University Press.
Tavidze, A. (Ed.). (2010). *Progress in economics research,* (Vol. 19). Nova Science Publishers.

Chapter 12
Whence Poverty

Abstract In this Chapter we will examine whether through the lenses of interdependence we can spot a society in which the rich are collaborating with the poor on the creation of the common good. The existence of poverty is undoubtedly a deep social wound. Can it ever be healed?

12.1 Introduction

Apart from laziness for those in poverty, the next explanation perhaps is to blame them for lack of education. How many BA are now unemployed and unemployable? The next most common, general explanation for the presence of overwhelming levels of poverty around the world is *scarcity* (of almost everything). It might be profitable to examine the latter explanation for the existence of poverty at closer range: Is poverty due to scarcity? We will find that, not scarcity, but fear of scarcity is the culprit. And fear of scarcity is created by inappropriate economic policies—policies rooted in existing institutions. More. There is much misinformation about the creation of wealth. Our plea: Can we call on Concordian economics policies to coordinate the actions of the rich with the actions of the poor?

12.2 Scarcity and Fear of Scarcity

Zillions of transactions that occur daily offer prima facie evidence that there is no such thing as scarcity in the world, nor does the firm expectation of entering into zillions of transactions tomorrow show evidence of scarcity.

And yet, in any economics textbook and in nearly every sentence in these books there is a subliminal—if not explicit—warning about scarcity. An official definition of economics remains "the science which studies human behavior as a relationship between ends and scarce means which have alternative uses."

Worse. Most any negative phenomenon in the economic world is attributed—again, explicitly or implicitly—to this imponderable factor, scarcity. High prices? Scarcity. Depressions? Scarcity. Inflation? Scarcity.

Consequently, there is a twist at the core of the functions of economiics. The concern of economists ought not to be with the size the resources available at any moment, but with the fairness of the distribution of available resources. Economists act as if they were technical engineers (as if they could increase real wealth); they ought to function more as moral scientists—as their illustrious precursors, up to Adam Smith, used to function. No, Adam Smith did not transform economics into a science. Economics is not a science today; economics is a mental discipline that has been in a state of crisis ever since Adam Smith published his famous book. As Philip Pilkington (2014), a brilliant British economist, has accurately pointed out: "Mainstream economics moves forward not through logical development and integration, but through forgetting".

As to the presence of scarcity in the world, we need to make a dispassionate analysis of three forms of scarcity: scarcity of natural resources; scarcity of sources of energy; and scarcity of money.

Left to her own devices, nature suffers no scarcity: Nature offers only superabundance. A codfish lays one million eggs at a time; a tree scatters thousands upon thousands of seeds in the wind. A tiny mustard seed yields a majestic tree. As a result of predator/prey relationships, there is sufficiency in nature.

What of energy? Looked at historically, it seems that as soon as one source of energy is depleted, inventive engineers and entrepreneurs find a new source. Wind and sun are the rage now. A grain of sand, if we believe in the equivalence of matter to energy, contains enough energy to keep us warm for a long time. But, it is said, at what cost? Thus, we ran headlong into the most cited form of scarcity ever, scarcity of money. Here indeed the discourse gets complicated because one objectively finds scarcity of money for most people and a superabundance of money for the few. The issue, then, is not scarcity of money but an inadequate distribution of money—and, indeed, an issue of prices. Someone famously said something like, "Keep costs low enough and I can buy the entire yearly production of a nation with one penny".

All this confusion happens in the economic discourse because phenomena are analyzed one at a time and not put all together in relation to each other. Walking on a mountain in Ecuador recently and seeing that every inch of the land was covered with superabundant vegetation, it became easy to dream of the day in which governments and corporations are to make the human stomach capable of digesting directly grass, rather than letting a cow transform grass into a steak. (This is a definite alternative to ongoing effert to produce "cultivated meat.") If governments and corporations were to systematically and responsibly invest in very long-term R&D projects, rather than being glued to the results of the next financial quarter and at best the next election cycle, dreams like these might become a reality in due time.

There is no scarcity of natural resources. The only (relative) scarcity is that of precious metals. And ever since time immemorial, people who want to control people have generally decided to use scarce precious metals as a base for the creation and distribution of money.

12.2 Scarcity and Fear of Scarcity

Money is so powerful an instrument that, to create a new and better world, some want to do away with it altogether. They confuse the thing itself with some of the nefarious uses that are made of it, chief among them is the use of money to control people. This use is not inherent to money, but a consequence of the scarcity of money, namely, the use of money to control people is inherent to the conditions under which money is created and distributed today. Contrary to much idealistic/unrealistic ideology prevailing today, money is a splendid thing. Indeed, properly used, in our age of individualism and human separation, money can become our best tool of community rebuilding. We have seen that financial independence for anyone and everyone lies in the interdependence of person to person.

Let us concentrate our minds, then, on the procedures for the production and distribution of money. Money used to be produced mostly using gold or silver or copper, because they are nonperishable materials. Scarcity and durability was a corrosive combination. It was up to the Chinese to break this gordian knot by creating paper money toward the end of the first millennium of Our Era, followed by the Colonists in the Commonwealth of Massachusetts in 1690. Benjamin Franklin took a hold of the issue, and never let it go. He fostered and, by gosh, won the War of Independence on this issue. "Taxation without representation" was not much more than an appealing slogan to be uttered upon demand. Benjamin Franklin carried the creation of money issue all the way to its inscription in Article 1, Sect. 12.8 of the United States Constitution. The entire effort fell into suspended animation when Alexander Hamilton, likely unawares, established the Bank of the United States on the European model, in which bankers create money for the benefit of friends and relatives first—and if crumbs fall off their table to feed the hoi polloi, that is truly beyond their power to control. It gives capitalists great satisfaction.

Keynes, of course, berated the "barbaric" tradition of creating money backed by precious metals and, eventually, even called for the creation of units of account named Bancors, which were designed to call attention to dangerous imbalances in international trade and thus facilitate the introduction of necessary corrective measures.

Concordian economics picks up on these historical threads and calls for the national bank—the Federal Reserve System (the Fed) in the United States—to create money (using superabundant paper and electronic—indestructible—digits in a ledger book) by issuing loans at cost—to public and private entities only for the creation of new real wealth. Thus, there will never be any scarcity, but always sufficiency of money. When the Fed creates money, not in relation to gold, not in relation to the hunger of voracious moguls, but in relation to the real needs and potentialities of the country, scarcity of money will be replaced with sufficiency. With public money, not created to satisfy the frenzy of consumer loans, but exclusively for capital expenditures, all the potential beneficial uses of money will be unleashed within the nation. More pointedly still, economists will finally be given an opportunity to learn how to let robots do the work of the slaves; and, if the ownership of the robots is equitably shared among all those who produce them, we are all finally going to gather the fruits of the digital age of abundance.

We must have peace and prosperity. We must solve the economic problem—not for its superficial financial aspects, and not even for the redemption of our past sins, but for the redemption of our current sins, for the deep moral and theological sins that we commit while trying to "make" a living. Look at the carnage, look at the moral mayhem that the scarcity of money and the hoarding of money and wealth in a few hands creates. We must solve the economic problem—not to "make" money, but for us to earn the kingdom of heaven on earth by practicing morality and the right theology. What a waste to spend one's life worrying and caring about money.

No scarcity, then, can be found of either natural resources, or energy, or money. And yet, and yet, fear of scarcity is forever going to remain the mother of all evil.

12.3 Fear of Scarcity as the Mother of All Evil

Fear of scarcity is the mother of all evil; see, Gorga (2016.). There is no scarcity of natural resources or energy or money, but *fear* of scarcity is real—as evidenced by the general condition of our age. The rich are in a constant search for subsidies and tax deductions; the middle classes are in a constant search for a job; the poor are in a constant search for entitlements. How can this condition be characterized? We need to pass from psychology to economics. Translating from the language of psychology into that of economics, fear of scarcity can be classified as *economic insecurity*.

What is the cause of this insecurity? The cause is not scarcity, but fear of scarcity; not a deficiency in Nature, but a deficiency in our intellectual structures that lead to deficient economic policies. This is the chain of causation that leads to economic insecurity. Fiscal policies whose inherent structure is to rob Peter to pay Paul, do not lead to economic security; arbitrary administrative decisions in too many facets of our economic life do not lead to economic security; most of all, a monetary policy that is designed to lend money to people who have money—and mostly "invest" this money in the purchase of financial assets, rather than in the creation of real wealth—this monetary "policy" does not lead to economic security. Pac Man practices of economic development do not lead to economic securit.

The greatest fear of all is generated by the incessant call for the redistribution of wealth. You never know when goons in legal suits—or IRS jackets—are empowered to take your wealth away. The Reader is begged to fill the gaps in this conversation: until prevalent practices prevail, the population has to accept the wisdom of President Biden. In his 2024 State of the Union Address, he stressed: "No billionaire should pay a lower tax rate than a teacher, a sanitation worker, a nurse!"

With the eventual implementation of Concordian economics, there will be no need for the redistributionist program. If people are free to produce and to own what they need, they will reduce waste, and will always find enough resources to satisfy their needs; population growth, which seems to threaten the natural balance of things, is "naturally" petering down in most of the world. When will we procreate only in relation to our ability to love?

Waste is an inherent problem with monetary policies built on debt, especially consumer debt. Much production occurs, not to create wealth, but to repay debt. The current cycle is to create debt to feed growth to induce more debt to feed more growth. This insane cycle is fed by the scarcity of money and its concentration into the hands of the few. This insane cycle will be broken if, as specified, loans are issued to create real wealth—not paper wealth—and the ownership of the new wealth is justly apportioned among all those who create wealth.

The issue is not scarcity, but fear of scarcity. Scarcity is a phenomenon invented by economists who have never set foot in a supermarket of developing countries, let alone developed countries. Economists, experts who are trusted to design fiscal and monetary policies, err twice on this issue: First, they base too many of their decisions on an entity that does not exist, scarcity; then, they do nothing to counteract a phenomenon that does exist, generated out of the creation of their favorite policies, economic **insecurity**.

Let us conclude this issue of overarching importance with this realization. When rows upon rows of buildings lie boarded up; when one third of the food supply goes daily into the garbage dump, it is not a question of scarcity of supplies. And, certainly, when the Fed stuffs billions of dollars into over bloated coffers, it is not a question of lack of money. The concern ought to be with the wise use of whatever resources are indeed available to us at any moment. There is no scarcity. There is only a misallocation of resources. Especially misallocation of financial resources. Scarcity is a hoax perpetuated by economists; economic science, by itself, is neutral on the issue. It would work just as well with assumptions of sufficiency, if not abundance. Another thought. Economists produce their theories as if they were market operators and they are deceived by their tools of suppy and demand. Contrary to the presuppositions offered by these tools, real market operators resist the temptation to offer more money to acquire available supplies. Conversely, real market operators resist the temptation to raise the price of their products for as long as they can. They prefer to shrink the amounts supplied: shrinkflation is a new word but an old practice.

12.4 How the Rich Make Themselves Richer

With passage of the 2019 GOP Tax Plan, we have witnessed one of the most disgraceful performances in the history of mankind; see, Gorga (2021a). Rather than taking care of those who go hungry to bed at night and have no shelter over their head in a bitter winter night, through manipulation of the Tax Code members of the U.S. Congress have voted for the forcible transfer to the 1% of the population wealth that has been created by others and morally belongs to others. Make no mistake, this is the eventual result of current decisions. If wealthy people pay less in taxes, other people will have to pay more. For confirmation, see the work of any student of capital gains taxes.

The Congressional frenzy occurred during the high holy days of Hanukkah and Christmas.

This was a period in which the religions were so enfeebled and partisanship so rampant that absurd blasphemy was proclaimed in defense of an accused child molester: A Google search confirms that not a pip was heard from the pulpit of any religion in revulsion against the implication that St. Joseph was a child molester. How could the religions find the moral fortitude to defend the poor and the homeless?

The passage of the GOP Tax Plan was a manifestation of sheer evil. The wicked were in charge. There is no other characterization of this charade-like abuse of the "fiscal policy" of our nation.

Yet, the shame in this action of the United States Congress lies not in the naked exercise of power; that is what immoral power does: It benefits itself and its friends.

It is the intellectual source of this shameless manifestation of sheer evil that is truly worrisome; the assault on the public trough was **justified** with a series of standard lies.

The lie is that "the rich make *us* rich"; the lie is that the rich *create jobs;* the lie is that the rich *create wealth.*

No. The rich make themselves richer.

The rich do not invest—they especially do not invest in risky ventures. On the contrary, being afraid of losing their money, they generally tend to hoard their wealth at home and abroad. Presdent Biden pointed this out in his 2024 State of the Union Address: "Wall Street didn't build this country! The middle class built this country! And unions built the middle class!" The bare truth in these matters is this: It is the poor, who, by their sheer power of consumption of wealth, make us rich. Production of wealth without consumption is unsustainable.

But more must be said. One thing is moral acquisition of wealth by the rich, and another completely different is the forced transfer of wealth from the poor and the middle class to the rich. There is much to be said on this form of capital accumulation. I will confine myself to the most evident one. For a complex number of reasons, the transfer of wealth from the poor to the rich is a **vain** type of action that in due time turns to the disadvantage of everyone. Syncretically, the Good Book writes that God punishes evil people by letting them fall into the "snares" they have created. What an elegant solution. See, Psalm 9:16.

How will the debacle occur, technically?

As a general sequence of events, we shall eventually see that the accelerating power of greed will raise values on the Stock Market a little higher. The rich people, being relatively few in number, will make those values unsustainable. The majority of the people, with their incomes shrinking especially because of the forced transfers of wealth from the middle class to the rich, will no longer be able to participate in Wall Street games. (Their tax deductions might at best take care of the cost of inflation). The collapse will inevitably come. It has always occurred in the past. How can it possibly be different this time around?

Unless we change our policies, inertia calls for a repetition of events. The rich will try to make themselves richer. But will they succeed? Is this possible or is it another figment of our imagination? The reality is different.

12.5 The Poor Make Us Rich

There is a reason why, after thinking and much publishing on Concordian economics for about fifty years, I never get bored.

I always find new wrinkles in this new/old paradigm of economic analysis. This is my latest surprise: The poor make us rich. See, Gorga (2021b).

Let me tell you how it came about.

I mostly stay away from any discussion about health care policy. It is such a tender subject.

But two weeks ago, because of the sense of urgency imposed by the proposed Graham-Cassidy Bill to "repeal and replace" Obamacare, I finally focused on it.

Gradually, I pierced through the air of unreality that, for me, envelops the subject of health care policy.

People on the Right express a concern for the negative psychological and sociological effect of spending money on the poor. In addition, they are mostly concerned about the rich paying for such expenses and, in equal measure perhaps, they are concerned about pushing the debt ceiling through the stratosphere of the trillions of dollars already spent that the nation does not have. (Yet, the 2019 tax grab made a charade of this good intention: because of the transfer of weath from the 99% to the 1%, the debt ceiling was fiercely pierced.)

People on the Left express utter disregard for the funds to be spent; for them, the debt ceiling be damned.

Do you see what is happening? Both sides, arguing at cross purposes, focus on money, not on people.

Helped by the relational nature of Concordian economics, I then focused on the flow of money as it relates to *all* the people involved in health care—not just the poor. This is what I saw.

The surprising end result from this analysis is that, far from "costing" the rich, it is the poor who make us rich—**provided we satisfy their needs**.

Should the consumption of the wealth of the nation ever come to a screeching halt, the rich would abruptly stop making money.

The poor, with their numbers and the satisfaction of the quantity of their needs, make us all rich. The rich do not have the numbers to consume the Gross National Product; it is the poor who by their numbers perform this essential function; see, Gorga (2015).

12.6 The Creators of Poverty

Some time ago, Gorga (1998), I published a piece in which I realized that the rich are not the creators of poverty; it is the **wicked** who create poverty. I found this to be a powerful discovery that freed me from many an error.

Ever since the publication of this piece I have discovered a few complementary truths: the rich are not the creators of jobs; it is the entrepreneur who creates jobs.

Giving tax deductions, grants, and subsidies to the rich in order to create jobs is a waste of money. Yet, the money is not only wasted; it compounds the weight of today's economic problems—that money does great damage by being a significant source of inequality.[1] Hence we increase the level of poverty in the nation.

12.7 The Rich Are *Not* the Creators of Poverty

I can hardly contain myself. After years of studying the issue at a not inconsiderable depth, I have found in an unsuspected source an insight that clears up the issue of the cause of poverty in a definitive and powerful way. The source of this insight is neither a treatise in economics, nor a work in sociology, nor a tome in the theory of justice. The source is a paper published in "*Spiritual Life*,"—a periodical of Carmelite spirituality—in the Fall of 1997. The author is Suzanne Mayer. The title is: "Songs of the City of God: Merton, Social Justice, And the Psalms".

The author prefaces her essay with this quote from Thomas Merton's "Bread in the Wilderness": "The Psalms are the songs of (the) City of God…. Singing them, we become more fully incorporated into the mystery of God's action in human history." Recalling that the Psalms are the "ancient prayers of Israel" ascending "like incense before the altar of God," she proposes to "explore 'the mystery of God's action in human history' through the vision the Psalms give of divine justice and through the covenant call to all humanity to enter into this process".

These are some of the Psalms she quotes. Ps. 10:2: "In arrogance the wicked hotly pursue the poor…" Ps. 37:14: "The wicked draw the sword and bend their bows, to bring down the poor and the needy…" How do you read these Psalms? I read them in this way: Poverty is created, not by the rich, but by the wicked. **What a liberating thesis**.

So often repeated, most of us have assumed it to be true. We have assumed that poverty is caused by the rich. Even I who, as those who have worked with me, ever listened to my words, or read any of my writings can attest, has never used one word against the rich, even I had never penetrated the issue as through this reading. In fact, most of my efforts were unfocused and must have seemed quixotic to many just because I have always refused to point the finger at "the rich".

Let us be honest. We have all assumed that poverty exists because of the rich. Indeed, have not many rich people themselves assumed that to be true? Certainly, society as a whole in its organized political effort has trained all its guns in that direction—and the reaction from the rich has, of course, been to resist that effort.

---

[1] Some solutions for economic inequality are these: Employee Stock Ownership Plans (ESOPs); Consumer Stock Ownership Plans (CSOPs); loans to entrepreneurs who produce real wealth, not to financial speculators; cancel unduly inflated debts; all-labor reward programs.

12.7 The Rich Are *Not* the Creators of Poverty

That most political discourse and action has for centuries been dominated by that assumption is not worth discussing at length. Much more interesting is another question. What is a fair assessment of the result of all that effort?

Do we not find that every now and then one faction wins a few painful battles, but that the war is constantly lost by all?

Are we not, generation after generation, faced with the same age-old problem of poverty? There are times when we become so exhausted by this burden that we refuse even to discuss it any more. But the problem remains stubbornly there. And it gnarls our soul. Not much joy, not much enjoyment of what we possess can be had, if we somehow keep in the back of our minds the suspicion that we have not done nearly enough to alleviate the pain and suffering of men and women who unwillingly live in poverty.

How can we tackle such an endemic condition? Is the situation hopeless? I believe that the first ray of light, and hope, can be grasped if we really try to learn about poverty, starting with splitting the problem into absolute and relative poverty. This is an important distinction. Relative poverty is the existential condition for which there will always be someone richer than others. The feast is a movable feast, indeed. That does not matter at all. Not one iota. What matters is that those who have less be not deprived of the conditions for a dignified and free life. When poverty of material conditions impinges on our freedom and our dignity, then we are suffering from absolute poverty. Then the quality of life of society as a whole is impoverished. Freedom and dignity are absolute qualities. No one can be deprived of them or we are all deprived of them—to say the least, we are all deprived of the joys of a guiltless life.

What changes when we distinguish between relative and absolute poverty? What changes when we make the wicked culpable for the existence of absolute poverty? Everything changes—and the problem becomes abruptly **soluble**. Let us look only at a few effects on us, through the lenses of some of the effects on the political stump and the religious pulpit.

Our political discourse changes. Our eyes are no longer focused on the behavior of the rich and the behavior of the poor. That polarization in our political life, with people taking sides between the two poles and making the other the enemy, vanishes. We all know the hatred generated by the "undeserving poor." How many pieces of legislation are passed on the strength of that hatred! How many punitive agencies exist in the vain attempt at enforcing those laws!

Though less spoken about, how much hatred is directed against "the undeserving rich"? Is not most of our tax code written on the assumption that the rich have taken something away from others? The wicked rich are most certainly engaged in those practices. But are all the rich wicked? *And are there not poor people who are wicked?* Our political discourse is purged of many impurities, and our political action becomes much more pointed, if we keep those two basic distinctions in the back of our minds. Our finger is pointed in only one direction, the proper direction.

The religious pulpit and the political stump can finally become allies—on an equal footing. The split that has plagued society, it seems forever, is healed. Ultimate goals remain different. One is concerned more with the metaphysical life and the other more with the physical life, but the struggle, in this life, on this earth, becomes one and the same: resistance against wicked actions.

Is it easy to identify the wicked? No. Absolutely not. As distinguished from the rich and the poor who can be easily identified, the wicked cannot be easily identified by others. But the wicked themselves know who they are. (At moments of deepest insight, we know that we are all wicked, at least sporadically, at least in part. In those moments we also know that some people do not know they are wicked: hence the need for moral and technical instruction, because without knowledge of good and evil, there is no "sin.").

The root to the solution of the problem of poverty is no longer found in punishment of the rich or punishment of the poor, or both. The solution can be found only in that eternal prescription for happiness: love your neighbor; love your God; and if you love them both, you will eventually cease to be wicked and you will even love yourself.

Thus the schism within the very soul of the religious people as well as the soul of the political people and, ultimately, the soul of each citizen is healed. The religious people can be concerned only with affairs of the moral life and the eternal life: they can eventually get out of "the social action." The political people can be concerned only with providing a framework for the "good government," namely the just government, within which we can take care of all our earthly needs. And we will all succeed. The political people will no longer be dealing with wicked people in sheep's skin coming out of the synagogues, the churches, and the mosques. The few—always few—vastly wicked people will no longer intermingle with the good people. They will isolate themselves; they will ostracize themselves. Only when self-purged, will they come back. Without insurmountable obstacles posed by the wicked, the majority of the people will satisfy all the needs that can and must be taken care of.

Poverty is a moral issue. As such it can be solved. But, then, just because poverty is a moral issue, do we not run against the hard fact that wickedness is an intrinsic part of human nature? I was myself under this impression until recently when, in a discussion with Father John Hughes of Fitchburg, MA, the issue was clarified for me. I pushed him to admit the inevitability of wickedness. But the goodness that is in him, resisted my push. He still declared himself optimistic that the human race will eventually shunt wickedness aside. It was then that it occurred to me. Yes, the potential for being wicked will always be with us. That is inherent in our human nature; otherwise we would not be free—free to choose between good and evil. But do we have to choose evil? Do we have to destroy ourselves in the process? Not at all. Our struggle will be to resist wickedness. Our past millennium has committed more wicked acts than all other millenniums combined, perhaps. We have had our fill. We can now gain control of ourselves and mold ancient aspirations into a Movement Toward Goodness (MTG). This is a challenging task indeed. We need all our wits to succeed.

12.8 Were I Wicked

Were I wicked, I would not specify with great precision who the wicked are: (1) landowners who do not want to pay a fair share of taxes on the value of their land; (2) central bankers who do not want to serve the public interest; (3) entrepreneurs who do not want to offer full compensation for services received; and (4) business people who want to gobble up the fruit of other people's effort. But that would be wrong: individually, each member of these categories of people are powerless; powerless to change the system. Who knows? The incorrigible optimist that is in me makes me hope that each one of these people will want to be powerful. Hence, they will join force to create the four Concordian economic policies that are destined to change the world. That is the power of interdependence.

12.9 The Rich Are *Not* the Creators of Jobs

It is the entrepreneur who creates jobs. Not the rich. Financial capital is wholly passive; indeed, physical capital is equally passive, unless it is invigorated by the entrepreneur. There are plenty of apples on the ground that gradually disintegrate. It is the entrepreneur, who may also be rich, but the entrepreneur—as entrepreneur—who gathers them, and by bringing them to market, transforms a natural product into a useful product.

Much might also be said in relation to the size of the enterprise. Small and medium-size enterprises create jobs. Not to put too fine a point on it, but large corporations tend to destroy jobs. With their penchant for consolidation of two or more enterprises into one, they are bound to reduce rather than enlarge the number of jobs available on the market. Another way large corporations tend to reduce jobs is by chasing the lowest wage markets, no matter where they are located, even if they are located not in one's nation but abroad.

12.10 Sundry Consequences

There are innumerable consequences that flow from these verities. We can look only at the most important ones here.

Tax Abatements, Grants, and Subsidies

Just remember this simple verity, the rich do not create jobs, and you know how to react when charlatans tend to convince you to give tax abatements, grants, and subsidies to large corporations, especially large financial, agricultural and industrial corporations, on the specious promise of the creation of jobs.

Will someone calculate the amounts? These are not empty words. They are words laden-full of dollars. If in doubt, just contemplate our financial landscape.

Is there any reason for the bail-outs and the ongoing bail-ins, at taxpayers' expense, for failing corporations other than the vain hope of the purported preservation and creation of jobs? Is there any other reason for paying interest on reserves, cash hoarded actually, held at the Federal Reserve System (the Fed)? Indeed, is there any other reason for the oil depletion allowance?

Jobs, (Living) Wages, and Technology

Jobs as a talisman? Why does the discussion of jobs carry such weight in a modern society? Why is it presented as the solution to most, if not all, our economic ills?

The topic of "jobs" is generally discussed separately from the topic of wages—especially living wages—and the topic of technology. Let us try to avoid this pitfall. Let us link these three topics together. A new world opens up to view.

Let us put it starkly. Wage increases are eaten up by rising prices; jobs are eaten up by technology. Wage raises followed by price increases make the world that much harder for the poor, those who are outside even the margins of the economics process; and the concentration of ownership of new job cutting innovations increases only income and wealth inequality.

This is a story that repeats itself. Remember Einstein's presumed definition of insanity (doing the same thing over and over again and expecting different result) and ask yourself: Should the unions ever again demand higher wages—and taxpayers demand jobs?

The answer is a resounding, no.

Is this a defeatist attitude? Far from it. Long story to be made short. Solutions are these: Taxpayers ought never to submit to the extortion of financial privileges on the promise of jobs; and unions should never push for higher wages. What are the real solutions?

Unions Should Push for Employee Stock Ownership Plans (ESOPs)

Employee Stock Ownership Plans (ESOPs) are growing by leaps and bounds. But more is to be done. ESOPs will grow steadily when, as suggested in the petition to restructure the procedures of the Fed that is now circulating on the Internet, the creation of new money is pursued only if it benefits all citizens of a nation. Once employees and workers become stockholders of the corporation in which they work, employees and workers can push for a fair distribution of profits: You see, wages are distributed *before* income is realized; profits, both as income streams and streams of capital appreciation are distributed *after* they are realized in the market.

And the Poor, What to Do with the Poor?

What is never realized is a third verity implicit in the present train of thought: The poor are an essential component of the economic process. The rich get richer with the increase of production and consumption of the Gross National Product. The rich do not have the numbers to consume the Gross National Product; it is the poor who by their numbers perform this essential function. Hence, apart from compensating workers and employees fairly, what is there left to do? The best is perhaps left. This is the creation of Consumer Stock Ownership Plans (CSOPs).

Can you imagine the world in which McDonalds, Stop and Shop, and Macy's at the end of the year distribute a fair portion of their income among the consumers who have been keeping them alive all year long? Another program worth exploring and implementing is the All-labor Reward Program: payment for housework.

An Analysis of Financial Wealth

This new world, the world of Concordian economics, will not come about until we run a deeper analysis of financial wealth. The long story, again, must be cut short. Here is its gist.

You and Joe have one million dollar each. You are equally rich. Joe's wealth eventually grows by leaps and bounds to 10 million dollars. Clearly, Joe is now ten times as rich as you are. But, by hook and by crook, you raise your financial wealth to 10 million dollars as well. You are now again as rich as Joe.

What has occurred—from a purely economic point of view—between the initial and the final position? Nothing has occurred. There has been only an accumulation of zeros. (Unless real wealth is created in the meantime; but this clause is cancelled by the reality that we are here dealing with financial wealth; the relation between creditor and debtor is strictly financial.)

Hence my second petition on the Internet to avoid a cataclysmic reduction of financial wealth by financial crisis, rather than systematic reduction of zeros. This is nothing more than the application of the ancient Mosaic Jubilee Solution.

Financial wealth is a pure accumulation of zeros. This is true for the global economy, not only the American economy.

References

Gorga, C. (1998). The creators of poverty. *Gloucester Daily Times, Symposium, 18*, A10.
Gorga, C. (2016). Fear of scarcity. *EconIntersect*, October 4. Available at https://econintersect.com/a/blogs/blog1.php/fear-of-scarcity. Accessed December 10, 2023.
Gorga, C. (2021a). How the rich make themselves richer. *EconIntersect, 6* November. Available at https://econintersect.com/pages/opinion/opinion.php/post/201801042127. Accessed December 13, 2023.
Gorga, C. (2021b). The poor make us rich. *EconIntersect*, 6 November. Available at https://econintersect.com/pages/opinion/opinion.php/post/201710101834. Accessed December 13, 2023.
Gorga, C. (2018). Scarcity and fear of scarcity. Mother Pelican. *A Journal of Solidarity and Sustainability, 14*(9). September. Available at http://www.pelicanweb.org/solisustv14n09page3.html Accessed October 21, 2023.
Pilkington, P. (2014). Authoritative arguments in economics. *Econintersect Blog, 9* November.

Chapter 13
Oh, the Bancor

Abstract In this Chapter we will try to put some content into a word coined by Keynes, Bancor. Not surprisingly, perhaps, we will find in it an extraordinarily rich content. Applied nationally, it will facilitate the application of Concordian Monetary Policy. Applied internationally, it offers us the framework of a new international order, the Bancor International Order (BIO). This is an Order that, if faithfully applied, will grant us not only justice but peace—even peace in Ukraine. Can BIO also create conditions of peace between Israel and Palestine?

13.1 Introduction

As a word coined by Keynes, the Bancor—the Banc d'Or—has fascinated many minds. It seems to hold such a promise! Can we extract all the good from it?[1]

13.2 Let Us not Pervert Keynes' Thought

In 1944, Keynes came to the Bretton Woods Conference to present his idea of the Bancor, a unit of account to be created by an International Authority to keep foreign exchange accounts always balanced so that trade could prosper among nations.

The co-convenor of the Conference, Harry Dexter White, had no ear for the Bancor. He was interested only in establishing the Dollar as the international reserve currency, a proposal that he was certain would be acceptable to the U.S. Congress.

The idea of the Bancor has been kept in subdued conversation among economists. Until now. Currently, that idea appears to be the core of a proposal that is presumed to be implemented in a few days by the International Monetary Fund.

Among others, James Rickards, an insider consultant and financial writer, has for some time been warning that a "Global Financial Elite" has the support of the IMF to a plan to replace the U.S. currency with a new "Distributed Ledger System" using

---

[1] A detailed advocacy of this policy is contained in a "Madison Document," Gorga (2017b).

© The Author(s), under exclusive license to Springer Nature Switzerland AG 2024
C. Gorga, *Concordian Economics, Vol. 2*, Springer Studies in Alternative Economics, https://doi.org/10.1007/978-3-031-54642-6_13

the IMF's "Special Drawing Rights" as a new "global reserve currency." That plan has not materialized yet, but presumably it is still under consideration. The plan is a perversion of Keynes' thought about the Bancor; see, Gorga (2019a).

The Bancor was supposed to be a unit of account, with no implicit exchange value.

13.2.1 *How to Set Things Right*

With three modifications, the Bancor can indeed set things right on the national and international scene. But do we know what is wrong on the international scene? We truly do not. The economics profession does not have the faintest idea about three prevalent choke points.

It is with the help of Concordian economics that we are going to identify these choke points. We shall see that Hoarding, Ownership, and misguided Bureaucratic Rules play an inordinate role in international—as well as national—affairs. Naturally. Their role in international affairs is much more detrimental and dangerous just for not having been identified by the economics profession.

Once we become acquainted with these not well-known factors it will be that much easier to identify the positive role that the Bancor can play in international relations.

13.3 Two Crucial Issues in Foreign Trade

Let us talk of two crucial issues in foreign trade. They are not examined because they do not exist in modern economic theory. The concern is about Hoarding and Ownership of wealth. They are hidden in plain sight. Until they are settled, all conversations about foreign trade create heat but not much light. Even to bring those issues to the fore, it takes a bit of doing. We have to wade through some deeply tecnical issues that make the substance if intenational trade economics.

Much of the conversation about foreign trade is concentrated on three controversial points: Who pays the tariffs? Who benefits from foreign trade imbalances? Who cheats?

The last question is most fascinating, but least relevant.

Apart from concerns about hoarding and ownership, not much new can be added to the fourth traditional question, "Who benefits from foreign trade?" In ideal, textbook conditions, if two nations engage in trade, they both benefit. Empirically, it is even possible to determine whether both nations benefit equally.

13.3 Two Crucial Issues in Foreign Trade

13.3.1 Who Pays for the Tariffs?

It is the citizens of the nation that imposes tariffs who pay the tariffs. It is they who are penalized. The goods they buy are more expensive than they would otherwise be.

13.3.2 Who Benefits?

Who benefits from tariffs? Once one goes beyond the simple fact that the government that imposes tariffs benefits, at least in the short run, the answer is complicated.

If national producers of goods imported are capable of exploiting the rise in prices of foreign products and are capable of producing goods of the same quality as imported goods, that nation clearly benefits, because tariffs create income and growth opportunities for locals. Yet, there are qualifications. If newly employed resources could be more effectively engaged producing different things, the advantage turns out to be illusory.

The damage inflicted upon the foreign country depends on the importance that foreign trade has in that nation. It also depends on their assumed inability to produce at lower cost, so to nullify the benefit to local nationals of the country imposing tariffs.

13.3.3 Long Run Issues

Long run consequences are hard to identify, because they depend on sets of movable parts. If tariffs on our products are imposed in retaliation, who among our exporters is penalized? Do we grant an incentive to our foreign competitors to leapfrog over current technology—so they might be encouraged to create entirely new technologies fit for the next stage of development?

Tariffs, in other words, can produce much churning within the two nations involved in trade. That is why wise economists have always opted for free trade: no tariffs; no trade wars.

The remaining issue then is: What are the effects of tariffs on the balance of payments?

13.3.4 Effects on the Balance of Payments

Effects of tariffs on the balance of payments can be positive or negative. The most interesting case to analyze is that of negative effects, because this effect immediately bifurcates—depending on the international status of currency used. To be specific, is the negative balance in "dollars"?

This is a crucial question. Most international trade is carried out in dollars. This is a huge issue. It has nothing to do with economic science; it is an issue of pure political and military power.

Crudely stated, when people of the world export their goods to the United States, the creator of dollars, countries of the world send us real goods produced by the sweat and tears of their workers—and the exhaustion of their natural resources.

We, in the United States, send them paper money and digital money.

This is a condition of enormous importance. It clearly explains the efforts of China trying to have their currency, the renminbi, accepted in international trade.

13.3.5 Two Crucial, Hidden Issues

There are two crucial issues that are absent from the current discussion on imbalances in foreign trade. Since we in the United States exchange paper and digital money for real goods, we are letting our negative balances grow so large that we periodically have to change the scale of our graphs to see those imbalances.

Who cares? Let them eat paper and digital money is the general posture. This is such a natural tendency; we are having such a free ride. Who would not exchange real goods for pieces of paper?

Those who are concerned about outrageous imbalances in foreign trade instinctively know that there is something rotten in Denmark.

Here is the rot: Hoarding of money in this country or, worse, abroad is extremely dangerous because its behavior is unpredictable. One thing is constant: It responds to the herd mentality. Once a leader sprouts, followers follow. Thus, it is just like in snow avalanches. The last snow flake that changes into ice creates an imbalance that sends a mass of snow downhill.

The second effect is the issue of Ownership. When Americans hear that the Rockefeller Plaza is in foreign hands, they gasp. Many other properties are in the hands of German, Japanese, and Chinese people. Even the Italians have acquired control of Chrysler.

That is the issue: control. Control over peoples' lives—through control of their property. Control can take one hundred subtle forms that go much beyond the scope of this presentation. This effect ought to concern each one of us greatly.

The fear of God might finally enter our psyche if we will ever notice this possibility: Because of their relatively small military and political power, Chinese people are still reluctant to use their economic power. They are hoarding dollars and are the major buyers of American bonds. What happens the day in which they say, "Enough already; either you do such and such (about foreign trade, for instance), or we demand an immediate exchange of bonds for dollars and our dollars for real estate and capital goods." The demand might be more burdensome, of course.

13.4 Fish Stocks and Our Balance of Payments

This looks like a diversion, but it is not. We mostly know that we have huge problems with our balance of payment. We have just seen that we tend to import real goods and are happy to pay for them in dollars. There are many issues here. For a great variety of reasons, we need to give a close look at the importation of seafood products. They are generally the third or fourth item on our list of imports. That alone should justify a closer look, but there are many important ancillary issues with which we need to be acquainted if ever hope to develop a sane and sound set of economic policies toward our friends and relatives abroad.

In the companion Volume 1 titled Concordian Economics – Tools for Economists and Social Scientists, we have seen how the way we deal with the family fisherman and family farmer and corner store owner is a deeply moral issue. It is called the "Free Rider Problem." Here we can see how moral issues come back to haunt us in a hundred hidden—but just—ways.

Our balance of payments is overly burdened by our consumption of seafood: We import approximately 90% of the seafood that we eat. Given our natural resources, we should be net exporters of seafood. We once were. American cod and dried codfish used to be world-wide staples.

Total value of edible and nonedible fishery imports in the United States was $35.8 billion in 2016. The total value of edible and nonedible exports was $21.3 billion. (https://www.st.nmfs.noaa.gov/Assets/commercial/trade/Trade2016.pdf).

The imbalance does not imply only a shipment of dollars abroad. It also implies a number of jobs exported, a number of jobs that could be created in this country, were we not to import that much more seafood than we export. And what about income not earned? The shameful levels of poverty that exist in the United States do not come from the sky.

13.4.1 Why This Imbalance?

Before answering this question, allow me to re-introduce myself. I have studied fisheries issues for about fifty years; I have published numerous papers and articles in fisheries development; I am the author (with Louis J. Ronsivalli) of Quality Assurance of Seafood (1988). Through this overall work we introduced fresh fish into the nation's supermarkets and per capita seafood consumption increased considerably. Hence, the imbalance in foreign trade.

The reason for the imbalance in our accounts with other nations is not due to lack of fish in our waters. Not to put too fine a point on it, the imbalance is due to misguided rules and regulations imposed by our National Marine Fisheries Service (NMFS) that prevent our fishermen from catching fish.

These rules and regulations are imposed to prevent overfishing, a potential exploitation of the fisheries to the point of endangering the existence of stocks of fish in the future. This is an assumption that is born out neither by science nor by the facts.

Most of the times, fishermen bitterly proclaim that there are fish in the oceans, but they are prevented from catching them by arbitrary rules and regulations promulgated by NMFS.

The mathematical formula on the basis of which NMFS makes its determinations contains all sorts of data, but no science. In addition to historical data, which are not valuable because they report past catches that are constrained by the given administrative rules and regulations, historical data are also ill recording the reality of fish stocks because of many unknowns in the number and types of discards. Data are based on crude estimates, and much ideology, but no science, because no science of fisheries stock assessments is known to NMFS.

Worse. Much data is procured through surveys. The science of surveys is pretty invaluable. You know the "universe," you select a small "sample" of the universe. You study the sample to know the universe.

In fisheries management, you do not know the universe. Current fisheries management ignores the reality. It uses data upside down. From the sample it wants to know the universe. The problem, of course, is that the universe is composed of the ocean—or the various oceans. This entity is huge, mostly unknown, and constantly changing.

Contrary to ongoing assumptions and practices, there is a science of stock assessments. This science represents the observed behavior of all biological species on land as well as at sea—even trees, it has been discovered, obey the same laws of nature. This science is represented by the predator/prey model, which has been explored ever since Lotka and Volterra demonstrated in the early 1900s that the periodic disappearance of anchovies in the Adriatic Sea was due—not to fishermen's overfishing—but to the abundance of their natural predators.

A study of New England Fisheries that I commissioned in the early 70s, while I was the Director of Planning and Economic Development of Action Inc. in Gloucester, MA, from Joe Wohl, a Draper Laboratory scientist who had contributed to sending a man to the moon, and safely back, shows that the mathematics of this science, nonlinear math as used in chaos theory, is extremely complex. And this complexity is one of the reasons why this science is not yet used by the National Marine Fisheries Service in its determination of stock assessments.

The dynamics of the biology of fish growth is evident to the mind that wants to see the reality: The larvae of bottom fish rise to the surface of the ocean for food (plankton) and light. In the process, they are met by the pelagics, fish that live in the middle of the water column, and are devoured. Those bottom fish larvae that survive, once they become codlings need to go down to their habitat to live among "friends and relatives" at the bottom of the ocean. And, again, codlings are met by the pelagics on the way down and devoured.

Biologists within NMFS have indeed found codlings in the stomach of pelagics.

It is this dynamics that dictates the existence of the predator/prey relationship. In this phase of the cycle, pelagics are predators and bottom fish are prey.

13.4 Fish Stocks and Our Balance of Payments

Once stocks of pelagics grow disproportionately, they collapse for at least two reasons: They become so dense that they are deprived of oxygen and beach themselves in huge quantities; their stocks also collapse for eventual lack of their primary food resource, bottom fish.

Once pelagics collapse, room is again created for the growth of bottom fish. In this phase of the cycle, bottom fish become the predators and pelagics the prey.

There are two more phases to the cycle: One, in which both predators and preys grow together; the other when they decline together. This is also the cycle of night and day, light and darkness. At sunrise and sunset, light and darkness are fused together—moving together toward light or toward darkness.

Thus, it is apparent that the geometry of the science of the predator/prey model, as it can be seen from the following diagram, is very intuitive. When mackerel (one of pelagic species) stocks go up, cod stocks go down. Predators at one moment become preys at another. The graph shown here is a two-phase diagram. A more complete diagram shows that there are two more phases to the natural cycle: To repeat, there is a phase in which both predators and preys grow together, and a phase in which both predators and preys decrease together (Fig. 13.1).

Clearly, it will take intensive study by NMFS to ascertain the current status of these biological cycles. And the cycle of bottom fish to pelagics is only one cycle that rules in the oceans: Another cycle is between birds and dogfish, for instance, as predators of pelagics and codlings that come to the surface of the oceans.

Clearly, there are also other forces that rule the biology of fish stocks: Ocean acidification and climate change are among them; fisheries managers do have to work with many other experts on important issues such as these.

Given these complexities, while waiting for detailed scientific studies along these lines, the science of fisheries stocks assessments can be reduced to this simple formula: NMFS should determine which ones are the abundant stocks of the moment, should inform fishermen of these findings, and then let the family fishermen freely harvest the abundant stocks. With the implementation of this simple, but far from

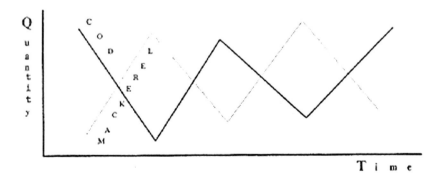

Fig. 13.1 A simplified predator/prey model

simplistic, rule we might be able to shake the shackles that today burden the family fisherman.

As pointed out in the companion petition that is circulating on the Internet (http://www.thepetitionsite.com/takeaction/241380953), which without prodding from me was in a short time signed by more than 550 people all over the world, the Magnuson-Stevens Fishery Conservation and Management Act (MSA), the Congressional Act that controls the fisheries, should be amended to allow family fishermen to freely harvest abundant species, while strict regulations should be prescribed—and enforced—for large corporate fishing concerns as well as for foreign fleets. Congress in its wisdom has already given NMFS the power, via import controls, to pursue both tasks for the avoidance of overfishing.

To penalize family fishermen for overfishing that is not done by them, but is done by natural predators of fish as well as by large corporate concerns and by foreign fleets, while responding to no scientific findings or biological needs, ends up destroying local employment and income of local fishing communities; and structural investments pursued over hundreds of years are, without any reason, going to waste.

If the fisheries industry should find the intellectual stamina to make an attempt to amend the MSA, the effort is not going to be a struggle against windmills. There is a good chance of success. The dictates of science might prevail over the dictates of ideology that during the last forty years have nearly destroyed our fisheries and the way of life of too many fishing communities.

The issues persist; the divisions persist. The New England Fisheries Management Council has just announced an 84% cut in the Haddock Catch quotas for Gulf of Maine stock. "We seem to find plenty, but they cant," said Terry Alexander, a Maine-based fisher who targets haddock and other species. "It's a disaster is what it is. A total, complete disaster"; see, Whittle (2023). The cultural bias in the presentation of the issues persists: the title of the piece is "Overfishing imperils haddock."

A silly question: why 84% and not 80 or 85%?

A not silly question: Is an 84% cut meant to destroy a fishery?

A final question: How can the few, very few, remaining fishermen cause as much damage as that evidently imagined by the current fisheries management?

* * *

What does this discussion have to do with the Bancor? There are many reasons for this discussion. The simplest one is this: Remember, the Bancor was conceived by Keynes as an instrument to smoothen imbalances in international trade. Well, one way to reduce imports is to increase local production. Yes indeed, one can increase local production of fish by changing NMFS rules that have strangled to family fishermen during the last forty years.

13.5 How to Solve the Many Money Woes of the World Using the Bancor

With three clarifications, the spirit of the Bancor may be revivified. First, taking a leaf from experience rather than abstract theory, as it was finally incorporated into the IMF's "Special Drawing Rights," the Bancor would have exchange value, a value ultimately determined by international financial markets.

Second clarification is that the Bancor ought to be created by each national Central Bank (not by the International Monetary Fund or any other supernational entity), so that we would have the American Bancor, the Swiss Bancor, the Chinese Bancor, etc. Let us temporarily call it the xBancor. Today's computers' power will easily let us ascertain the value of each Bancor at each moment in time.

The third clarification is most important. Each national Bancor would have to be created and distributed in accordance with Three Rules developed within the context of Concordian monetary policy. The Bancor should be issued as a loan:

1. only to create real wealth of tables and chairs, not to purchase financial instrument;
2. to individual entrepreneurs, co-operatives, corporations with ESOPs in their constitutions, and public agencies with taxing power so that the loan can be repaid;
3. at cost.

Money, even digital money (digital money is already here), created in accordance with these rules is not centralized and it is highly unlikely it could easily be completely traceable and programmable by any Puppet Masters. These characteristics are, of course, contrary to the scary, likely scenario that is being painted by many "insiders" who are familiar with ongoing plans of the International Global Elite who want to reach very deeply into everybody's pocket—who presumably also want to control mind and actions of everybody on earth.

Come to think of it, to guard against the coming of such a horrible world a final solution might lie within the accounting system. While the local bank issuing the loan must keep an account of each transaction, there is no need for the Central Bank to keep track of it. There are a hundred ways of mixing names and amounts through which anonymity at the Central Bank level might be legislatively assured.

13.5.1 When Should the xBancor Be Created?

The xBancor should be created as soon as possible; as soon as a national—and international—discussion occurs to gain acceptance of this financial instrument. But not later than a few hours after the next financial crash occurs.

13.5.2 What Value Should Be Assigned to the xBancor?

Each xBancor should be created at par value with each existing national currency: thus, 1 U.S. US Bancor = $1.00; 1 Swiss Bancor = 1 Swiss Franc; 1 Chinese Bancor = 1 renminbi.

Yes, the value of each Bancor would be allowed to fluctuate as the value of today' currencies fluctuates.

Yes, we would then have a **world currency**—but it would be wholly controlled by each national government.

13.5.3 What Is the Role of the IMF and the World Bank in a Bancor Regimen?

The Role of the IMF and the World Bank in a Bancor regimen remains precisely as it is today. Indeed, if the IMF should feel the need to use its privilege to create Special Drawing Rights, it could continue to do so. It would appear that there would be no need to even change the name of its financial operations. The IMF would continue to create SDRs. There might not even be the need to call these financial instruments IMF Bancors or any other such denomination.

13.5.4 What Are the Benefits of Creating Bancors?

To penetrate the value of creating a Bancor regimen we have to determine the timing of its creation. The major distinction is creation before the next Stock Market crash or after the Stock Market crash.

BEFORE THE CRASH. If the Bancor regimen is created before the crash, there would be ample opportunity to fully explain and to plan ahead for each and every detail of this regimen; ample opportunity to avoid potential pitfalls; ample opportunity to debate pros and cons.

AFTER THE CRASH. If the Bancor regimen is established soon after the crash, what will be avoided is the catastrophic collapse of the value of, likely, all national currencies—as well as the collapse of the value of all financial instruments.

13.5.5 Short-Term Effects

Short-term effects can be rather easily determined. The opening of the national credit flow to satisfy the needs of the agricultural, commercial, and industrial enterprises implies that, provided the Bancor regimen is established in a truly timely fashion, a collapse of the financial world will not affect the world of the real economy one iota.

Another Great Depression will be avoided. And this disaster will be avoided without shifting the burden on to exhausted taxpayers and/or unexpectant bank depositors. Or more simply, but perhaps more insidiously, without shifting the burden on the over-inflated accounts of Central Banks.

Unless a Debt Jubilee is proclaimed in accordance with Moses' injunctions, the least damage that we are inflicting upon the real economy by overburdening the accounts of Central Banks is an opportunity cost. We have no appetite; we have no resources for maintaining our public infrastructure in order. Even after the recent $2.9 billion influx of federal funds and during the current ravages of inflation, the United States of America is fast plunging the maintenance of its public infrastructure to a level that used to be the shame of developing countries.

The collapse of the financial world will, of course, have some major implications for both the workers within that world and the stockholders and bondholders depending on that world. These are people who might see the value of their portfolios reduced even to zero. Provided their portfolio is diversified, financial ruination will not totally engulf them.

People who will lose their jobs will have the opportunity to make one of at least three choices: They might choose to retire prematurely; they might start the business operation of their dreams; or they might find employment with local banks that are expected to prosper under a Bancor regimen.

13.5.6 Long-Term Effects

Long-term effects of a Bancor regimen are much more difficult to pinpoint. Given that the creation of Bancors is determined in accordance with firm needs of the people requesting Bancor-denominated loans, the overall economy is set on a steady course.

Given that the distribution of Bancors is determined in accordance with the value people contribute for the creation of national wealth, the overall economy is set on a just course.

Being set on a steady and just base, the overall economy is set on a lasting course.

13.5.7 Is There an Ecological Side to This Proposal?

The ecological benefits of this proposal are quite numerous but rather imperceptible at first sight. To evaluate them, one needs to be clear-sighted as to the dangers of world-wide financialization. How many trees are felled world-wide, not to create real wealth, but to pay outstanding debt? How many necessary public works are not installed because their financial cost is too high? In between, how many products are consumed, not because of physical need, but psychological irrepressible urges that pop up under prevailing monetary rules? Only waste dumps know.

13.6 Conclusion

The overall assessment of creating and distributing Bancors following rules determined within the context of Concordian monetary policy is this: We shall pass from a world in which money controls people to a world in which people control money. Not simply within each country, but world-wide—all at once.

Let a Concordian Bancor regimen come: The sooner the better. Let the collapse of the modern financial world come: The sooner the better.

We are tired of waiting for a just and steady world of economic affairs.

Acknowledgments I owe a debt of gratitude to Harry Bego for allowing me to use his TExtract program.

References

Gorga, C. (2023) What to do if the stock market crashes? *TalkMarkets*. Retrieved December 6, from https://talkmarkets.com/content/us-markets/what-to-do-if-the-stock-market-crashes?post=126594

Gorga, C., & Ronsivalli, L. J. (1988). *Quality Assurance of Seafood*. Van Nostrand Reinhold.

Gorga, C. (2017b). A proposed congressional joint resolution for peace and prosperity. *Madison, The Open Gov Foundation*. Retrieved December 12, 2023 from A Proposed Congressional Joint Resolution for Peace and Prosperity | Madison (mymadison.io). "Madison Document"

Gorga, C. (2019a). Let us not pervert Keynes' thought. *TalkMarkets*. Retrieved December 6, 2023 from https://talkmarkets.com/content/economics--politics/let-us-not-pervert-keynes-thought?post=245291

Gorga, C. (2019b). Two crucial issues in foreign trade. *TalkMarkets*. Retrieved March 25, 2023 from Carmine Gorga Blog | Two Crucial Issues In Foreign Trade | Talkmarkets

Gorga, C. (2021). Three steps to unify the country. *EconIntersect*. Retrieved September 6, 2023 from https://econintersect.com/pages/opinion/opinion.php/post/202001190038

Gorga, C. (2022a). The Bancor as an instrument of national and international peace. A piece in search of a publisher Retrieved August 2022 from Bancor as an Instrument of National and International Peace

Gorga, C. (2022b). The economic content of the 'our father' prayer. **MOTHER PELICAN** *A Journal of Solidarity and Sustainability, 18*(1). Retrieved November 10, 2023 from Available at http://www.pelicanweb.org/solisustv18n01page18.html

Krugman, P. (2023). The Weird New War on 'Woke' Money. New York Times. Retrieved October 25, 2023 from https://www.nytimes.com/2023/04/07/opinion/desantis-digital-currency-florida.html

Rodrick, S. (2020). *An Introduction to ESOPs*, NCEO, National Center for Employee Ownership, 19th Edition. Retrieved April 2020 from An Introduction to ESOPs | NCEO

Urbina, I. (2023). A brief history of a problematic appetizer. *New York Times Guest Essay*. Retrieved October 22, 2020 from https://www.nytimes.com/2023/10/22/opinion/calamari-squid-restaurants-china.html?smid=nytcore-ios-share&referringSource=articleShare

Whittle, P. (2023). Haddock, a staple Atlantic fish, is in decline off New England, regulators say. *News Center Maine*. Retrieved October 25, 2020 from https://www.newscentermaine.com/article/news/local/haddock-fishing-maine-new-england/97-e2037311-8ba8-450d-b493-cbd8680f1478

Chapter 14
Economics of Justice and Peace in the World

Abstract The Bancor is an instrument of justice. Peace follows justice, especially economic justice. As its primary function, the Bancor can—ought? must?—be used as an instrument of national and international peace. Let us briefly see how.

14.1 The National Scene

A revelation. I am not sure when that happened, but a short while after I conceived of the essential characteristics of the Bancor, a revelation occurred to me. The revelation is that the Bancor can become not simply a world currency but can become the fulcrum of an International Order of Justice and Peace. All it takes is the adoption by other countries in the world of the same rules as those for the creation of the US Bancor.

If that happens we create a Bancor International Order (BIO); see. Gorga (2022)– not as an external impistion from any source, but spontaneously.

All that it takes is for all countries, or as many countries as possible, to adopt the same rules when they create a national Bancor. All it takes is for the IMF or any other international body to certify that such and such a country has indeed adopted these rules for the creation and distribution of their national currencies, namely to issue loans:

i. Only for the creation of real wealth of tables, chairs, and foodstuff;
ii. Only to individual entrepreneurs, cooperatives, corporations with an ESOP in their constitutions, and to public entities with taxing powers; and
iii. Loans at cost.

Thus, we may have the Dollar-Bancor, the Yen-Bancor, the Renminbi-Bancor, whose relative values can be instantaneously discovered at any moment in time, thanks to the powers of modern computing technology.

It would be nice if every country in the world were also to accept in short order the wisdom of a Mosaic Jubilee and cancel all debts every seven years—plus perhaps adopt all other economic rights and responsibilities recommended by Concordian economics. But the adoption of all Concordian practices might be too much to expect at first. As adumbrated in my work, such a broad adoption might be too much even for the United States. Perhaps nations will come around to it when they see the enormous benefits of these policies whenever applied wherever applied.

Bancors ought to be free to be exchanged for real wealth in any part of the world, thus the Hegemony of the Dollar, which is decreasing in any case, will come to an **[automatic end.]**

And the silent, relentless, often destructive competition between the Dollar and the Renminbi will be transformed into a healthy competition along positive paths, with benefits to be enjoyed by all.

Somehow, we have to wake up to the reality that competition leads to violence; that self-reliance leads to violence; that Rationalism leads to violence: I AM NUMBER ONE. Relationalism is the answer. Interdependence is the answer.

The creation of the Bancor International Order (BIO) may be institutionalized under the supervision of the International Monetary Fund, whose function will be limited to certifying that each national Bancor has indeed been created following the Three Rules of Concordian monetary policy. Participation in the BIO ought to be automatic, but as any other organization in the world, BIO might want to establish its own internal rules. Thus, countries could be invited to participate, for instance, provided they meet certain requirements.

The Three Rules for the creation and distribution of money are eminently rules of economic justice. Financialization has been the creator of many injustices. Concordian monetary policy slows it down.

Following the first Rule for the creation of Bancors, i.e. "creating and distributing money only for the creation of real wealth," the Fed and other Central Banks will abate the deficiencies of financialization: creating money to create money. Wall Street can continue to thrive by borrowing private money, namely by accessing the private loan market.

Following this first Rule, public money will be diverted from Wall Street to Main Street. All the benefits of decentralization will be reaped by the country as a whole. Local Banks, being the ultimate originators and administrators of public money on behalf of their clients and the nation as a whole, will reacquire their traditional roles of sensitivity to the local needs of local entrepreneurs.

In addition, directing public money toward Main Street immunizes the country against any calamitous collapse of Wall Street; see, e.g., Gorga (2017).

Following the second Rule—issuing loans to individual entrepreneurs, cooperatives, corporations adopting an ESOP for their growth, and public institutions with taxing powers—the Fed and other Central Banks will accomplish a number of goals at the same time. They will favor the creativity and initiative of the people, all the people of a nation; they will spread the currently concentrated ownership of corporations among all their workers and employees; spreading the ownership of tools, gadgets, robots, and AI among the people, the Fed and other Central Banks will favor the industrialization, rather than the financialization of each country.

Following this Rule, the Fed will consolidate the power of the ESOP Movement. A few years ago, the number of people belonging to an ESOP in the United States became larger than the number of people belonging to Labor Unions; see, e.g., Rodrick (2020). Unions should be encouraged to tie their membership dues, no longer to higher wages, but to a fair distribution of ownership of the corporation in which their members work.

The call for higher wages is a self-defeating strategy. Higher wages are followed by higher prices. To think otherwise, is to believe in fairy tales; history tells us the truth. Has there ever been any protracted absence of this sequence? Workers do not gain much in the process; yet people on fixed income are squeezed by inflation. Unintended cruelty is imposed upon the poor. The only beneficiaries of the policy of higher wages tend to be local and foreign competitors. Thus, workers even lose their jobs in the process.

Following the third Rule—issuing loans at cost—the Fed and other Central Banks (mostly public agencies), will reduce the cost of the production of real wealth and thus influence the inflation of prices of capital and consumer goods.

* * *

Mirabile dictu, as the reader of this work knows well, in 2015 these proposals were presented to the Fed, and the Fed graciously responded, Durr (2016): "Given your proposal (for a new monetary system), I suggest that you contact your state and federal representatives." Scarcity of time and financial resources has allowed me to follow this suggestion only haltingly.

Once the three rules are in place, it will be much easier, perhaps even automatic, to implement the other recommendations of Concordian fiscal, labor, and industrial policies.

14.2 The Bancor as an Instrument of National Peace

As an explicit conveyor of economic justice, the Bancor will instantaneously become an instrument of domestic peace—in whatever country following these Three Rules is the Bancor issued. Much has been said about inequality and poverty and political instability. A few years ago, Gorga (2021), I distilled the issues in a few paragraphs that I am paraphrasing here:

There is a whole array of injustices that must be set aright—in America as well as in most other countries of the world. Set these injustices right and you solve many problems of inequality and poverty and political instability.

We have to understand that the affections that hold together MAGA (Make America Great Again) People, people who on the basis of hopes and promises swing their allegiance from one political party to another in America, are the resentments and the afflictions that society inflicts upon them.

Owners of large tracts of land are strangling the cities and corralling large masses of (MAGA) people into overcrowded lots.

MAGA People's lives are being eviscerated when money is lent to people with money on easy terms and the people without money are left to pay outrageous interest.

MAGA People's lives are being eviscerated by robots that take their jobs, their livelihood, away.

MAGA People's lives are being eviscerated whenever two mega corporations are glued together; then the few gain more power and the people within and without both corporations suffer many afflictions. Are there similar groups in other countries of the world?

The Bancor created and distributed in accordance with the Three Rules of Concordian monetary economics, especially if aided by the other Concordian economic policies, will do much to alleviate problems of inequality, poverty, and political instability.

Social unrest will gradually become a thing of the past.

14.3 The International Scene

An injection of moral fortitude in our political discourse will gradually transfer the benefits to be obtained pursuing the creation and distribution of the Bancor from the national to the international scene, the area for which the Bancor was originally conceived.

The institution of the Bancor is an eminent institution of economic justice. And we know that with justice comes peace. If the institution of the Bancor is indeed going to create domestic peace in the United States, is it not reasonable to expect similar results when the Bancor is instituted in other countries of the world?

With some to-do, the answer is positive; knowing the needs of the players helps.

The Bancor can become an instrument of international peace.

A rather immediate danger, the danger of nuclear holocaust, can be met with an efficacious solution, a Grand Design. President Biden, it is suggested, can offer the end of the Dollar Hegemony, a great desire of President Putin, for an end to the war in Ukraine.

Some Readers already know what will President Biden get in return.

This bargain can be constructed out of the monetary policy that results from Concordian monetary economics extended to the creation of the Bancor International Order (BIO). Any nation that follows the same Three Rules for the creation and distribution of their national currency, three rules of economic justice, can be certified by the IMF to become a member of BIO, provided certain other conditions are met; provided, for instance, it ceases any belligerent action.

The historical and intellectual background for this proposal I have found in an article published by Stephen Kinzer in the Boston Globe of October 16, 2022. The resolution of the Cuban Missile Crisis shows that it is possible to strike a deal with Russia. Especially when survival hangs in the balance.

14.4 The Grand Bargain

When, in Gorga (2022), I conceived of the Bancor International Order (BIO), I was not aware of President Vladimir Putin's rage against the "unipolar" world of U.S. dominance of world markets; see, Kottasova et al. (2022).

President Putin's words deserve to be known: "When they won the Cold War, the U.S. declared themselves God's own representatives on earth, people who have no responsibilities – only interests. They have declared those interests sacred. Now it's one-way traffic, which makes the world unstable" (ibid).

Now that that rage is in the news, it might be easier to start an open discussion of these issues. President Putin is partially right. The United States has achieved dominance in world markets, but not since 1991 with the collapse of the Soviet Union, and not through the presence of military bases that encircle Russia today. The U.S. dominance of world markets was established in 1944 through the Bretton Woods Agreement to which Stalin was invited to participate and refused; that dominance was established by the obligation of every nation to carry out international trade (almost exclusively) in dollars; see, Steil (2013). Technically, up to 1971 all currencies were pegged to the dollar and the dollar was pegged to gold, convertible at the rate of thirty-five dollars an ounce. The value of the dollar has been free floating ever since.

Russia regretted her decision not to participate in the Bretton Woods Agreement that established the International Monetary Fund and the World Bank. Under the guidance of President Putin, Russia today might not miss a second chance to become a full partner in international financial agreements.

Stalin might have ultimately been hampered from participating in the Bretton Woods Agreement by a churlish Marxist bias against money.

Mr. Putin seems to be free of such a bias; he clearly loves money for himself and his friends.

But one condition to enter BIO ought to be imposed on Russia, as on any other belligerent country: Russia must end the war in Ukraine.

The Bancor International Oder might then become an instrument of immediate peace, peace where it is greatly needed, in Ukraine.

Ever since these pages were written, a horrible conflict has developed in the Holy Land; might a well-crafted BIO also create conditions of peace between Israel and Palestine?

14.5 The Bancor International Order as the End of the Unipolar World

Peace in Ukraine might be achieved because it satisfies President Putin's rage about the complexities of unipolar word of US dominance of international trade. To repeat, when I conceived of the Bancor International Order (BIO), I was not aware of President Putin's rage against the "unipolar" world of U.S. dominance of world markets.

Now that that rage is in the news, it might be easier to start an open discussion of these issues.

For the Bancor International Order (BIO) to become an instrument of peace in Ukraine, it means that the United States, more specifically, the U.S. Congress, must make peace with relinquishing the dominance of world markets that it achieved in 1944.

Before rushing into judgments, the U.S. Congress and the American people ought to become acquainted with the price of this dominance. This price, for some obvious but devious reasons, has been carefully kept under wrap.

An open discussion of this issue might make clear, not so much the benefits, but the hidden price paid for that dominance. If we follow some of the intricacies of international trade, we realize that America is suffering from a dangerous trend: the gradual transfer of the control of her physical assets to foreign nations.

14.6 AGAIN: The Price of U.S. Dominance of World Markets

As I first pointed out in TalkMarkets, we must examine two crucial issues in foreign trade; see, Gorga (2019). They are not examined because they do not exist in modern economic theory. The concern is about hoarding and ownership of wealth; one was expunged from polite discourse by Adam Smith, the other by Thomas Jefferson in the same year. They have become hidden in plain sight. Until they are settled, all conversations about foreign trade create heat but not much light.

Hoarding of money in this country or, worse, abroad is extremely dangerous because its behavior is unpredictable. One thing is constant: It responds to the herd instinct. Once a leader sprouts, followers follow. Thus, it is just like in snow avalanches. The last fleck of snow that turns into ice creates an imbalance that sends a mass of snow downhill.

The second effect is the issue of ownership. When Americans hear that the Rockefeller Plaza is in foreign hands, they gasp. Many other properties are in the hands of German, Japanese, and Chinese people. Even the Italians have acquired control of Chrysler. That is the issue: control. Control over peoples' lives—through control of their property. Control can take one hundred subtle forms that go much beyond the scope of this presentation. This effect ought to concern each one of us greatly.

The fear of God might finally enter our psyche in the United States if we will ever notice this possibility: Because of their relatively small military and political power, Chinese people are still reluctant to use their economic power. They are hoarding dollars and are the major buyers of American bonds. What happens the day in which they say, "Enough already; either you do such and such (about foreign trade, for instance), or we demand an immediate exchange of bonds for dollars and our dollars for real estate and capital goods."

Yes, let us trade the existence of the unipolar word for peace in Ukraine.

14.7 Louis D. Brandeis on Compromise

Louis D. Brandeis said this on compromise: "I don't believe in compromises—but I do believe in the full play of forces and in giving my opponent what he wants if not inconsistent with what I want, and particularly if what he wants is something I want to get rid of."

Let us get peace in Ukraine and let us give President Putin the end of the unipolar world.

The world will get a fervently desired peace in Ukraine; the United States will get rid of two hidden, dangerous forces unleashed by the practices of the unipolar world: great hoards of dollars in foreign hands and the insidious habit of selling the ownership of our assets to foreigners.

14.8 An Unexpected Benefit

In a BIO regimen, an unexpected benefit of immense importance will automatically occur: the bloated influence of the military-industrial complex will be deflated–in the United States as well as the rest of the world. Peace and security march together. Security cannot be but mutual.

14.9 Can the Bancor International Order Be Created?

We have all the tools to create the Bancor International Order (BIO). It should be created. But it will not be created without intense scrutiny in this chapter.

The sooner the scrutiny starts the better. The more complete the better. In addition to the right of access to national credit that has essentially been treated in this chapter, the full project of economic justice recommended by Concordian economics includes the treatment of 1. The right of access to land and natural resources, 2. The right to the fruit of one's labor, and 3. The right to the enjoyment of one's property. See, e.g., Gorga (2008).

The advantages of a Bancor International Order are too intense to be explored here. The project of economic justice is capped with the acceptance of the wisdom of a systematic Mosaic debt jubilee. Two asymmetric stances will be outlined.

If the BIO is established and President Putin accepts the invitation to participate, peace in Ukraine will be at hand. A stop will be put to the waste of human, natural, and even military resources worldwide. The danger of a WWIII will be averted.

A hidden benefit will accrue to the United States: Through the intricacies of international trade, America is gradually losing control of her physical assets to foreign nations. This surreptitious development will gradually come to a screeching halt if the BIO is established.

14.10 A Look Forward

Will Concordian economics be applied? For many consilient reasons, the answer is a definite yes.
    When will it be applied? i do not know the answer to this question.
    You do, dear Reader.

Appendix on Immigration

Problems of immigration are very much like problems of poverty. Their cause might be vastly diffrenet, but their solution is identical. Once the problem of immigration has reached such proportions that cannot be solved by "private" means anymore, than the solution is identcal. Solutionn can be found only by changing the institutions. Useful ideas might be found among the soltions presented in these two volumes.
    The institutions to be changed are the institutions in countries that force human beings to abandon their homeland in desperate search for a new satisfying life abroad.
    Certainly, much study needs to be devoted to the reforms needed for each country in the world. Many international organizations ought to redouble their efforts. The general proposition is this: Each country ought to try to implement new policies. Old certainties are collapsing.
    Because of her history and some contemporary predicaments, the United States has a special duty. It should control the operations of her citizen in foreign countries, especially those operations that affect local natural resources. It should openly lead in finding democratic solutions abroad: now this is no longer a matter of rhetoric; now it is almost a matter of survival. Sorry, Professor Tucker. Saudi Arabian oil is not ours.

References

Durr, J. (2016). *Personal communication to Carmine Gorga, September 14.* Public Affairs Office of Board of Governors of the Federal Reserve System. https://1drv.ms/w/s!AgFxYQBpjmMFj06wiz_G_fkJWeWO

Gorga, C. (2008). Concordian economics: Tools to Return Relevance to Economics. *Forum for Social Economics,* May. Reprinted, with a new Introduction, in *Mother Pelican: A Journal of Solidarity and Sustainability, 11*(2). Retrieved December 6, 2023 from http://www.pelicanweb.org/solisustv11n02page4.html

Gorga, C. (2017). What to do if the stock market crashes? *TalkMarkets.* Retrieved December 6, 2023 from https://talkmarkets.com/content/us-markets/what-to-do-if-the-stock-market-crashes?post=126594

Gorga, C. (2019). Two crucial issues in foreign trade. *TalkMarkets.* Retrieved March 25, from Carmine Gorga Blog | Two Crucial Issues In Foreign Trade | Talkmarkets

Gorga, C. (2021). Three steps to unify the country. *EconIntersect.* Retrieved September 6, from https://econintersect.com/pages/opinion/opinion.php/post/202001190038.

References

Gorga, C. (2022). The Bancor as an Instrument of National and International Peace, A piece in search of a publisher. Retrieved December 6, from Bancor as an Instrument of National and International Peace.docx

Kottasová, I., Pokharel, S., Radina, G. (2022). CNN, "Putin lambasts the West and declares the end of 'the era of the unipolar world.'

Rodrick, S. (2020). An Introduction to ESOPs, NCEO, National Center for Employee Ownership, 19th Edition. Retrieved April 2020 from An Introduction to ESOPs | NCEO

Steil, B. (2013). *The Battle of Bretton Woods: John Maynard Keynes, Harry Dexter White, and the Making of a New World Order*. Princeton University Press.

Conclusion

A brief recap. Hoarding is the Pivot in the History of Economics. Adam Smith inaugurated modern economics by removing Hoarding from the discussion of social, economic, and political affairs. Without the understanding of Hoarding, economics gradually lost relevance. We allow the individual person to hoard more and more wealth by *legally* taking it away from what is built by the many. And then we beg the rich to give a pittance to the poor through moral extortion: "if you do not give me to give to the poor, you are a bad person."

With Concordian economics, Hoarding is returned to the economic discourse; and the understanding of Harding leads to the recovery of the Aristotelian/Aquinian project of economic justice. With Concordian economics, the construction of economic justice is completed by adding the plank of Participative Justice to its structure. We all have the right to participate in the economic process, none of us is a slave (or ought to be a slave) any more. This way we will create all the wealth that we need, all the wealth that we want.

Scarcity is a figment of the economist's imagination.

This is what takes place under the guidance of economic justice. No more will MAGA People be corralled into tights quarters; no more will MAGA People be denied access to loans or granted loans only at exorbitant interest; no longer will MAGA People receive insufficient wages and be deprived of a share of the capital appreciation they have created; no more will MAGA People be losing their job sites to local or foreign competitors who reduce wages to a pittance.

In this construct, MAGA People compose 99% of the population.

And the 1%, under the aegis of social justice, is not fairing much better. How would you like to live under the incubus of a Stock Market plunge somewhere in the world. What if you have borrowed money to acquire that standing in the market?

Within the constraints of minstream economics, the rich beg for subsidies and tax deductions; the middle classes beg for a job; the poor beg for shelter and bread.

Economic justice is not a literary abstraction, but a need of the human soul. Practicing economic justice one fills his or her soul with jubilation, not only because one emerges from the shell of the self, but because one establishes firm, satisfying relations with The Other. To practice economic justice is to escape from Solipsism, as the danger of Secularism. This is the work of reconstruction of the Polis; this is the work needed to create the Civilized Society, a reconstruction based on a growing understanding of Self and Others.

All is accomplished through Love, because justice is a virtue. And the virtues cannot be exercised in isolation. Either they are all exercised or none is. It takes love to receive and to give economic justice.

It is then, as Saint Thomas Aquinas reminded us, that we achieve the "peak of power," power over ourselves. Only then can we influence the actions of other people, if we ever want to.

In his 2024 State of the Union Address, President Biden has reported that "A record 16 million Americans are starting small businesses and each one is an act of hope." Think if these businesses--and all bsinesses to come--were created through access to national credit. Think if, through ESOPs, they were to extennd ownership to all their workers and employees. Think if they were to procure their loans at cost. Think if they were to institute a CSOP in their operations.

Think if the President had asked the Unions to demand, not higher wages, but a fair share of ownership. Think is the Preident had asked the Unions to apply the Brandeis Rule.

Think if the Predent had asked Municipal Assessors to raise taxes on land and natural resources, whille lowering taxes on buildings and labor income.

Perhaps the most important benefit of Concordian economics will be gathered in the associated fields of Jurisprudence and Political Science. Concordian economics resolves the ancient, perennial issue of how "can the rich and the poor be enabled to act as political equals." The short-form answer is this: The best form of government is the one that governs on the basis of **self-imposed** (hence democratic) **rules of economic justice**. In this system, The Government—after much vetting—*declare*s a set of economic rights and responsibilities to be shared by the entire nation and leaves The Market free to *exercise* those rights.

Ideally, the vetting will converge on the creation of the set of economic rights and responsibilities enunciated throughout the work on Concordian economics. The I and The Other will no longer be strangers; they will no longer be fighting fors upremacy. They will discover that ONE DEPENDS ON THE OTHER.

The work of Interdependence does not stop there. The full revelation, the full construction of Concordian economics occurs within the embrace of the Interdependence of everything with everything else. Indeed, guided by the intellectual needs of Concordian economics we have transformed the entire field of Retionalism to Relationalism.

Starting from the equivalence of Production to Distribution to Consumption of wealth, it takes but a step to fall into the embrace of the equivalence of matter to energy to spirit. With this equivalence we can finally obtain a full dance of Econ-Ecol in our private, concrete, earthly gardens. Once within the earthly gardens, we will discover their connections with the ethereal gardens through the equivalence of Being Becoming Existence. And so on, and so forth.

"You have been endowed from your birth with princely gifts; in eternal splendor, before the dawn of light on earth, I have begotten you" Psalm 110:1–5, 7.

Index

A

Access to land and natural resources, 43, 183
Access to national credit, 14, 15, 44, 55–57, 59, 69, 70, 87, 109, 121, 129, 134, 135, 142, 145–148, 189, 196, 198, 199, 203, 226–228, 230, 265
Accumulation of wealth, 4, 100–102, 111, 142
Adam Smith, 2, 5, 17, 37, 38, 60, 64, 68, 84, 100–107, 109, 111, 112, 126, 154, 181, 194, 196, 234, 267
Afflictions, 26, 182, 261, 262
Affluent, 18, 26, 71, 72, 153, 161, 183, 228
African nations, 199, 200
American Colonists, 55, 56, 102, 109–111
Aquinas, 2, 36, 60, 62, 68, 100–104, 111, 112, 122, 223, 268
Aristotle, 2, 36, 60, 62, 68, 100–104, 111, 112, 122, 196
Augustine, 2, 100–104, 111, 112

B

Bancor, 27, 132, 145, 198, 235, 247, 248, 254–257, 259–265
Bancor regimen, 256, 257
Borrowers, 12, 71, 93, 96, 117, 131

C

Capital credit, 71, 94, 132, 169, 227
Capitalism, 15, 16, 53, 60, 61, 85, 181, 194, 200
Capital loans, 12, 159

Cash, 7, 18, 64, 79, 80, 82, 83, 89, 90, 94, 105, 116–119, 145, 153, 154, 158, 159, 171, 197, 243
Central Banks, 29, 44, 84, 132, 134, 150, 158, 160, 256, 260, 261
Charity, 44, 45, 101, 120, 150, 197, 223, 228
Chinese people, 250, 264
Chocolate bar, 107, 114, 154, 155
Common wealth, 59, 70, 121, 133, 134, 137, 149, 171
Communism, 194, 200
Community, 11, 37, 38, 43, 49, 58, 69, 119, 129, 133, 137, 138, 142, 149, 153, 156, 157, 160, 161, 173, 176–178, 180, 187, 188, 192, 193, 197, 198, 207–209, 226, 227, 230, 235, 254
Commutative justice, 36, 40, 109, 155, 196, 221–223, 225, 226, 230
Compound interest, 94, 95, 130, 159, 169
Concordian economics policies, 58, 233
Concordianism, 5, 18, 51, 66
Concordian monetary economics, 262
Concordian monetary policy, 9–11, 14, 27, 48, 100, 102, 105, 106, 109, 111, 121, 168, 169, 247, 257, 260
Concordian world, 139, 140
Consumerism, 132, 153, 160, 161
Consumer loans, 12, 159, 198, 235
Consumer Ownership Plan, *see* CSOPs
Consumers, 10, 12, 14, 15, 26, 52, 70, 71, 80, 81, 83, 93, 94, 103, 106, 107, 131, 132, 139, 143, 144, 148, 160, 161, 169, 180, 195, 202, 210, 220, 226, 236, 244

Control, 17, 57, 65, 69, 71, 93, 100, 101, 104, 105, 111, 141, 142, 148, 149, 155, 171, 173, 174, 176, 181, 183, 196, 201, 210, 225–229, 234, 235, 242, 250, 255, 257, 264, 265, 266
Control people, 57, 234
Creation and distribution, 148, 259, 262
Creation and distribution of money, 27, 71, 119, 169, 234, 260
Creation of jobs, 13, 243
Credit, 10, 12, 17, 42, 44, 45, 56, 57, 59, 70, 71, 86–88, 90, 91, 93, 94, 104, 105, 109, 116, 117, 119, 129, 134, 135, 137, 138, 140, 143, 145, 148, 169, 171, 183, 200, 226, 229
Crisis, 1, 5, 7, 53, 55, 56, 82, 84, 86, 87, 107, 125, 126, 131, 139, 153, 154, 161, 173, 181, 218, 234, 244, 262
Consumer Ownership Plans (CSOPs), 15, 70, 81, 83, 94, 143, 144, 192, 239, 244
Cubans, 197, 199
Currency, 56, 86, 103, 110, 111, 115–119, 128, 134, 247, 249, 255, 259, 262

D
Dead economists, 16, 93
Death of money, 79
Debt, 4, 12, 24, 28, 37, 59, 70, 82, 83, 90, 91, 95, 96, 130–133, 145, 146, 149, 157, 159, 168, 169, 222, 236, 239, 256, 257, 265
Debt jubilee, 4, 12, 18, 28, 37, 70, 96, 132, 157, 159, 256
Digital money, 250, 255
Distribution, 3, 4, 8–10, 36, 38–40, 59, 62, 81, 83, 100, 113–115, 129, 135, 143, 144, 154, 155, 168, 171, 176, 177, 191, 195, 217, 219, 221–224, 228–230, 234, 235, 244, 257, 261
Distribution of ownership rights, 48, 154, 173, 217, 219, 223, 229
Distribution of wealth, 143, 236
Distributive justice, 36, 40, 62, 155, 222, 230
Doctrine, 33, 35, 36, 39, 40, 61, 62, 64, 220–222
Doctrine of Economic Justice, 33, 35, 36, 40, 61, 62, 221
Dollars, 84, 91, 117, 131, 133, 237, 243, 244, 249, 250, 263–265

E
Economic freedom, 12, 58, 68, 138, 146, 147, 175, 228, 229
Economic inequality, 16, 99, 180
Economic insecurity, 2, 7, 236, 237
Economic justice, 2, 5, 29, 33, 34, 36, 39–41, 45, 60, 61, 66–69, 71, 72, 109, 112, 146–148, 155, 158, 167, 172, 175, 181, 196, 199, 203, 217, 220, 221, 223, 225, 228–230, 261, 265, 267, 268
Economic process, 3, 4, 26, 30, 38, 40, 41, 102, 107, 109, 113–115, 118, 120, 126, 140, 144, 149, 154, 155, 158, 182, 196, 197, 219, 222, 228, 230, 231, 244, 267
Economic rights, 29, 30, 33, 34, 41, 42, 47, 51, 54, 58, 60–62, 64–67, 69, 71, 72, 109, 112, 120, 140, 155, 156, 168, 170, 183, 184, 189, 192, 196, 198, 217–220, 224, 225, 228, 229, 259, 268
Economics of Justice and Peace, 259
Economic system, 1, 4, 7, 38, 39, 53, 54, 60, 65, 84, 85, 113–115, 117, 120, 135, 140, 146, 170, 218
Economy, 6, 7, 16–18, 52, 54, 68, 72, 80, 85, 87–89, 112, 115, 135, 139, 141, 143, 144, 150, 157, 159, 171, 172, 191, 192, 227, 244, 256, 257
Employee Stock Ownership Plan, *see* ESOPs
Entrepreneurs, 9, 14, 15, 44, 47, 59, 81, 82, 119, 135, 137, 148, 157, 189, 192, 197, 198, 201–203, 228, 229, 234, 255, 259, 260
Equivalence, 2, 36, 39, 40, 114, 176, 198, 218, 219, 234, 268
Employee Stock Ownership Plans (ESOPs), 9, 14, 18, 44–46, 57, 59, 70, 83, 87, 120, 135, 137, 143, 157, 189, 192, 197–199, 201, 202, 210, 226, 239, 243, 244
Ethics, 100, 103, 217–220, 223, 230
Ethics in Concordian economic practices, 218, 223
Ethics in concordian economics, 217
Ethics in Concordian economic theory, 218

F
Financial independence, 39, 153, 156, 158–161, 168, 169, 210, 235
Fluoridation, 185–188

Index

Free rider problem, The, 38
Function of money, 115, 120, 155

G
General Theory, 7, 38, 52, 93, 113–115

H
Higher wages, 8, 83, 144, 173, 243, 261
Hoarding, 1, 4–7, 13, 17, 37, 43, 89, 93, 104, 105, 108, 133, 170, 199, 218, 219, 226, 248, 250, 264, 267

I
Inequality, 16, 17, 36, 38, 71, 72, 129, 170, 171, 174, 180, 239, 261, 262
Injustices, 25, 29, 63, 65–67, 72, 88, 89, 182, 260, 261

J
Jubilee Solution, 95, 130, 131, 133, 244

K
Keynes and Hayek, 2, 13, 16, 51–53, 55, 57, 60
Keynes Model, 38, 39, 48, 113, 154, 218

L
Land Tax Values (LTV), 56
Land values, 48, 56, 172, 173
Large middle class, 100, 101
Legal representation of real wealth, 115, 116
Loans, 9, 10, 12, 17, 18, 44, 56, 59, 69, 70, 81, 87, 93, 100, 104–106, 117, 119, 135, 137, 141, 144, 145, 156, 159, 183, 189, 197, 199, 227, 236, 259, 261, 267

M
Middle classes, 16, 26, 102, 111, 127, 146, 147, 183, 236, 267
Monetary system, 4, 10, 28, 29, 56, 109, 120, 128–130, 135, 137, 141, 145, 146, 148, 157, 168, 261
Money and wealth, 30, 115, 236
Money supply, 59, 118, 129
Moral issue, 224, 242, 251

Mother Nature, 176, 185, 186

N
Natural allies, 137, 138
New real wealth, 18, 44, 57, 65, 69, 142–144, 235

O
Old economists and bankers, 140
Ownership rights, 3, 30, 65, 105, 107, 114, 154, 173, 195, 196, 217, 220, 224, 229, 230

P
PacMan Economy, 17, 18
Paper money, 116, 137, 235, 250
Participative justice, 40, 108–110, 155, 196, 221, 222, 225, 230, 267
Peace in Ukraine, 247, 263–265
Peak of power, The, 122, 204
People controlling money, 4
People control money, 57, 148, 257
Piece of paper, 116, 224
Price of land, 11, 191, 192
Private money, 139, 143, 148, 149, 260
Privileges, 34, 35, 47, 65, 66, 71, 72, 146, 148, 200, 201, 243
Problem of poverty, The, 241
Project Financial Independence, 153
Promulgation and administration of justice, 171
Property rights and entitlements, 225
Proposals, 23, 29, 67, 79, 125, 134, 150, 159, 160, 173, 261
Public capital, 81
Public interest, 46
Public money, 10, 48, 128, 143, 145, 192, 260
Public money for public works, 145
Public policies, 99, 105
Public works infrastructure, 199
Purchase of consumer goods, 12, 44
Purchase of goods, 44
Push for higher wages, 8
Push for high wages, 8

R
Raising Steve Jobs, 88
Rational justification, 106

Rational plan of systematic reduction of debt, 146
Rational reason, 114
Real economic growth, 157
Real estate, 203, 250, 264
Real explanation, 129
Realization, 11, 64, 101, 136, 237
Real wealth of tables and chairs, 156, 255
Reasoning, 2, 58, 126, 128, 141, 142, 204, 219, 224, 227
Recommendations of Concordian economics, 56, 156, 193
Redistribution, 135, 146, 148, 171, 236
Relation of complementarity, 6, 39, 108
Relation of equivalence, 109
Relation to gold, 147, 235
Removing Hoarding, 267
Reward of not-hoarding, The, 93
Revised Keynes' Model, 38, 113, 218
Right of access, 43, 44, 55, 56, 59, 66, 69, 70, 109, 121, 129, 134, 135, 148, 203, 222, 225, 226, 265
Right of access to land and natural resources, 43, 69, 196, 199, 203, 225, 228, 265
Right of ownership, 43, 45, 58, 65
Role of Governments, 67, 68
Role of Hoarding, 5
Rules of logic, 6

S

Saving and investment, 6, 39
Scarcity, 5, 29, 41, 137, 147, 149, 181, 200, 201, 233–237, 267
Scarcity and fear of scarcity, 233
Scarcity of money, 29, 141, 234–236
Scarcity of sources, 234
Scarcity of sources of energy, 234
Science of fisheries stocks assessments, 253
Services of labor, 64
Simple Interest, 95, 159
Smith's goal, 104
Sober people, 17, 100, 101, 104
Socialism/Communism, 181
Social justice, 34, 64, 67, 68, 194, 220, 240
Social programs, 24
Social scientists, 121, 122, 251
Spiritual Life, 240
Splinter programs, 107, 126
SRD, *see* Systematic Reduction of Debt
SSRN AllTime Author Citations ranking, xiv
Stable monetary system, 145

Stable system, 54
Stop Inflation Cold, 8
Structure of economic justice, 67, 106, 108, 109, 222, 223
Structure of Keynes' model, 218
Structure of macroeconomics, 113
Subjective micro theory, 52
Supermarkets, 90, 177, 251
Supernational entity, 254
Surplus value, 73
Systematic Mosaic debt jubilee, 265
Systematic Reduction of Debt (SRD), 132
Systems analysis, 186

T

Taxes on land and natural resources, 17, 18, 43, 46, 57, 58, 69, 170, 230
Theory and policy, 108, 195, 196
Theory and practice of interdependence, 5
Theory of distribution of ownership rights, 217, 218
Theory of Interdependence, ix
Theory of justice, 41, 61, 62, 71, 240
TIME BOMB, 169
Too-big-to-fail corporations, 130

U

Unipolar world, 263, 265
Unpaid work, 89
US dominance of world markets, 263, 264
Use of money, 103, 104, 141
Use of money to control people, 141, 235
Use of national credit, 44–46

V

Value of housework, 87, 88
Value of land and natural resources, 43, 226
Value of money, 12, 59, 109, 129, 131, 139, 226
Values of ownership rights, 217, 219, 220
Values of real wealth, 52, 92, 120

W

Wealthy people, 130, 131, 237
Workers, 8, 9, 36, 45, 56, 58, 70, 73, 81, 84, 85, 109, 143, 144, 149, 158, 171, 173, 174, 187, 222, 227–230, 244, 249, 257, 260, 261
Work for corporations, 183, 188